THE ARTIST'S METHODS
AND MATERIALS

'*There is a logic of colours*' (*Cézanne*)

CÉZANNE (1839–1906)
The Clockmaker

MARIA BAZZI

The Artist's Methods
and Materials

TRANSLATED BY
Francesca Priuli

JOHN MURRAY
Fifty Albemarle Street London

English translation

John Murray (Publishers) Ltd
1960

Printed in Great Britain by
Butler and Tanner Ltd. Frome and London

Ego vere utar via veteri, sed si propriorem in-
venero, hanc muniam. Qui ante nos ista moverunt,
non domini nostri, sed duces sunt. Patet omnibus
ars nondum occupata. Multum, ex illa etiam
futuris relictum est.

SENECA, *EPIST.* XXXIII

Foreword

The true assessment of the value of a work of art is very rarely made during the life of the artist. He may or may not make a reputation during his lifetime but it is always left to posterity to make a true evaluation of his contribution.

It is certainly very difficult to judge the merits of the majority of the works produced by the younger artists of today as so many of them are producing paintings which bear no relationship to anything done in the past.

As a teacher of many years' experience I know that the present-day student is out to create a quick and sensational effect, and he has neither the patience nor the desire to study the technique of his job. I would say that the general rule amongst younger artists is to look down on technical accomplishment as something to despise. I am not prepared to pass a judgment on what is receiving praise or being acclaimed as great art today. Like most artists I am really interested only in the kind of work that I do myself.

Judgment or no judgment, there is one thing certain. Such is the lack of regard paid to painting technique by the younger generation that within a very few years from now pictures painted today will have disintegrated and fallen off the variety of unsuitable surfaces on which they were painted. The mixture of unsuitable materials causes the paint to crack and discolour in a very short time. There will be very little left to posterity to enable assessors to give a value to the present-day contribution to art.

This book which I have read is one that should be in every studio and school. It should be studied and memorized. If I were teaching painting, this is where I would start my students off. One cannot teach art but one can teach and explain techniques. This is the most useful book of its kind that I have ever read.

JOHN SKEAPING

Contents

xi

Illustrations and Painters

xiii

Introduction

Many artists of today are so preoccupied with aesthetic formulas that they seem to have forgotten that a painting is not
merely the result of theories but is made with materials as well
—organic and inorganic—and that the life of the picture
depends on their chemical changes and reactions. It is necessary
to select very carefully the materials with which supports,
grounds, pigments and varnishes will be combined to avoid the
danger of decaying, darkening, warping and blistering. It is
therefore indispensable for an artist to have a good knowledge
of the technical aspects of painting, for only then will he be
able to achieve the fullest expression of his possibilities, at the
same time creating a work which will last.

It is particularly important that a work of art should be protected from decay, for art, although an individual expression of
genius, belongs to human history and should be handed down
with the greatest care to future generations.[1] Careful technique
does not hamper freedom of artistic creation, as some people
believe. On the contrary, if the artist has absolute confidence in
his control of technical processes, he can express his inner vision
with more breadth and spontaneity.

If we consider how quickly modern pictures show signs of
deterioration in comparison with the paintings of the old
masters, which seem wonderfully immune from decay, we
might conclude that materials once used are no longer available. And yet, not only are they available but many modern
pigments, adhesives and thinners are far better than the old
ones. Nevertheless the fact remains that the artist of today does
not always know which materials to choose or how different
materials should be combined. Nor is he always able to dis-
tinguish between sound materials and the cheap, short-lived
substitutes now on the market.

Too often the painter does not grind his own colours, and buys his supports, varnishes and thinners already prepared, without knowing anything about their nature or composition. An artist who does not prepare his own pigments does not know how they can blend and he is probably unaware of the fact that some are radically altered merely by contact with a metal spatula. Moreover, painters seldom realize that alterations in tone are more often caused by the binding media than by the colour pigments themselves.

In the old days artists in the course of their training acquired knowledge and formulas which were the outcome of the experience of centuries and which guaranteed the durability of a painting; they bought their materials in a raw state at the apothecary's shop, and knew how to test their quality. In those days long years of technical experience and manual practice of art were required, in the course of which mind and spirit acquired a particular habit of professional honour and conscientiousness.[2] If the artist of the present day does not make a thorough study of the technical aspects of painting, this is not only due to new aesthetic concepts but to the fact that materials now available are not always pure and lasting; hence the technical difficulty which lies between the conception of an idea and its realization is greatly increased. This is why contemporary artists consider the study of painting technique a hindrance to self-expression.

In ancient times the technique of painting was closely linked not only with chemistry or alchemy, and medicine, but also with religion and philosophy. Since all knowledge was considered to emanate from a divine source, science and art, inspired by the spirit, were necessarily bound up with technique, which was the outcome of practical experience. In Egypt every discovery concerning art or science was submitted to the priest for approval and only then inscribed on the temple columns: these inscriptions bore no signature, since knowledge was considered impersonal. Ancient authorities, such as Iamblichus, mention the stelae of Hermes, on which all science was inscribed. As well as these, the astrologer Manetho mentions sacred books preserved within the temples. This is confirmed by early Greek alchemists such as Olympiodorus.

Later on in the Alexandrian Era, both artists and craftsmen began to collect systematically all the knowledge connected with their trades which had previously been kept secret by the priests. Treatises and encyclopedias, generally known as Hermetic books, now became popular: one example is the Leyden Papyrus, a compilation of formulas of the 3rd century before Christ. These formulas, written in Greek, are connected with the so-called Chemistry of Moses.

Clemens of Alexandria also quotes one of these encyclopedias.[3] The most varied technical notions were mixed up with invocations to gods or demons, with conjuring formulas, with alchemistic recipes for transforming base metals into gold and silver, with advice for falsifying metal alloys or precious stones. All these notions were fused and confused, often full of copyists' mistakes and complicated by obscure symbols, so that they became nearly indecipherable when the oral tradition died out.

We should not be surprised, therefore, that in the Book of Enoch the origin of science is ascribed to demons exiled from Heaven,[4] because in the Alexandrian age the precepts of art and science were bound up with magic and alchemy. The same substances (*pharmaka* and *venena*) were used for painting, healing and poisoning, and for making magic philtres.[5] Minerals were studied with the object of extracting colours and producing metal alloys, as well as substitutes for these alloys; coloured glass was used to create the enchantment of mosaic, and imitation gems.

In Greece, however, artistic and scientific knowledge was not compiled and controlled by the priests but was in the hands of philosophers such as Plato, Aristotle, Democritus[6] and Theophrastus, all of whom pursued knowledge methodically and freely transmitted it. Even the physicians became so interested in artistic questions that they neglected the studies strictly relevant to their calling and were duly reprimanded by Hippocrates.[7]

In the course of time the learning which sprang from Chaldea, Babylon and Phoenicia and matured through contact with the Hebrews, the Greeks and the Egyptians reached Rome during the Imperial Age, and was translated into Latin. Yet emperors and men of science alike did not welcome this new knowledge and indeed opposed it as it was tinged with occultism. Imperial edicts were issued, causing the destruction of most of these books.[8]

Since technical rules were mixed up with heterogeneous information and further complicated and obscured by magical and alchemical formulas, a great part of the practical tradition of painting was lost. Although Pliny was acquainted with the oriental works brought back by Ostanus and with Hebraic notions on the magical arts, he declared them all false and branded their practitioners as charlatans. However, following his natural bent for exact science rather than for abstract theories, he systematically extracted all the information relating to techniques and materials formerly used in science, art and industry, and compiled it, omitting all symbolic references. Pliny's work was to earn him a position of great authority during the Middle Ages. It is when writing on medicine that he also mentions oils and resins useful for painting. As will be described later on, it was from Pliny that students of technical problems, such as the Van Eycks,[9] were to derive innovations in painting technique. Not only did the Roman naturalist hand on precious rules for mural painting, but he also wrote a description of plastering and binding media (derived from Vitruvius) to be used in both tempera and encaustic painting. In the Roman period one might also mention Dioscorides, Pedanius, Galen, and the medical books quoted by Ætius and by Paulus Ægineta, which also yield some information on the materials used for painting.

With the fall of Imperial Rome and the rise of the Church the sciences and arts began to flourish in monasteries, where monks devoted themselves to scientific studies. Like the priests of ancient Egypt, members of the Church now took up the pursuit of knowledge; but whereas in Egypt the priests kept their science secret and revealed it only to a few sworn initiates, the monastic orders gave freely of the knowledge they had rediscovered and carefully tested. They put the fruits of their research at the disposal of the artist, but they had no desire to earn praise or money, only to help human progress and thus 'give honour and glory to God, from Whom all art proceeds'.[10]

When, in order to restore the lost traditions, the monks

4

started to gather and piece together the scraps of knowledge that had been dispersed, they faced an exceedingly difficult task. For when the School of Athens had died out after Justinian's Edict and the famous library of Alexandria had been destroyed, only Byzantium survived. It was here that the greatest collection of alchemical treatises of the Middle Ages was brought together between the 7th and 10th centuries. This sacred art was sought after by the Arabs and Greco-Alexandrian knowledge thus passed to Syria, where chemistry made great progress under the Abbaside rule.[11] Thence chemical and alchemical treatises were, at a later date, brought to Spain, where they were translated into Hebrew, Provençal, Castilian, and later into Latin. These translations in turn circulated throughout France, Germany and Italy.[12]

At the end of the 6th century the iconoclasts and later the Moslems drove a large number of Byzantine artists to seek shelter in Italy. These artists, monks and laymen alike, settled mainly in Monte Cassino, Ravenna and Venice, and brought with them their Byzantine techniques and formulas. The tradition of the practical craft of the old Roman artists still survived here and there in the studios and was handed on to Carolingian painters.

About the 12th century the main centres of these scientific studies were in Piedmont, Lombardy and Venetia. As in Alexandrian times, treatises and encyclopedias abounded, and again we note that manual practice was strictly allied with both scientific and mystical theories. The greatest variety of recipes, dealing with metallic alloys, dyes, colours, soaps and glass-making, was collected from different sources, without any attempt at systematic arrangement.[13]

In every monastery there was a spicery where the monks who were interested in painting pursued their chemical studies, so when art once again became the province of laymen the best painting materials were still prepared in the monasteries.[14] Technical knowledge spread even further when painters began to form confraternities, generally named after St Luke.

At the end of the 13th century the Florentine Guild of Physicians and Apothecaries[15] comprised not only the painters but also the wax and oil dealers, and the shield and panel

5

manufacturers as well. The fact that simple craftsmen for-gathered with artists and scientists made for the best results in art. Painters were able to get the most reliable advice from the physicians, and at the same time could choose the best materials from the apothecaries, also learning how to recognize good workmen.

Although painting had by this time gradually been separated from alchemy, it was still connected with medicine. Physicians, theologians and philosophers, following the path of St Albertus Magnus, Roger Bacon and Saladino d'Ascalo, were exceptionally active in scientific research. Physicians were scholarly men, since they had to hold a degree in philosophy, grammar and art.[16] It was only natural that painters should ask them to explain the ancient texts of Dioscorides, Galen, Marcellus and Hippocrates; Cennino Cennini acquired his knowledge of oil depuration from these authors. Antonio Veneziano while studying the laws of herbs in Dioscorides became so interested in their wonderful properties that he finally abandoned the art of painting to become a physician. Cennini's treatise on painting is extremely valuable to us: it sums up mediaeval knowledge and describes clearly and simply the pictorial craft. Thanks to him we know the methods used by Giotto and his school. During the Humanist period there were considerable changes in the technique of painting: the art of illumination gradually died out, oil painting began to replace tempera, encaustic technique was neglected and fresco replaced mosaic. Once again, as in ancient Greece, it was no longer the Church but the physical and natural sciences and philosophy which regulated the artistic sciences.

In the 15th and 16th centuries, while ancient texts were still studied,[17] innovations and new experiments were carried out. We find books of recipes—compiled on the lines of the Alexandrian Encyclopedias—such as the manuscripts of Bologna, Strasbourg, the Marciana Library and Padre Alessio the *Gesuato*; at the same time original works by Lomazzo, Vasari and Leonardo appeared, in which new problems were studied and technical innovations described.

Descriptions of varnishes and colours appear in the medical books of Mattioli, Cardano and Fioravanti, and physicians continued to give their professional advice to painters. There

6

are many instances of artists and physicians who were friends: Leonardo and Marc Antonio della Torre, Correggio and Giambattista Lombardi, and, later on, Van Dyck and Theodore de Mayerne are a few examples.

A new spirit of individualism arose towards the end of the 16th and the beginning of the 17th century, and the *bottega*, where there had once been a complete spiritual harmony in the creation of art, now ceased to exist. No longer did one master try to pass on clearly and fully the tradition which had been handed down to him. The *bottega* gave place to the school and the academy. Hand-in-hand with the new individualism came the individual method and the personal point of view, and professional jealousy also made its appearance.

In 17th-century books on art—with a few exceptions such as the treatises by Armenini and Padre Pozzo—recipes for impasto and for other materials are no longer taught. In their place we find lively arguments between the exponents of individualism and those of tradition, between representatives of the North and those of the South, between the upholders of spontaneity and those of fixed rules, and between the naturalists and the mannerists. A typical description of these controversies is to be found in a satire by Salvator Rosa. Armenini relates that many Roman painters with whom he was acquainted were excellent draughtsmen but were at a loss when it came to using colours properly. He attributes this ignorance to the carelessness of their teachers and to professional jealousy.[18]

When international art-dealing began about the middle of the 17th century, a new problem arose: that of authenticity. Baldinucci and Rosa write that fakes were very frequent in their time, as well as false attributions. The treatises of this period were often written in the form of dialogue, fable or allegory, and usually dealt with classifications of artists according to artistic merit and market price. They also gave advice on matters of artistic taste and on how to detect fakes, and often a glossary of technical and manual terms was included.

About this time *L'arte de la Pintura* appeared, an important work by Francisco Pacheco, which clearly draws on the teachings of Dürer, Leonardo and van Mander. Soon afterwards Palomino Velasco wrote his *Museo Pictorico*. In England, France, Germany and Flanders, many short treatises were written, dealing with miniature painting, varnishes and the new watercolours.

It was widely observed that oil paintings produced at the close of the 17th century and throughout the 18th darkened considerably. However, instead of seeking the reason in defective technique and the improper use of materials, artists experimented with new methods to obtain clear and luminous tones. Treatises were written on these new methods, as applied to pastel, watercolour, and enamel and ivory miniatures. There were also some attempts to revive the ancient technique of encaustic painting. But these writings are very superficial, and we even find works which set out to teach the reader how to become a painter in three hours—without touching on drawing or any theory of colours.[19]

But there is one work of this period which stands out: a French encyclopedia by an unknown author, published at Avignon in 1737, upon which many other authors have drawn. Like the ancient Egyptian and mediaeval books of recipes, it collects various teachings and indeed includes much material from Padre Alessio's compendium. The anonymous author makes a noble attempt to further sound technical notions based on the neglected ancient tradition, but his was a voice crying in the wilderness.

Towards the end of the 18th century absurd innovations were attempted, one of the most illogical being 'Eludoric painting'.[20] Its technique consisted in submerging the canvas in a basin of water and applying the paint under water, the impression being that all excess oil would be removed from the colours and that one could see the final effect of the picture as if it were under glass.

There still continued to be a lively interest in encaustic painting. Indeed, for over a century artists and men of science, priests and noblemen continued to argue over the composition of ancient encaustic. In most cases their individual ideas, amateurish methods and lack of philological and chemical knowledge produced a chaos of theories and recipes and caused the ruin of a number of paintings. However, De Montabert produced an interesting work on ancient techniques. Although this is valuable as an historical document it contains such

8

erroneous conclusions that artists like Prud'hon, who relied on De Montabert's opinions, produced pictures which cracked and grew dark in a very short time.

At the end of the 19th century art and science had parted company for so long that any poor painter who tried to learn his technique from books found himself confronted with conflicting opinions, untested recipes and unobtainable substances with obscure names. Many of the materials suggested could not be blended and used as they lacked tractability, permanence and covering power. Fortunately the study of painting technique gradually began to take shape again.

The merit for having started to collect and translate old manuscripts which clearly set forth historical sources must go largely to Sir Charles Eastlake and to Mrs M. Merrifield. We owe serious writings on the subject to Sir Alexander Church, Ernest Berger, Eibner, Vibert, Max Doerner, A. P. Laurie, Dinet, Raelman and, in more recent times, to Maroger, H. Hubbard, Maximilian Toch and Hilaire Hiler. It is, however, regrettable that some of these authors have such preconceived ideas about temperas and oils, and particularly about emulsions, that they have almost twisted the historical evidence to prove their unjustified assumptions. Even more recently some very scholarly works have appeared, conceived and written in a purely scientific spirit by Ralph Mayer, Thompson Varvey, R. J. Gettens and George Stout.

The object of this manual is to make available a ready reference to basic recipes, both ancient and modern, which will be easy to consult. As a restorer I have been in a position to study the diseases of pictures at first hand and to explore the possibilities of each medium in practice at the same time as testing its permanency.

I do not propose to deal with theories about colour scales or about aesthetics since these cannot be permanently established. But I have gathered together that which does not change through the ages and which has been transmitted from one generation to the next: a certain amount of practical craftmanship, as necessary to the painter as harmony is to the musician and prosody to the poet.

9

PART ONE

THE ARTIST'S MATERIALS

I

Surfaces for Easel Pictures and their Preparation

From the earliest times wood, stone, leather, metal, parchment and paper have been used by the artist as supports for easel pictures. At first wood was the most commonly used material, later, canvas.

PANELS

Panels were mostly of poplar, oak,[1] white poplar, or chestnut. Only in rare instances were they made of resinous wood: careful artists, such as the Flemish masters, used to remove all gum and resin from the wood before priming, since these substances warp the panel, making the colours flake and crack. They therefore left their oak panels (oak was most frequently used in Flanders) immersed for a long time in running water to free them from an excess of tannin and resinous substances.

Nowadays there is an excellent method for treating wood. The panel is subjected to hot steam, which renders it less sensitive to variations of temperature. The steam takes out the resin and causes the albuminous bodies to coagulate, thus avoiding, or at least diminishing, those dangerous tensions of the fibres which make oily grounds and colours crack. Another precaution recommended is soaking the wood with strong smelling essential oils, or with special preparations which prevent woodworm.[2]

An oak panel by Van Eyck,[3] protected on the back by a composition of gesso, glue and tow, subsequently coated with black varnish, is still immune from woodworm and the paint is smooth and perfectly preserved.

We therefore recommend treating panels on the back and sides with a damp-proof coating such as a thickly applied mixture of common oil paint and varnish, glossy or mat lacquers like Duco, or cement and other similar preparations.

The need to protect the back of a painting has been proved to be of the utmost importance. Many triptychs which have stood for centuries in damp churches present a central panel (painted on one side only) which has suffered from rot or woodworm and is warped and flaked, whereas the two side panels (painted on both sides) are perfectly preserved and smooth.

The woods most frequently used nowadays are dark walnut, cedar and teak. A panel made of one of these is more suitable than canvas for painting with an egg or oleo-resinous base.

PLY-WOOD

Each layer must be laid with the grain at right angles to that of the previous layer. The most suitable woods are those of a light colour (poplar, lime, plane, chestnut). The grain should not be strongly marked as in time it may show through the paint. Ply-wood should be primed with a thin coat of glue and gesso, with a coat of tempera, or with diluted varnish. It should never be prepared with oils, varnishes with a lacquer base, or oil colours, all of which in time darken the tones.

HOW TO PRIME PANELS

In ancient times the manner of preparing panels with gesso was similar in all countries to that described by the monk Theophilus and by Cennino Cennini. The wooden boards, free from knots and irregularities, were smoothed with a plane; then all grease was removed and the various boards were joined with a glue made of cheese and lime. Fixed bars to hold the boards in position were avoided as they would have made the wood split; nails were short so as not to reach the priming since, being subject to rust, they would in time force it up and cause it to flake off. Then the panel was lightly sized and the joins were covered with strips of fine linen carefully glued down. Some artists covered the whole panel with canvas or with tanned leather.[4] When the first coat of glue was absolutely dry a coat of gesso and glue was applied. After a few days all rough-ness was scraped off and a second coat of gesso, more finely ground, was applied with a bristle brush and finally smoothed with the palm of the hand. The panel was then left for a few minutes. When the preparation had almost dried, and there was very little moisture left, up to eight successive coats of gesso and glue were laid on with a bristle brush. The panel was then left to dry in the shade in the open air and was finally rubbed down with a scraper until the surface was as polished as ivory.

CANVASES

Some writers, misinterpreting Vasari,[5] have attributed the invention of canvas supports to Margaritone d'Arezzo. Actually the practice is very ancient since it is mentioned by Pliny, Juvenal and Boethius;[6] a Mount Athos MS deals at length with special very liquid preparations made with gesso, soap, honey and glue for use with canvases stretched on frames. This custom was brought to Italy by Byzantine artists and spread throughout the country.

Canvas, which at first had been glued to panels, was now stretched on frames, making it possible to produce works of huge dimensions which could easily be moved. At first canvas was treated with gesso and glue in the same manner as panels, with a coarse undercoating and a polished layer on top. Very soon, however, these preparations deteriorated, since the canvas contracted and the preparation itself lacked elasticity. The Venetian painters knew how to make thin, elastic primings, which enabled the pictures to be rolled up without suffering any damage. Very often the canvas would be lightly smeared with a glue of starch and sugar and then with a thin coat of gesso and glue.[7]

Later, so as to work more quickly, artists used oily grounds.

15

This was a most unfortunate innovation, for these preparations not only made paintings darken but caused very severe cracks as well. In the 17th century there was a vogue for red and brown grounds which absorbed the mid-tones and increased the shadows, altering the values of colours.

In the 17th century painters also took to adding litharge to the oil to make the ground dry more quickly. This produced a new type of deterioration, because litharge does not mix with the other ingredients of the ground and in time forms granulations which deform the picture.

These oily preparations were not applied directly to the canvas, as the oil would have eaten into the fibre. Vegetable glues were interposed, but as these were inherently hygroscopic, the preparations and colours on pictures stored in damp places gradually decomposed, which resulted in many pictures disintegrating altogether.

At the end of the 18th century French artists experimented with various types of ground containing honey and wax but very soon stopped using these materials because of their poor qualities. They found it was better to use instead a preparation consisting of an emulsified oil paint mixed with an equal quantity of the same pigment kneaded with water.[8]

White grounds made of gesso and glue are still the best as they do not alter the tone and colour values of a picture;[9] if used on canvas they should be spread very thinly.

One can verify at once whether a canvas has been badly primed with gesso and glue. At the slightest rub or graze the priming cracks or comes off as dust, according to whether there is too much or too little glue in the ground. A canvas prepared with oil will last many years before cracks appear, so an artist cannot, by rubbing the canvas between his fingers to test the elasticity of the priming, make a satisfactory examination before beginning to paint, as he can with a canvas prepared with gesso.

How to Prime Canvases

A canvas should be made of linen or hemp; if it is entirely or partly made of cotton it will stretch and crack and, moreover, will not hold the priming well. Silk[10] is an extremely poor support for painting because in time it splits and disintegrates. Something new has recently appeared on the market in America—a canvas woven with glass or nylon fibres; but this has already proved to be a very fragile surface.

To prepare a canvas, wet it and allow it to dry. Stretch on a frame, then paint it with a light coat of glue. The following day the canvas should receive a coat of gesso. Allow a few hours to pass and then apply a second coat, with the brush strokes at right angles to the previous ones. While this coat is still damp smooth with a spatula to make it adhere thoroughly and fill up all the interstices of the canvas.

Fine canvases only need a light priming. Coarse ones will require two coats of gesso and glue, but not more, or they will harden and turn rigid. If one adds a little skimmed milk to this preparation the priming becomes more elastic and the danger of cracks is avoided.

The edges of wooden frames should be bevelled; if left sharp they may cut into the painting. Wedges must be placed in the corners so as to make it possible to tighten the canvas if it stretches. A very good practice is that of lining the canvas primed with gesso with one treated with oil, as this affords protection against damp.

Some painters are in the habit of preparing their canvases with the colours left on their palettes. This residue of almost dry and lumpy paint, mixed with oil and varnish, is spread thickly on the canvas and the picture is condemned from the start to go dark and flake rapidly. In addition, oil, which dries slowly, forms an elastic layer under the painting. When this eventually dries, the paint applied over it cracks.

If an artist through laudable thrift regrets having to throw away the colours left over on his palette, let him use them, diluted with a little oily varnish, on the backs of panels to protect them from woodworm and damp.

Some painters smear the reverse of their canvases with wax and resin as a protection against damp, but this system is not recommended since it tends to make the canvas go slack and form humps.

METALS

Metal supports are seldom used nowadays, probably due to high cost, weight and the impossibility of smoothing them if they become deformed.

But formerly this type of support was popular. Cennini tells us that iron was used,[11] and perhaps the custom derived from the practice of painting armour. Brass,[12] tin, silver,[13] and, most of all, copper, were also used, as Vasari, Leon Battista Alberti and Leonardo report.[14] It also appears that the Flemish masters painted on slabs of gold, thinking that this would ensure permanent durability. But their paintings perished when they were stolen and melted down for the sake of the precious metal.

The use of iron was discontinued because paintings deteriorated through the formation of rust. Copper, which was greatly in vogue during the 17th century for small pictures, *fondelli*, little portraits, and so on, is no longer used as it is often spoilt by streaks of verdigris.

Artists painted directly on these metal sheets, without priming with gesso: they merely smeared the surface with garlic juice to make the colours grip. In some cases the sheet metal was given a very thin coat of a brown or grey oily preparation.

Recently W. Ostwald of Munich has recommended aluminium as a surface on which to paint. He asserts that this metal, when exposed to the air, forms a waterproof, transparent skin on its surface to which the paints adhere tenaciously so one can use oil colours without any priming whatever. This is of interest, since there is a demand for sacred pictures from religious missions, especially in Africa, where every painting on wood or canvas is rapidly spoilt by atmospheric conditions.

MARBLE, STONE

Slabs of veined marble were often used for painting little scenes and landscapes in which the veins were used to obtain cloud or wave effects. Oil colours were used on stone, especially on the columns and walls of churches, and we shall discuss these in connection with mural painting. Many painters used slabs of slate, but this was soon discontinued as they proved too heavy and brittle, and often disintegrated because they contained nitre.[15]

LEATHER

We have information about paintings on leather by Byzantine artists.[16]

At the time of Theophilus, leather, preferably horse-hide, was stretched on panels before priming with gesso, perhaps to avoid the gesso cracking where the boards joined. Leather and all tanned hides in general offer an elastic support which paint grips well, but as it was expensive and the seams showed through the gesso it did not have a lasting vogue and was soon replaced by canvas.

Nevertheless leather was widely used in Russia and was treated with the juices of herbs to render it immune from worm.

CARDBOARD

Cardboard is a good and inexpensive material for small paintings, as long as it is thicker than $\frac{1}{10}$ in. It must be prepared on both sides as it is extremely sensitive to damp. First it must be smeared with thin glue. This coat is generally not sufficient to insulate the painting from the impurities contained in the cardboard and a second priming of gesso and glue must therefore be applied, with the brush strokes across those of the first. Oil preparations should not be used on cardboard: the one currently used in China and described on page 29 is much better. On the back of the board one can use enamel, cement preparations or hot paraffin wax as a protection against damp.

CARDBOARD COVERED WITH CANVAS OR PAPER

The best glue for attaching canvas to cardboard is flour paste. When the canvas is smoothly stretched on the board, put it to dry under weights. The canvas should overlap the board by a few inches all round so that it may be folded over and fixed down on the reverse with fish glue. The surface is then primed with gesso and glue.

Cardboard can also be covered with Watmann or Canson paper, previously prepared with casein. The result is a light, mat and dry painting. In former times the paper was prepared with a solution of tragacanth.

ETERNIT

Experiments have recently been made with slabs of eternit, a synthetic material which is not deformed or warped by damp. It can very easily be prepared with gesso and glue and can be painted on with both oil and tempera colours. Some artists cover slabs of eternit with a light plaster so as to provide a basis for easily handled murals. Oil colours should not be applied directly on to eternit; priming is necessary to insulate the colours, which would otherwise rapidly darken and become dull.

De Chirico recommends linoleum and oil cloth, but these materials are dangerous as they become hard and coriaceous and crack easily.

MASONITE OR PRESDWOOD

Modern artists, especially in America, make use of this material as a painting surface, since it is firm and keeps its shape well. It is best prepared with a gesso priming. In order to obtain perfect adhesion all traces of grease must be removed with a wad of cotton wool saturated with a mixture containing 2 parts of spirit and 1 part of ammonia. When dry, smooth with emery paper, then apply the priming as you would for preparing panels and cardboard. Paper or canvas may be glued on before priming. Masonite is made of compressed wood fibres and when waterproofed with paraffin wax stands up well to damp, does not warp or crack. In America large boards are glued down on to wooden trellises, as if they were panels, to keep them flat.

PARCHMENT

It is possible to paint directly on parchment with oil colours, as the ancient painters did, or pastels may be used, but one must first roughen the surface by rubbing it with pumice stone. This produces an excellent surface.

To paint with watercolours or to illuminate, the parchment should be mounted on a stretcher, or on cardboard in the same manner as paper used for watercolour painting.

All grease must first be removed with ox gall mixed with a little alum, or with glue and honey, which make the colours grip.

IVORY

For miniatures choose bluish ivory with a smooth grain. If the ivory has turned yellow, treat it with hydrogen peroxide and place in the sun. Rub down with emery paper and then with pumice and cuttle-bone. Ivory should first be lined with white paper, affixed with very transparent flour paste or with gelatine glue, and then with strong, thin cardboard. Next, dry between pieces of blotting paper under pressure. Remove any grease with ox gall or very dilute ammonia. The surface should not be touched by the fingers as they will leave spots of grease to which colour will not adhere.

PAPER

To be able to paint on paper with oil [17] or tempera colours one has only to coat it with a solution of tragacanth dissolved in water (see pp. 73, 111–12) or with diluted tempera colour. If the paper is to be used for an oil painting, it is advisable to mount it on cardboard with a vegetable glue.

The choice of paper is of great importance in watercolour painting: it should be made with rags of lisle and not with cotton fibre or wood pulp, since paper of an inferior quality destroys all depth of tone, and goes yellow and brittle in time. The paper should not be too porous and should be glued carefully to avoid stains. To remove all possible traces of grease, sponge with a solution of ox gall or very dilute ammonia before beginning to paint. If the paper has been badly glued it should be covered with a coat of very light glue (4 per cent) fixed with a formalin solution (4 per cent).

Paper can be mounted on cardboard, on a frame or on special stretchers.

For gouache painting the procedure is the same as for watercolour.

Paper for pastels should be rough and coloured. It can be made rougher by giving it a coat of light glue mixed with pulverized pumice and clay. Two coats of this should be applied, crossing the brush strokes. When dry it can be smoothed with cuttle-bone. This preparation can also be applied to cardboard, canvas and wood.

RECIPES FOR
OTHER PREPARATIONS

A. P. Lauries's Recipe for Priming a Panel [18]

'A panel was sized and coated with one coat of Ripolene enamel. When dry the surface of the Ripolene was sandpapered and unprimed canvas attached to the surface, in one case with a strong carpenter's glue and in the other case with casein. In both cases the canvas was found to be firmly attached, and on being forcibly torn off left the glue and the casein attached to the Ripolene surface. Such a canvas so attached gives a capital surface for a gesso priming of either size or casein. This combination of wood and canvas is the most reliable backing for a picture which we can obtain out of known materials.'

Priming for Tempera. John Duncan, R.S.A. [18]

'Well seasoned mahogany is used for the panel, and the refined gelatine used for micro-cultures is used for the glue.

Eighty sheets of this gelatine are dissolved in a pint of warm water as quickly as possible, care being taken not to boil the solution. The panel is wetted and a piece of muslin glued on to it.

The gesso-grosso is prepared by mixing plaster of Paris with this glue to a consistency which can be plastered over the panel with a trowel. This is given two days to dry and is then scraped down with the edge of a three-cornered file.

The gesso-sottile is prepared by mixing thoroughly one pound of plaster of Paris with one gallon of water. This is frequently stirred at first and then kept for a month. The water is then drained off and the gesso collected in a cloth, the water squeezed out, and then mixed with the glue in about equal volumes. Eight thin coats of this are laid on with a brush and the panel is left to dry for four days. The surface is then rubbed down with fine sandpaper, and in some cases it is burnished with an agate. It is then coated with two or three coats of weak size to make it non-absorbent. The back of the panel is also roughly coated with gesso.'

HOLMAN HUNT'S PREPARATION [18]

'Select a prepared ground originally for its brightness, and renovate if necessary with fresh white when first it comes to the studio; white to be mixed with a very little amber or copal varnish. Let this last coat become of thoroughly stone-like hardness. Upon this surface complete with exactness the outline of the part in hand. On the morning for the painting, with fresh white from which all superfluous oil has been extracted by means of absorbent paper, and to which again a small drop of varnish has been added, spread a further coat very tenderly with a palette knife over the part of the face work, and of such a consistency that the drawing should faintly shine through. In some cases thickened white may be applied to the pieces needing brilliancy, with a brush and the aid of rectified spirits. Over this wet ground the colours, transparent and semi-transparent, should be laid with light sable brushes, and the touches should be made so tenderly that the ground below shall not be worked up, yet so far noticed to blend with the

23

superimposed tints as to correct the qualities of thinness and staininess which over a dry ground transparent colours used would inevitably exhibit.

Painting of this kind cannot be retouched except with an entire loss of luminosity.'

Carlos Merida's Priming[19]

'For a half a square yard of canvas:
Bring 2 half-glasses of water to a boil, add:

Glycerine	35 drops
Honey	20 ,,
Whiting	6 handfuls
"Fishtail"	7 sheets.

The fishtail is a prepared glue sold in the United States under that name.'

Goupil's Preparation[19]

'Goupil uses a ground composed of:

Gelatine	1 part
Glue	1 part

dissolved in skimmed milk in proportions so that it will be thin, but slightly syrupy. Whiting or zinc white in powder is then mixed in; the first coat is given thinly and the second rather more thickly. Not over three coats should be used, for fear of cracking.'

Louis Hess's Recipe for Priming[19]

'4 oz. fine slaked dental plaster,
1 teaspoonful of parchment glue
1   ,,   of cold unboiled milk.

Grind in, and then grind in 1 teaspoonful long oil varnish (boiled linseed oil).

If the paste is too thick, add 1 teaspoonful of water and the varnish afterwards. Then add 4 or 5 drops of ammonia to eliminate possible acids.

24

By substituting whiting for the plaster, and ordinary glue for the parchment glue, this ground becomes quite simple to make.'

RALPH MAYER'S PREPARATION [20]

Among the preparations described by Ralph Mayer we recommend the following, which is simple to make and flexible.

4 oz. of rabbit skin glue
¾ pt. of water

Soak for twelve hours to let the preparation rise. Dissolve at a low temperature and remove from fire before it boils. Pour into a receptacle containing chalk dust and stir until the paste is smooth and even; if necessary, pass through a sieve. The gesso when used should be a creamy, fluid paste.

MAX DOERNER'S PREPARATION [21]

Dissolve 2½ oz. of glue in ¾ pt. of water and prepare as above. Apply this glue to the canvas or panel, and leave to dry: one day will be enough in summer, but two or three days must be allowed in winter. If the canvas becomes slack, stretch it again on the frame.

Add plaster and white zinc to this glue and make a smooth, creamy paste; if too thick a little more gum solution should be added. Apply with a paint brush and allow to dry. The canvas should retain its elasticity even after the application of the second coat. If this ground is found to be too absorbent, allow it to dry and then paint over it with the glue solution. After a few days smooth the surface with very fine sandpaper, cuttlebone or powdered pumice.

PREPARATION CONTAINING OIL [22]

Prepare glue as in previous recipe (2½ oz. of glue to ¾ pt. of water) and apply to canvas with a paint brush.

When thoroughly dry spread the following paste, also with a paint brush: 1 part of zinc white, 1 part of plaster and 1 part

25

of glue, thoroughly mixed; then add 1 part of oily varnish and work with a spatula to a smooth consistency.

When this ground has dried, apply a second, taking care to obtain a smooth surface.

This second coat dries more slowly than the first. Polymerized oil, or *Stand Oil*, which is linseed oil washed and purified in the sun, may be substituted for oily varnish. Nut oil and poppy oil should not be used as they dry too slowly.

If a less absorbent ground is desired, the gesso ground should be rubbed down when dry and brushed over with a mixture of 1 part of glue and 1 part of oily varnish. This ground containing oil yellows slightly with time but regains its whiteness if exposed to the sun.

Preparations containing oil must be left to dry in the light for months before use.

PREPARATION WITH CASEIN BASE

Casein grounds are extremely hard and rigid and should therefore not be used on canvas but on wood or paper and cardboard. Casein tempera [23] to be used for priming should be prepared by diluting 1 part of tempera in 4 parts of water. This should be applied in a very thin coating.

EGG GROUNDS

These grounds are difficult to make successfully, since the oily content of eggs makes the preparation go yellow, and if used in excess causes the priming to flake. It is better to use a diluted coat of any of the emulsions recommended for tempera colours than a preparation containing yolk or albumen (very brittle).[24]

PREPARATION WITH PASTE

Some painters use a rye paste to make a gesso ground, with 1 part of rye flour to 15 parts of very hot water mixed to a smooth consistency. The ground thus obtained is similar to that described on page 16.

Grounds containing rye paste are very elastic but become

26

brittle with time and as early as 1598 Volpato noted their fragility.[25] Many oil paintings by Venetian masters have this type of ground and are cracking and flaking, especially if they have hung in damp places. Sometimes the whole painting can be lifted off simply by washing with pure water.

Some painters prefer a very diluted starch paste to the one made with rye flour.

COLOURED GROUNDS

The slight tempera colouring which some painters have used with their gesso grounds from the earliest times should not be confused with the red and brown *mestiche* (oily preparations) whose defects I have already mentioned. This light and transparent tinting had the advantage of making the grounds less absorbent. Galen (Book X) reports this practice and says that painters used cold tones of green, blue and brown as the whiteness of the gesso strained their eyes. Books of recipes give this procedure throughout the Middle Ages, and the 'protoplasmo' mentioned by the monk Dyonisius is the *verdaccio* of which Cennini speaks.[26] Unfinished pictures prove that this was generally practised. Two unfinished pictures by Michelangelo, 'Madonna and Angels', and 'Christ deposed from the Cross', show that a light wash of green earth was applied as a ground for flesh tints. The initial stage of an unfinished picture by Garolfo in the Galleria Capitolina shows a green coat applied evenly to the whole canvas and not merely under the flesh tints.

The slightly grey gesso grounds used by Rubens have preserved all the brilliancy of his colours. He obtained them by mixing plaster and glue with a little finely ground charcoal.

HOW TO MAKE NON-ABSORBENT GROUNDS

To paint with tempera and colours thinned with varnish or light varnish glazes, it is necessary to prepare a non-absorbent surface. The canvas or panel prepared with gesso must be evenly sprayed with an atomizer with one of the following solutions:

27

Skimmed milk
Light solution of glue containing $\frac{1}{10}$ of alum
$4\frac{1}{2}$ per cent formalin solution
Thinned tempera

It is dangerous to add honey, syrups, gum, soap and glycerine, since these are hygroscopic substances and cause mildew and flaking. Avoid all grounds with an oil or oily varnish base as they darken the colours; also avoid all varnishes with a base of collodium, cellulose or celluloid dissolved in acetone, even if these preparations have been made elastic by the addition of castor oil. None of the lacquer and spirit preparations recommended by Hilaire Hiler and some German scholars should be used either. Although they make the ground damp-proof they prevent the colours from adhering properly and the painting becomes very fragile.

Tudor-Hart's system of waterproofing grounds is to mix 1 part of zinc white ground in oil and 1 part of white mixed with egg emulsion (see p. 117). Water is then added to increase the volume of the mixture by one half.

A thin coat is applied first, and when perfectly dry a second, crossing the brush strokes.

After a few days the surface is smoothed with pumice and polished with a slightly damp rag.

GROUNDS FOR OIL OR TEMPERA PAINTING ON PAPER

Herman Sachs recommends the following for priming:

$\frac{1}{2}$ part of plaster
$\frac{1}{2}$ part of zinc white
1 part casein glue

to which have been added from 2 to 5 per cent of glycerine or castor oil to give elasticity.

PRIMING WITH SKIMMED MILK

Paper can be prepared by applying two coats of skimmed milk which close the pores of the paper and make a pleasant and inexpensive ground.

CHINESE PREPARATION FOR CARDBOARD

Two or three coats of this priming render the cardboard as hard as wood and give it great stability. It is excellent for preparing the backs of cardboards and panels.

> 27 parts ground slaked lime
> 3 „ alum
> 20 „ well emulsified fresh blood.

Pig's blood is considered the best.

INEXPENSIVE PREPARATION FOR CARDBOARD

Herman Sachs recommends an inexpensive way of priming cardboard panels so that they do not absorb oil and tempera colours excessively.

Paint twice with a solution of 2 parts water and 3 parts sodium silicate.

PRIMING WITH A CELLULOSE BASE [27]

Ralph Mayer cites experiments made in America with cellulose which have not proved satisfactory. Cellulose insulates the colours too much from the ground and prevents their adhesion. So far, the results of the experiments have been inconclusive.

MIXTURES AGAINST WORM

Before applying gesso grounds it is well to disinfect the panels so as to make them immune from worm.

Any of the following mixtures can be used:

(a) A solution of alcohol and corrosive sublimate (6 per cent) applied to the back of the panel;

(b) Decoctions of tobacco or aloe with a small quantity of water, applied hot several times on ordinary panels; one coat only of the solution, cold, on ply-wood as the moisture might cause the layers of wood to come apart;

(c) *Carbolineum*, an oil of pitch, is thinned by heating and applied to the back of the picture. This preparation has the defect of darkening the wood. Other colourless preparations of pitch, such as creosote, can be used with excellent results, but unfortunately smell unpleasant;

(*d*) Chinese wood oil applied to the back of the panel makes the wood as hard as stone and worm-proof;

(*e*) Essential oil of pyrethrum mixed with oil of turpentine and paraffin oil (1 part pyrethrum, 5 parts turpentine, 5 parts paraffin oil) is an excellent worm killer and preventive. So are trichloretan, tetrachloretan or exachloretan mixed with paraffin oil which prevents complete evaporation and also helps to discourage wood worm. None of these preparations penetrates below the surface of the panel and they make the wood more inflammable;

(*f*) The following is a good old recipe: 12 oz. essence of turpentine, ½ oz. aloe, 1 oz. camphor, 77 grains of santonin, melted over a low fire and applied warm to the wood;

(*g*) D.D.T. or similar substances, such as Bosan C, can be applied to the back of the panel.

Preparations made with water can be applied to both sides of the panel: those made with oil or with essential oils should be applied only to the back, or the gesso ground will not adhere perfectly.

EQUIPMENT FOR PAINTING

PALETTES

Walnut is the best wood for palettes.

The palette should be rubbed down first with powdered pumice and then rottenstone—not olive oil.

It is important to saturate the wood with oil and varnish. Care should be taken to allow every coat to dry and harden before applying the next. A mixture of hot oil and copal varnish is better than pure oil.

Palettes should be kept scrupulously clean. Dry colour should be removed every day. There is nothing worse than painting with colours which have formed thin elastic skins; they make the picture go dark and produce cracks and lumps. Some modern artists use white porcelain palettes even for their oil colours.

Enamel, tin or porcelain palettes are recommended for tempera colours. Do not use aluminium palettes as the colours are affected and darken, especially if they contain varnish or vinegar.

BRUSHES

It is extremely important to keep brushes in good condition. Old brushes well kept are much more supple and useful than new ones. They must be kept scrupulously clean. In cleaning they should be rubbed gently so that the bristles are not torn or removed. If washed only with oil of turpentine they will remain hard and sticky; and if left to soak in turpentine for a long time the bristles will soften and twist. They should be dipped in turpentine or in paraffin oil immediately after use and dried with a rag to remove all excess paint. They should then be dipped in warm soapy water and rubbed between the fingers so that the soap forms a little foam, then rinsed and the operation repeated until they are perfectly clean. The brushes should now be dried with care and left in the air for some hours to allow all moisture to evaporate. If they are made of animal fur such as badger or sable, they should be kept in tin boxes containing camphor or herbs to prevent moth.

Brushes which have been used for tempera or watercolour should be cleaned with soapy water and then thoroughly rinsed. Some painters apply olive oil to their brushes to keep them soft, but this is very bad practice: the oil never dries and causes deterioration in the paintings for which they are used.

If the brushes become stiff through being left dirty or soaked with varnish or resins, they will regain flexibility if dipped in amyl acetate and then washed with a mixture of spirit and oil of turpentine.

SPATULAS

There are two types of palette knife: for handling the pigments and for painting. Both types must be made of flexible steel, horn, ivory or wood, but those for painting must be much more pliable.

The old masters used the palette knife for painting with encaustic, and it is also used by modern painters who dislike a smooth finish. Rembrandt accidentally discovered this technique when he could not find the brush he needed. Reynolds in the *XII Discourse on Painting* adds the comment that 'chance in the hands of a man who knows how to make use of it, often produces daring and singular beauties'.

To clean spatulas after using them, rub first with a rag slightly moistened with turpentine and then with a dry one.

2

Grounds for Mural Painting

Walls can be either brick or stone. Old walls must be absolutely dry and without trace of nitre; new walls should be allowed to dry thoroughly in the air before plaster is applied. If traces of saltpetre are found, the only solution is to build a facing of bricks just in front of the wall to be decorated, leaving a space between wall and facing in which the air can circulate.

The system recommended by Vitruvius and Pliny is still the best way to protect a painting from damp in a wall. It was followed in Santa Maria Antiqua and consists in applying a mixture of lime, pozzolana, tufa and broken tiles to the wall before the roughcast was put on. A smooth stone wall should be roughened with a hammer to give the roughcast a good hold.

The wall should be well moistened with water before applying the roughcast as this has no grip on a dry surface.

Brick walls require more moisture than stone walls. Sometimes it is enough to damp the wall the day before but at others it is necessary to damp the wall repeatedly for a whole week.

PLASTERS AND ROUGHCASTS

The lime to be used for frescoes must be slaked at least one year before use. There are limes of various types: 'fat' lime, 'thin' lime and hydraulic lime.

Fat lime swells a great deal when soaked in water and consists of very pure oxide of calcium. It is calcined in an oven and when well cooked is light and melts quickly in water. If over-cooked, it melts slowly and is not slaked easily; badly cooked, it remains heavy and is difficult to slake. This is the lime most commonly used for fresco painting. It is well to slake it as soon as it has been calcined and then put it through a very fine silk sieve.

Thin lime, or lime of the Dolomites, contains a good percentage of magnesia (from 30 to 40 per cent) which reduces its cohesion and makes it very soluble in water. When soaked, this lime increases very little in volume. It has the advantage of allowing the painter to work more slowly than when using fat lime; plaster made with this lime remains fit to paint on for about fifty-six hours. The ancient frescoes of Southern Tyrol and Austria which are so well preserved were made with this lime, but modern paintings for which the same mixture has been used have deteriorated at once because the air, today, is no longer free from coal smoke and sulphuric acid, which badly affect the colours during the drying process.

Hydraulic lime hardens rapidly under water. Some painters have used it for frescoes with satisfactory results, but they have had to restrict their palettes as many colours refuse to set, or deteriorate, when in contact with this lime.

How to Slake Lime

According to Armenini quicklime should be brought to the boil and then dried in the sun on bricks. Others bury this lime in a pit for years: if buried in sandy soil the plaster becomes more cohesive. The Romans used to add vinegar to hasten the slaking process.

Gian Battista Alberti gives this advice: 'Do not put too much water with the quicklime all at once as it must be slaked slowly, wetting it over and over again until it is saturated. It should then be stored in a rather damp and shady place without adding other ingredients, and covered on top with a light layer of sand, until in time it ripens and turns somewhat liquid.'

Sand

Sand should be siliceous and river sand is the best. It should be free from pyrites, iron and salts of mica since these cause the mortar to scale off, nor must it contain clay which causes

34

cracks. The sand should be washed until the water remains clear. It should be of an even grain: the coarse quality is suitable for fat lime, and the very fine for thin or hydraulic lime.

Pozzolana

In ancient times pozzolana was used instead of sand. This produces a mixture of extraordinary solidity but is very difficult to apply, so it is generally kept for the roughcast.

Straw or Vegetable Fibrous Substances

A very ancient practice is to add vegetable fibrous substances to plaster to give it elasticity. In the palace of Amenhotep III at Thebes filaments of marsh plants are found, and chopped straw or tow in other Egyptian plasters. A thin coat of gesso has been applied over this and painted either with gouache or with tempera. In the Indian paintings at Ajanta and the frescoes of China and Japan rice chaff and dung have been mixed with the mortar. The Benedictines and the monks of Mount Athos have spread in the West the custom of mixing in fibrous materials which make the plaster dry more slowly, allowing more careful work. After applying a plaster containing fibrous materials it is necessary to wait a couple of days before painting, but this type of plaster provides a surface which can be painted on for four days—longer than is possible on ordinary plaster. Colours applied during this time do not become friable.

Water

This must be pure spring or river water—not stagnant—and must not contain salts or traces of metal.

Roughcast (Arricciato)

This is the coarse and rough layer applied directly to the wall in order to hold the plaster. It is generally made of 1 part slaked lime and 2 parts sand. Water is added and the mixture kneaded until it becomes stiff and smooth. It is kept for several days in a cool place away from the light. Cennini warns that it should not be used immediately as it is too fiery. If it hardens too much, thin with water when necessary.

The mortar is thrown on to a wet wall with a trowel and is then smoothed. If a second coat of mortar is applied, take care to wet the first coat. In ancient times the outlines of the cartoon were traced on to the roughcast and then filled in with green earth or some other monochrome. Nowadays the roughcast is not thicker than $\frac{3}{8}$ in. Many painters spread the plaster on the roughcast when the latter is still fresh, while others allow it to dry and then wet it before applying the plaster and sometimes roughen it with a scalpel to obtain better adhesion.

PLASTER (INTONACO)

This is a much finer mixture which sometimes contains marble dust as well. Use equal parts of lime, sand, marble dust.

For 'buon fresco' painting, plaster should be applied only to the section that can be covered during the day. For 'secco' and other types of mural painting, the whole surface of the wall is plastered. The coat of plaster should be thin and smooth and no thicker than $\frac{1}{4}$ in. for 'buon fresco'. Smooth it with a trowel, or, better, with a marble roller as Vitruvius recommends, or with a glass bottle as they do in the Trentino and in Tuscany. If the plaster contains quartz neither a roller nor a bottle will stain it as a metal trowel does.

Originally the painted wall had a perfectly smooth surface, but after Padre Pozzo's experiments artists began to use his granulous plasters. A painting on this type of surface is very luminous when viewed from a distance. This is an excellent system for decorating vaults and cupolas but it is less suitable for vertical walls as the rough surface catches the dust.

MURAL PAINTING ON LOOSE PANELS

Hermann Sachs[1] tells us how to make loose plaster panels for murals. The surface area should not exceed 21 sq. ft. Mix

1 part of Portland cement, 1 part of sand, 1 part of very fine gravel with water to a very stiff consistency. There are two ways of making this composition into slabs.

WITH STEEL FRAME

Make a steel frame and stretch on it a net of galvanized steel wire (ordinary steel frames and wire must be made rust-proof by varnishing with minium). Place the frame on a table and apply the mixture $\frac{3}{4}$ to $1\frac{1}{2}$ in. thick. Smooth and level and leave to stand for a couple of days. Then scrape the surface with a metal comb and roughen so that the next coat of plaster will grip well. After a fortnight apply the plaster which can be painted 'a fresco', 'a secco' or with tempera as required.

WITH WOODEN FRAME

A wooden frame can be used with steel wires stretched across it to form a trellis. This is prepared in the same manner as the steel frame.

PANELS WITH PLASTER BASE

Mix 2 parts of plaster of Paris with 1 part of gravel and sand, wetting with a watery glue solution, and pure water. Place in a wooden mould on varnished iron frames $1\frac{1}{4}$ to $1\frac{1}{2}$ in. thick. Half an hour later roughen the surface with a metal comb and if necessary moisten it. This is ready for painting about ten days later.

MURAL DECORATION ON CARDBOARD[2]

Frescoes or decorative temperas can be painted on cardboard, provided it is at least $\frac{1}{4}$ in. thick. Mount the cardboard on a wooden frame and prime on both sides with hot glue and then with the following mixture:

1 part of glue ($6\frac{1}{2}$ oz. glue to $1\frac{3}{4}$ pts. of water)

1 part of plaster of Paris
2 parts of fine quartz sand.

A coat 2 to 5 mm. thick is applied and smoothed to a level surface. This is a light and cheap surface, suitable for painting with casein, shiny stucco, 'buon fresco' and 'secco'. This mixture can also be applied to eternit, masonite and so on.

PAINTING ON CONCRETE

Only oil colours can be used on concrete, which must be treated to prevent alterations of the pigments. A watery solution of chloride of zinc is therefore applied; this also serves to harden the surface.

It is also possible to prepare the concrete by washing it with a solution of ammonia salts and water; while the wall is still wet apply two coats of oil colour thinned with oil of turpentine.

Before beginning to paint it is advisable to apply two coats of a solution of bisulphite of calcium to ensure that any colours thinned with fatty varnishes will adhere.

3
Pigments

It seems that the earliest painters knew only four colours:[1] a white, which had the character of carbonate of calcium, a yellow ochre, a red ochre and a black. The Egyptians, like the Romans at a later time, had a very rich range of brilliant colours of both mineral and organic source, since they used vegetable dyes for textiles.[2] In his *Treatise on Stones*, Theophrastus of Ephesus[3] gives a list of various pigments, and mentions sandarac and orpiment (sulphide of arsenic), natural and burnt ochre, smalt blue, lapis lazuli and vermilion.

In the Middle Ages new vegetable colours were invented which were chiefly used for illuminating. These colours were most beautiful and extremely subtle, but they were discarded in the 19th century as painters no longer believed that they could stand up to the light. At that time these colours had lost their original stability because of careless preparation and also because they were mixed with fatty oils which cause alteration, whereas the varnishes and balsams originally used gave protection. The absence of all traces of vegetable colours in the works of Leonardo and Rubens [4] has been taken as a proof of their fugitive quality, but in fact their disappearance is due more to restorers than to the influence of light or atmosphere. The old recipes still produce very beautiful transparent colours, useful for glazing tempera, watercolour and gouache paintings.

In theory even variation of tone can be obtained with very few basic colours, but in practice a palette with a large number of tints allows the painter to produce infinite and delicate harmonies of colour with greater speed in execution.

In our day the artist has at his disposal more solid colours than those originally known. Chrome greens, cadmium reds

39

and yellows and titanium white can be mixed with perfect safety to produce new shades; they have taken the place of copper greens, cinnabar, orpiment and white lead which, unless definite precautions are taken, turn dark and cannot be mixed together.

The iron derivatives, such as the Mars colours and the ochres are fast to light and can be mixed with each other and with white lead. It is obviously necessary to avoid mixing them with those colours which alter in contact with a metal palette knife, such as Naples yellow and cobalt violet. Other mineral colours, the oxides of chrome, cobalt, cerulean, ultramarine and ivory black become stable if rendered inert by long calcination.

ALTERATIONS OF TONE

Darkening or changes of tone may have various causes:

CHEMICAL REACTIONS

These reactions are produced when certain colours are mixed, for example, vermilion (sulphide of mercury) mixed with white lead (carbonate of lead) forms a black sulphide of lead. Such reactions take place very slowly if the colours involved require a long contact before being affected, or if they have been mixed with preserving substances like oil, resins or balsams, while colours ground with water change very quickly.

The following combinations affect colours which are stable in themselves:

White lead with:

        Saturn red (Red lead)
        Lakes
        Chrome yellows
        Paris blue (a weak variety of Prussian blue)
        Ultramarine

Cerulean with:

        Saturn red (Red lead)

Ivory black
Indian red

Light cadmium yellow with:
Saturn red (Red lead)
Red earths
Cobalt violet

Medium cadmium yellow with:
Raw and burnt earths
Cobalt violet

Cadmium orange with:
Burnt sienna

Ultramarine with:
Aureolin
Saturn red (Red lead)

The shades obtained by mixing cadmium yellow with emerald green are stable only if mixed with zinc white. They otherwise become garish and the emerald green tends to predominate, disturbing the colour scale.

FADING

Fading and discoloration take place if the artist has used colours sensitive to light which are generally vegetable colours. According to Eibner (*Chemiker Zeitung*, 1911), zinc white causes the following colours to fade when exposed to light: Chrome yellows, zinc yellows, Paris blue and ultramarine.

The ancients used to cover colours with a tendency to darken, like cinnabar, with a transparent coat of colours known to be fugitive, such as the lakes, thus preserving the intensity of tone.

DARK FOUNDATIONS

Foundations made with red or brown earths, especially if ground with oil, absorb the mid shades in a very short time and alter the values of *chiaro-scuro*.

41

Many substances cause pigments to darken. Cooked oils and resins of poor quality have this effect and their use has caused many pictures to darken. Litharge not only darkens the picture but also roughens the surface.

DAMP AND MILDEW

Certain colours, such as the cobalt greens, deteriorate quickly as a result of mildew and damp.

HOW TO TEST THE PURITY
OF COLOURS

There is no need for a laboratory or costly apparatus to analyse the main colours,[5] as only the following substances are necessary, and they are common and easily procured:

> Strong white vinegar
> Kitchen salt (saturated solution)
> Oxalic acid (saturated solution)
> 'Aqua forte' (1 part nitric acid, 5 parts of water)
> Carbonate of soda (saturated solution)

The only instruments required are a spirit lamp, a few glass pipettes, filter paper and a spoon, which must not be tin-plated.

The colour must be pulverized. To test an oil colour, place a small quantity in a glass with benzine and change the liquid several times to remove all fatty substances, then dry with blotting paper. To test tempera or watercolour, wash the colour several times with water and then dry it. The liquid must remain colourless to prove the absence of aniline. Emerald greens, cobalt, ultramarine and the lakes—which are finely ground—should be left for several weeks before pouring off the benzine or water. The powder is so fine that for a long time it remains suspended in the liquid and colours it. Advice for these tests is given in the tables which follow with reference to each colour separately.

Another simple and practical way of examining colours and mixtures is to make long brush strokes of colour, both pure and mixed, on a piece of canvas prepared with gesso. Then cut the canvas into two pieces and when thoroughly dry put one piece into a dark place, preferably a cupboard, and expose the other to strong light, possibly to sunlight. After six months or a year compare the two pieces and discard the colours which have deteriorated.

To test colours for frescoes place a little colour in a linen bag, bury it in slaked lime and leave it for a few weeks. Then compare this with colour which has not been treated to see if there is any change.

Sometimes expensive colours like the cobalts, cadmiums, ultramarines and so on, are falsified with aniline dyes. This is easily detected by placing a little colour on a piece of white paper and leaving it for one day. If the halo formed by the oil is coloured, aniline is definitely present.

TABLES OF MINERAL COLOURS

TABLE 1: WHITES

COMPOSITION	PROPERTIES	USE
White lead (Flake white, ceruse, Crems white, London white, *blanc d'argent*, etc.) Basic lead carbonate	Very poisonous; great covering power and is a good drier. Turns dark when exposed to the air or to sulphur fumes. Should not be used with the lakes which it discolours, or with cadmium yellows, vermilion and ultramarine which it alters.	Should be used only for oil, varnished tempera and encaustic painting. Should not be used with ordinary temperas especially if they contain vinegar, fresco, watercolour, pastel. *Test:* Place a small amount in nitric acid: it should dissolve completely. A residue betrays the presence of sulphate of lead.
Freeman white Sulphate of lead.	Permanent; its behaviour in impasto still to be studied.	Experiment.
Zinc white (Chinese white)	Non-poisonous; mixes well with other pigments. Does not have much covering power and dries slowly. Unless of excellent quality, tends to crack when used in thick impasto. Loses this tendency when mixed with vermilion, cinnabar and the cadmiums.	Used for all easel painting. *Test:* Must dissolve completely in vinegar or dilute chloride. Effervescence indicates chalk. Residue indicates presence of kaolin.
Titanium white Titanium dioxide, Oxide of titanium	Non-poisonous: a newly introduced pigment which has excellent qualities. Unless carefully prepared tends to separate from oil.	For all types of painting except pastels and murals. Hilaire Hiler reports that 28 million dollars have been spent in America to produce a perfect titanium oxide for painters.
Tungsten white	Unsuitable.	Do not use.

TABLES OF MINERAL COLOURS

COMPOSITION	PROPERTIES	USE
Antimony white	Unsuitable.	Do not use.
Bismuth white	Van Dyck experimented but discarded this pigment as it darkens rapidly.	Do not use.
Barium white (Barite, baryta white, heavy spar, permanent white) Barium sulphate	Non-poisonous, not affected by atmospheric agents, but has little covering power.	Should not be used alone but mixed with flake and zinc white, and with the lakes in decorative paintings.
Litophone Mixture of barium sulphate and zinc sulphide	Turns black as an effect of light and damp.	Do not use.
Dutch white or Hamburg white Mixture of white lead and barium	Doubtful solidity.	Experiment.
Lime Oxide of calcium	Is obtained by heating the mineral in special ovens; exposed to the air absorbs carbon dioxide. Combines with water producing heat and forming slaked lime or hydrated calcium.	Slaked lime is used in frescoes for roughcasts, plasters and *bianco San Giovanni*. Quick or slaked lime is used to make stucco, emulsions and temperas. Quicklime prevents oil of turpentine from going thick and frees it from fatty contents.
White clay (Meudon white, Spanish white, etc.) Calcium carbonate	Solid, non-poisonous, does not cover.	Serves for tempera with glue, in making pastels, stuccoes and grounds.
Gypsum white Calcium sulphate	Absorbs moisture turning into hydrated calcium sulphate. Can be very finely powdered; used in gilding.	Serves to make gesso priming for panels, canvases, to fill where colour is missing, to make stucco.
Kaolin (English kaolin, Vicenza earth) Hydrated aluminium silicate	Is mixed with white lead and oil to make grounds. Talc is also a silicate white.	Used for watercolours; for glaziers' glue; talc is used in making crayons and to remove excess grease from pictures.
Marble white	Made with very white Carrara marble pulverized and put through a very fine sieve.	Is added to lime in making plaster and to some colours to lighten them for fresco painting. Also useful in grounds with casein base on which oil colours produce a mat effect.

TABLE II: YELLOWS

COMPOSITION	PROPERTIES	USE
Bismuth yellow Bismuth chromate	Unstable.	Do not use.
Chrome yellows Lead chromate	Poisonous. Turn dark in contact with the air.	Do not use.
Naples yellow (Mineral yellow, Merimée yellow, Thénard yellow, etc.) Lead antimoniate	Is discoloured by contact with metal spatulas and palettes.	Can serve for fresco if well prepared; for oils and tempera if well varnished.

TABLE II: YELLOWS (cont'd)

COMPOSITION	PROPERTIES	USE
Greenish Naples yellow	Turns black.	Do not use.
Pinkish Naples yellow, or brilliant yellow	Permanent if carefully prepared.	Experiment.
Cadmium yellows Cadmium, cadmium sulphides	Poisonous. Darken all colours with lead base, and especially tempera colours. Lose this defect if prepared with oil and varnish. Are stable if well prepared and have a range of beautiful shades from lemon yellow to deep orange. Light cadmiums are often adulterated with flowers of sulphur and become harmful to pictures. Should therefore be tested by experiments.	Excellent for all types of painting if made by reputable firm. *Test:* Dissolve the cadmium in 4 times its volume of nitric acid. The liquid should be milky; if greenish, chrome is present; if red, cinnabar.
Zinc yellow Zinc chromate, zinc and potash bichromate	Unstable.	Do not use.
Barium yellow (Mutrie or lemon yellow) Barium chromate	Does not cover. Stable if used for oils, unstable in watercolour as affected by air.	Do not use.
Massicot	Poisonous, goes black, cracks; once used as siccative.	Do not use.
Mosaic gold Tin sulphide	Goes black.	Do not use.
Orpiment Arsenic sulphide	Very poisonous, unstable.	Do not use.
Turner's yellow (Mineral yellow, Montpellier Cassel yellow)	Poisonous, unstable.	Do not use.
Strontian yellow (Strontium chromate)	Very stable if well prepared.	Suitable for easel painting. *Test:* Should dissolve perfectly in 10 times its volume of nitric acid.
Mars yellows	Very solid. Tone does not deepen when mixed with oil as it does with ochres. Mars brown, red and violet are obtained by calcination.	Suitable for all types of painting.
Cobalt yellow or Aureolin, Potash and cobalt salts	Very transparent, can be used instead of Indian yellow and yellow lakes.	Suitable for watercolour; if used for oil painting must be used with varnish or with a siccative as it dries badly when pure.
Transparent yellow Nitrite of potassic cobalt and alumina	Similar to cobalt yellow, excellent if mixed with green.	Like cobalt yellow.
Yellow ochres (Roman ochre, golden ochre, Oxford ochre, Spanish ochre, etc.) Earth colours, containing clay, limestone, iron hydroxide	Yellow and golden ochres are permanent; lemon ochre harmful as it is a hydrated iron sulphate. American yellow ochres contain 70 per cent barium sulphate. A beautiful orange ochre is *grès de Théviers,* a very solid colour.	Well prepared and washed, for all types of painting.

TABLE III: REDS

COMPOSITION	PROPERTIES	USE
Red ochres (Venetian red earth)	Very solid and permanent. Mixed with white lead produce beautiful shades.	For all types of painting.
Armenian bole	Iron oxide, clay, calcium silicate, magnesia in various proportions.	Mixed with deer's suet or soap and red earth for preparing ground for gilding.
Cinnabar (Vermilion) Compound of mercury and sulphur	Extremely poisonous. Goes black through influence of air and of lead colours.	To be used with caution in oil painting and in well varnished tempera.
Cadmium red Cadmium selenide and cadmium sulphide	Very solid, permanent and not affected by light.	For all types of painting. Experiment with frescoes.
Potter Rose	So called because it was invented during 19th century by a potter in Staffordshire by calcinating tin oxide, lime, chrome oxide. Stable and opaque.	For all types of painting.
Minium (Saturn red) red oxide of lead	Poisonous. Turns dark when exposed to air and light.	Do not use.
Realgar Arsenic sulphide	Very poisonous.	Do not use.
English red *Indian red* *Scarlet* and *Mars red*	Very solid: their shades vary according to degree of calcination; strong colouring power.	For all types of painting. *Test:* Must dissolve completely if placed in boiling hydrochloric acid.

TABLE IV: GREENS

COMPOSITION	PROPERTIES	USE
Cadmium green Mixture of yellow cadmium and emerald green	A superfluous colour as it can be mixed by the artist on the palette.	Experiment.
Celadon green Anhydrous green chromic oxide	A silvery green, which mixed with white lead produces beautiful cold tones.	For all types of painting. Experiment with frescoes.
Lamorinière green Anhydrous green chromic oxide and alumina	Substitutes green earth and can be mixed with all colours.	For all types of painting. Experiment with frescoes.
Emerald green (Viridian, Guimet green, Pellettier green) Hydrous green chromic oxide	Very poisonous, solid, unalterable.	For all types of painting. Experiment with frescoes.
Uranium green	A rare colour, solid but not much used.	Experiment.
Copper green Copper acetate	Poisonous, tends to darken.	As an oil colour it becomes stable if mixed with a balsam.
Veronese green or *African green* Basic copper arsenate	Extremely poisonous. Can be mixed with white lead, strontian yellow and cobalt; is affected by zinc white.	Is used in oil and tempera, well varnished and mixed with balsams and resins.

46

TABLE IV: GREENS (cont'd)

COMPOSITION	PROPERTIES	USE
Cobalt green *Rinnman's green* Cobaltous oxide and zinc oxide	Very poisonous. Has good covering power. Very sensitive to damp which causes it to darken.	For easel painting. Experiment with frescoes.
Ultramarine green	Durable and inert; not much used.	Used chiefly for watercolour.
Green bice *Bremen green* *Earth green* Oxides, hydrate of copper	Change tone.	Do not use.
Malachite green	Obtained from the stone. Solid, suffers from emanations of sulphuric acid. Should not be used with cadmiums or with egg tempera.	For all types of painting. Mix with caution.
Veronese green earth	Excellent for tempera, less good for fresco, not much good in oils.	For tempera, pastel, encaustic; with caution in mural painting
Prussian green Double salt of iron cyanide and cobalt	Affected by light.	Do not use.
Scheele's green (Mineral green, Swedish green)	Goes black.	Do not use.
English green *Milory green* *Green cinnabar* Mixtures of chrome yellow and Prussian blue	Unstable compounds.	Do not use.
Schweinfurt green (Vienna green) Copper arsenate	Goes black. Poisonous.	Do not use.
Arnandon green Chrome phosphate	Unstable.	Do not use.
Manganese green *Cassel green*	Alters.	Do not use.

TABLE V: BLUES

COMPOSITION	PROPERTIES	USE
Cobalt blue (or *bleu de Thénard*) Cobalt oxide and alumina	Excellent colour discovered by Thénard in 1802.	For all types of painting. *Test*: If pure remains unaltered when placed in solution of nitric acid.
Ultramarine (*lapis lazuli*) Natural and artificial	The natural colour is extracted from lapis lazuli. The artificial one obtained by Guimet in 1828. Solid, stable, not affected by alkalis. Discoloured by weak acids. Should always be washed first in hot water and then in cold before grinding. Should not be mixed with white lead.	Natural variety is excellent for all types of painting except fresco. Must not be used with temperas containing vinegar. Artificial variety is also a good colour and can be used as the natural sort. *Test:* Natural variety melts in nitric acid without residue. Artificial variety should dissolve when placed

TABLE V: BLUES (cont'd)

COMPOSITION	PROPERTIES	USE
		(1 part) in saturated solution of oxalic acid (10 parts) without residue.
Azzurra della Magna (*cendrèe*, mountain blue, copper blue, blue bice) Chemical formula imperfectly known	Stable. The ancient recipe is lost.	Can only be used in oil painting if mixed with varnish and oil of spike. Was and is used for all types of painting.
Prussian blue (Chinese blue, Antwerp blue, Berlin blue) Compound of iron and cyanogen	Is affected by light and alkalis. Dries badly when used for oils; is discoloured by lime if used in fresco. Mixed with cobalt produces a watercolour which is discoloured in the light but regains its tone if placed in the dark.	Do not use.
Cerulean blue Cobalt and tin blue	Solid and permanent. Substitutes generally heavy and opaque.	For all types of painting.
Academy blue	Mixture of ultramarine and emerald green. Can substitute Prussian blue having the same tone. Solid.	For all types of painting. Experiment with frescoes.
Smalt blue	Used by the Egyptians. Ancient formula lost. The one recently found by Prof. Fouquier has little tinting power.	Experiment.

TABLE VI: VIOLETS

COMPOSITION	PROPERTIES	USE
Cobalt violet Cobaltous oxide arsenate	Must not be used with metal palettes or spatulas. Solid.	For all types of painting. Experiment with frescoes.
Mars violet	Very solid.	For all types of painting.
Manganese violet or *Mineral violet* Manganese phosphate	Solid.	For all types of painting. Experiment with frescoes.
Cassium blue Gold and tin oxides	Permanent but lacking brilliancy.	Excellent for enamel.
Violet ultramarine	Solid but difficult to find.	Experiment.

TABLE VII: BROWNS

COMPOSITION	PROPERTIES	USE
Cassel brown Lignite	Cracks when mixed with white lead.	Do not use.
Van Dyck brown (calcined ochres composed at times from organic matter) Unstable chemical composition	Very solid if well prepared. Has good covering power and dries quickly. Discard if slow in drying as this reveals presence of bitumen.	For all types of painting. Experiment with frescoes.
Cappagh brown (Veronese brown, Caledonian brown)	Practically impossible to find pure; dries perfectly, is very solid; often adulterated with mixtures of calcined ochres and Van Dyck brown.	Experiment.
Mineral bistre Hydrated manganese oxide	Transparent, has no body.	For drawing, watercolour and miniature.

TABLES OF MINERAL COLOURS

TABLE VII: BROWNS (cont'd)

COMPOSITION	PROPERTIES	USE
Bitumen, Asphaltum or Mummy	One of the most dangerous colours. Damages pictures beyond repair, causing them to darken and crack badly with ever-increasing fissures. Never dries completely.	Do not use.
Transparent brown or Vibert brown	A modern substitute for bitumen.	Experiment.
Brussels brown (bone brown)	Not permanent.	Do not use.
Florentine brown (Copper, iron cyanogen)	A transparent colour of great beauty. Not perfectly permanent.	Experiment. So far only used in oils.
Burnt umber Burnt Sienna Brown ochre	Have the same properties as the raw earths.	For all types of painting. Tend to darken in oils.

TABLE VIII: BLACKS

COMPOSITION	PROPERTIES	USE
Russian black Venice earth Rome earth black	Have the same properties as other earths.	For all types of painting.
Manganese black	Used during the 19th century.	No longer marketed, so it is impossible to try out.
Graphite Black lead	Stable and excellent in mixtures.	Used only for drawing and to make pencils.

TABLES OF CARBONS—VEGETABLE COLOURS

TABLE IX: CARBONS AND COLOURS PRODUCED THROUGH CALCINATION

COMPOSITION	PROPERTIES	USE
Ivory black Burnt ivory Bone black Calcined bones	Pliny attributes the invention of this colour to Apelles. Tends to separate from water: for murals should be applied with lime water or tempera. Dries slowly if used with oils and should be mixed with varnish, resins or siccatives.	For all types of painting.
Vine black Oak black Peach black Lampblack	Oak and vine black are bluish; mixed with white are suitable for painting skies. Peach black made with calcined peach stones gives false tones especially in mixtures. Lampblack is permanent and is the most transparent.	For all types of painting.
Horn white	A solid white which does not affect the lakes or colours affected by white lead.	Used by the old masters for tempera, especially in Flanders.
Pearl white Calcined oyster shells	Excellent colour for fresco; is found in frescoes at Pompeii.	For mural painting.

TABLE X: VEGETABLE COLOURS

COLOUR	PROPERTIES	USE
Gaude yellow	Extracted from *reseda luteola* by boiling with water and alum. Precipitation is caused by addition of a solution of potash. Strain and wash while warm.	For easel painting with water.
Gamboge Gum resin	As watercolour it is spoiled when exposed to air. Must be mixed with balsam or resin for oils. Excellent for wax painting.	For easel painting, especially for glazing.
Avignon grain or *Stil de grain*	Extracted from the berry and seed of *pixacanta*, species of kerprun found near Avignon. Colouring substance is fixed on alum earth. Precipitate and fix again on alum.	For watercolour, miniature, tempera. For oils if mixed with balsam. Good for encaustic, never for murals.
Saffron	Discoloured by light.	Do not use.
Terra merita *Curcuma longa*	Also called Indian saffron: recipe given by Leonardo in cod. Atl. fol. 244, B side.	For miniatures and watercolour.
Camomile *Sunflower* *Ginestra tinctoria Celidonia* *Aloe*	Transparent yellows discoloured by light. Flemish masters put aloe in amber varnish to obtain golden light.	For miniatures and to colour varnishes.
Madder lake *Lacque de garance* *Crimson lake* *Rubens lake*	The best lakes are extracted from roots and coloured woods. Should not be mixed with white lead.	For all types of painting. Only for 'secco' in murals.
Poppy red	Extracted from dried poppy petals placed in spirit (Leonardo Vinciano MSS B fol. 3 back). Very fragile.	Do not use.
Chica red	Extracted from leaf of American chica plant. Not very stable.	Experiment.
Indigo	Extracted from leaves and bark of Indian leguminous plant. Boil in water to purify and add to spirit. Dry, place in muriatic acid to remove earth residue and iron oxides. A substitute was obtained from *woad* (*isatis tinctoria*).	For easel painting with water. Is found in Flemish and Dutch pictures in perfect condition, mixed with resin.
Cornflower blue	Extracted by soaking dried petals in spirit. Unstable.	Do not use.
Brown Stil de grain	Extracted from *berberis vulgaris* joined to Avignon grain, ashes of wine sediment and solution of alumina sulphate; more solid than yellow *Stil de grain*. The recipe is given by Tingry.	For easel painting with oil; a resin or balsam must be added.
Bladder green	Extracted from *rhamnus frangula* by pulping berries and cooking until liquid becomes viscous: add alum, water and a little lime.	For easel painting as watercolour and for encaustic.
Iris green *Violet green* *Stramonium* *Tobacco* *Spanish ennel green*	Extracted from pressed petals, mixed with water and alum. Heraclius says that a fine green is obtained by adding lime to the pressed petals.	For watercolour and miniatures. Called *Sap green* by the trade.

TABLES OF ORGANIC COLOURS, ANILINES, ETC.

TABLE XI: ORGANIC COLOURS OBTAINED FROM ANIMAL SUBSTANCES

COLOUR	PROPERTIES	USE
Purple from *murex*	The ancient recipe is lost. Murexide is artificially made from uric acid.	Used in ancient times for dyeing textiles, for the *purpurissum* which was applied for glazing as a lacquer mixed with egg tempera on crimson or blue grounds (Pliny).
Cochineal carmine	Discoloured by light.	Do not use.
Indian yellow (*purée*, Prusi) Euxantic acid and magnesia *Peruvian yellow*	Mixed with oil is soluble in water, so balsam or varnish must be added. Does not alter in light. Extracted from the urine of camels or cows fed on mango. Unobtainable nowadays, it is substituted by Peruvian yellow prepared by Depouilly treating uric acid extracted from guano. Commercial product often adulterated with poor quality lakes.	For all easel painting.
Sepia extracted from ink bag of the cuttle-fish	Cuttle-fish from the Atlantic produces blackish colour; from the Adriatic a good brown	For watercolour and drawing.
Eggshell white	Pulverize the shell and boil in water with a little quicklime. Wash, pulverize again, dry in sunlight. Very stable.	Used for mural painting and for temperas with colours affected by white lead.

TABLE XII: ANILINES AND ALIZARINS

COLOUR	PROPERTIES	USE
Geranium lake *Thyre rose* *Brilliant red* *Violet lake* *Purple red* *Paris violet* *Transparent lake* *Black lake*	Anilines, artificial colours extracted from coal-tar. Unstable in light.	Do not use.
Azo or *Spectrum red* *Mineral lake* *Marigold yellow* *Blue lake*	Alizarins obtained synthetically from anthracite; not sufficiently tested.	Experiment. Blue lake is solid and a substitute for Prussian blue.

COLOURS RECOMMENDED FOR THE VARIOUS TECHNIQUES

The following is a list of some colours recommended by Ralph Mayer:

FOR OIL PAINTING

Whites: Zinc
White lead
Titanium

Blacks: Ivory, lampblack
Mars black or iron oxide

Reds: Light and dark cadmium
Alizarin
Mars red
Venice red earth

Blues: Ultramarine
True cobalt
Cerulean

Greens: Emerald green
Oxide of chromium
Turquoise and cobalt greens
Ultramarine green

Yellows: Light, medium and dark cadmium
Orange cadmium
Naples yellow
Yellow ochres of different shades
Raw sienna
Aureolin
Strontian and barium yellows

Violets: Violet alizarin
Cobalt and manganese violet
Mars violet

Browns: Raw umber
Burnt umber
Burnt sienna

Whites: Chinese
Titanium

Blacks: Ivory, lampblack
Mars black

Reds: Light, medium, dark cadmium
Alizarin
Iron oxides (Mars, Venice, Indian red)

Yellows: Light, medium, dark, orange cadmium
Mars and ochre yellows
Raw sienna
Aureolin
Strontian and barium yellow

Blues: Ultramarine
True cobalt
Cerulean

Greens: Emerald
Oxide of chromium
Green earth
Cobalt, turquoise and ultramarine greens

Violets: Cobalt and manganese violet
Violet alizarin
Mars violet

Browns: Raw and burnt umber
Burnt sienna
Brown alizarin
Burnt green earth

FOR TEMPERA

We recommend the same colours used for oil painting, excluding white lead but including green earth.

Used by modern artists:

Whites: San Giovanni white
Neutral fixed white

Blacks: Mars black
Lampblack

Reds: Natural and artificial iron oxides

Blues: True cobalt
Cerulean

Greens: Emerald green
Oxide of chromium
Cobalt green
Green earth

Yellows: Mars yellow
Yellow ochres
Raw sienna

Violets: Mars violet
Cobalt violet

Browns: Turkish raw and burnt umber
Burnt green earth
Burnt sienna

4

Glues and Oils

ANIMAL AND VEGETABLE GLUES

If an animal and a vegetable glue are mixed together, the substance obtained is much more adhesive and elastic than either of its components separately. Glues are damp-proofed by adding oil and resin; and they can be more easily mixed with resin if a little borax and alkali are added. The presence of vinegar and acids makes glues unsuitable for the carbonates, ultramarine and white lead. Salts prevent perfect cohesion; glycerine causes mildew.

ANIMAL GLUES

Carpenter's glue: too rigid, should not be used for pictures or grounds. Makes mastic or stucco and is used to size panels.

Flanders glue: less adhesive than carpenter's glue, also less rigid.

Totain or Cologne glue: made from clippings of animal skins.

Fish glue: this and the totain glue are of great value to painters. Both are very adhesive, elastic and almost colourless.

Gelatine: the type used for microcultures, very transparent and colourless, recommended for tempera and grounds.

Casein: very adhesive but rigid, should be mixed with other substances to acquire elasticity. (See *Tempera*, p. 135.)

Albumen: forms a very rigid glue, soluble in water, glycerine and in spirit.

VEGETABLE GLUES

Flours and starches boiled in water produce a very sticky substance called vegetable glue.

The addition of garlic juice and resins increases the adhesiveness of these glues. To prevent or delay putrefaction oil of cherry laurel, camphor or cloves is added while the glue is boiling.

POTATO GLUE

Potatoes boiled in water for a long time form a clear and adhesive gelatine. Mixed with pigments it makes an excellent tempera; mixed with dry chalk it makes mastic or stucco. It can also be successfully used for tempera mural painting. (See *Tempera*, p. 131.)

DEXTRIN GLUE

Should not be used either for painting or for grounds as it is too rigid and causes cracks. It is extracted from starch by means of acids and is therefore dangerous as the acids affect many colours. It is used to prepare certain watercolours. (See page 106.)

RECIPES FOR GLUES

Animal glues are left for twelve hours to swell in equal parts of water. More water is then added until the right consistency is obtained. They should be cooked over low heat and *not* allowed to boil as this diminishes their adhesiveness.

SECCO SUARDO'S ELASTIC FISH GLUE

Melt 12 parts of isinglass in 12 parts of water over low heat. Stir constantly and add 4 parts of molasses. Remove from flame and add 1 part of ox gall. Place the glue in an iron vessel and allow to evaporate without boiling until it thickens, then leave to dry. The glue has the consistency of indiarubber and lasts for years.

When needed, melt a piece in warm water to the desired consistency. It is very adhesive and elastic and clings to any surface, even if greasy.

To be used for priming and in restoring.

Parchment Glue

Boil 100 parts of small parchment clippings in 300 parts of water until the mixture has shrunk to one tenth of its original volume. Strain through linen. With the addition of honey this is used for tempering colours. (See *Tempera*, p. 129.)

Glove Skin Glue

Boil 1½ oz. of small clippings of white skin in 1¾ pts. of water until the mixture has shrunk to one sixth of its original volume. Strain. Used for priming and for tempera.

Glue with Oil of Turpentine

Excellent and very sticky. It is made as follows:

19 oz. of totain glue are left to swell in an equal amount of water

3 oz. of fish glue
3 oz. of gum arabic }each dissolved in 10 oz. of water

Add 154 grains of Venice turpentine, 154 grains of ethereal oil of turpentine and 309 grains of pure spirit. Diluted with water to the desired consistency it is used for grounds and to consolidate paintings.

Non-putrefying Glue

Soak 3¼ oz. of isinglass in 19 oz. of water and melt; then add 3¼ oz. of white vinegar, using a double boiler. Add 3¼ oz. of alum and 8 oz. of spirit and allow to cook for fifteen minutes. When required dilute with water. (Remember that glues containing vinegar should not be mixed with temperas with a carbonate base.)

Starch and Turpentine Glue

This is an excellent glue which dries rapidly and is very suitable for priming. In 1¾ pts. of water boil

3¼ oz. of starch
1¾ oz. of isinglass
1¾ oz. of purified Venice turpentine.

Starch Glue

Mix and cook equal weights of water and starch. Dilute with hot water and make a transparent jelly. Rice starch makes the same type of glue.

Casein Glue

Take 309 grains of casein and 62 grains of borax, and shake up in a few spoonfuls of water. After a few hours add enough water to form a dense syrup.

Chipolin Glue (for Wood and Cardboard)

In 2½ pts. of water boil three heads of garlic and a handful of wormwood leaves until the liquid is reduced to 1¾ pts. Strain through linen and add ¾ pt. of parchment glue, a handful of salt, 1½ gills of vinegar and boil.

This glue is used to size panels and cardboards. It disinfects them and gives a good surface to hold a gesso and glue ground. It was popular in France during the 18th century for priming lacquered panels.

Other recipes for glue are to be found in the chapter on *Tempera* (p. 129).

OILS

All text-books for artists divide the oils used for painting into: *fatty or fixed oils* (of vegetable origin); *essential oils* (extracted by distillation from petroleums or plants); *empirheumatic oils* (obtained from wax and camphor); *animal oils* (of which only egg oil, tested by Vibert and Eibner, is of interest).

FIXED OILS

These oils oxidize in contact with the air. This process can be hastened through the use of siccatives but these may have bad effects on the picture as they may cause darkening, especially if they contain lead. Oils should be purified, that is, freed from mucilage and acidity. Acid oil is dangerous, especially for colours containing alumina, such as the lakes: it forms a tacky, non-drying substance, difficult to spread with a brush.

Before using the oil it is advisable to test it with a piece of litmus paper which will turn red if there is any acidity.

Fixed oils are affected by the moisture in the air, as was proved by Prof. Laurie's experiment. He mixed some transparent crystals of copper sulphate both with fixed oils and varnish. These crystals are a blue-green colour owing to the water they contain. He began by removing all traces of water by pulverizing the sulphate and exposing it to heat, thus obtaining a white powder. Painting with this substance he obtained a white opaque enamel. The painting was then exposed to steam and in a short while the sulphate, combining with the water, went back to its original blue-green colour. He repeated the experiment with the powder mixed with varnish and found that even varnish was affected by humidity. On the other hand resins and balsams dissolved in essential oil resist the action of damp for a long time.

For this reason unstable pigments were protected in ancient times by the addition of a little balsam (Venice turpentine and Strasbourg turpentine).

NUT OIL

This is cold pressed from well-dried nuts. It dries more slowly than linseed oil but has the advantage of not turning yellow so easily. It is specially suitable for use with the lakes.

LINSEED OIL

For painting one should use cold pressed linseed oil. It dries quickly but goes yellow in time and easily turns rancid. It forms a layer of solid paint which has less tendency to crack than that made with nut or poppy oil.

POPPY OIL

This oil is extracted from poppy seeds, and is the least

59

viscous and cleanest of all oils. Although it takes a very long time to dry, it has the advantage of not turning rancid easily. It is excellent in emulsions with glues for tempera. This oil is hot pressed and all mucilage eliminated. It is discoloured by colours with a lead base.

OTHER FIXED OILS

Almond and *olive* oils should be avoided as they do not dry. Nor have good results been obtained from the oils of *sunflower* (used in Russia), *soy bean*, *Chinese wood* and *hemp*.

Castor oil is used by some artists in very small quantities to give elasticity to spirit varnishes and to dammar and mastic varnishes. The proportion is from 2 to 5 per cent.

Stand oil, or polymerized oil, is prepared (especially in Holland) by boiling linseed oil so as to free it from air, or by drying it in the sun without allowing it to oxidize. This oil is thick and dries slowly. It is excellent in emulsions with yolk of egg or diluted with essential oil of turpentine.

It increases the brilliance of varnishes and media made with a Venice or Strasbourg turpentine base since it blends well with these ingredients.

TESTING FIXED OILS [1]

Very often the linseed, nut and poppy oils sold to the artist are adulterated with poor quality seed oils or with fish or mineral oils. To test the purity of an oil place a small quantity in a glass test tube and examine it as follows:

First test: Place 3 or 4 drops of oil in spirit to which a little potash has been added. Bring the liquid to the boil and add about $\frac{1}{4}$ cu. in. of distilled water. If the solution remains clear the oil is pure.

Second test: Boil 5 parts of oil with 1 of washing soda. If any fish oil is present the liquid will turn red.

Third test: Put 3 or 4 drops of sulphuric acid into a small quantity of oil. Shake the test tube well and leave to settle. The liquid will separate forming two layers, one oily and one acid.

If it is real linseed oil and pure, the oily layer will be orange. If it is poppy oil, it will turn dark cherry red; if it is nut oil a darker red. The acid layer must remain unchanged and colourless.

PREPARATION OF FIXED OILS

Leonardo recommends that when preparing nut oil the skin of the kernel should be removed since 'this skin separates from the oil and floats to the surface of the painting causing changes'.[2]

He also describes the preparation of oil for tempering colours: 'Choose the best nuts, shell them and put them to soak in clear water in a glass jar, changing the water whenever you see it becoming clouded. It may be necessary to do this seven and even eight times. After a time the nuts disintegrate when stirred and form a milky pap. Place this in dishes in the open air and you will see the oil float to the surface. To collect it in a perfectly pure and clean condition, twist pieces of cotton wool and place one end in the oil, letting the other end hang over the edge of the plate above a vessel placed about two inches below the level of the oil in the plate. Little by little the oil will rise through the cotton wool and will drip into the vessel. This oil will be most pure, the sediment remaining in the dish. All oils are naturally clear and it is the manner of extraction which may change them.'[3]

Oil for Painting

'To make oil suitable for painting purposes:[4] 1 part of oil, 1 part of "first" turpentine and 1 part of "second" turpentine.' To make this mixture of oil and resin recommended by Leonardo, extract and purify oil according to the preceding recipe and add 1 part of distilled turpentine and 1 part of Venice turpentine rather than the 'second' turpentine which is merely soft pitch. Leave the mixture in the sunlight to amalgamate well. This oil gives an enamel-like quality to colours and dries quickly. The resin content protects various pigments which cannot be used with oil in a pure state.

61

'Now I will also here teach how all colours are to be tempered with oil, better and (more) masterly than other painters; and in the first place how the oil is to be prepared for the purpose, so that it may be limpid and clear, and that it may dry quickly. . . .

'Take the oil of linseed or of hempseed, or old nut oil, as much as you please, and put therein bones that have been long kept, calcined to whiteness, and an equal quantity of pumice stone; let them boil in the oil, removing the scum. Then take the oil from the fire, and let it well cool; and if it is in quantity above a quart, add to it an ounce of white copperas; [5] this will diffuse itself in the oil, which will become quite limpid and clear. Afterwards strain the oil through a clean linen cloth into a clean basin, and place it in the sun for four days. Thus it will acquire a thick consistence, and also become as transparent as a fine crystal. And this oil dries very fast, and makes all colours beautifully clear, and glossy besides.

'All painters are not acquainted with it; from its excellence it is called oleum preciosum, since half an ounce is well worth a shilling; and with (this) oil all colours are to be ground and tempered. All colours should be ground stiffly, and then tempered to a half liquid state, which should be neither too thick nor too thin.

'These are the colours which should be tempered with oil: vermilion, minium, lake brasil, red, blue bice, azure, indigo, and also black, yellow, orpiment, red orpiment, ochre, face brown-red, verdigris, green bice, and white lead. These are the oil colours and no more. Here observe that these colours are to be well ground in the oil and at (last) with every colour mix three (that is, a few) drops of varnish, and then place every colour by itself in a clean cup, and paint what you please.' (Eastlake's translation of the 15th-century manuscript.)

Daniel Seghers' Oil for Painting

The characteristic crystal-clear brilliance of his colours was due to the use of nut oil boiled with a little Strasbourg turpentine.

Old and thickened oil dries better and is more solid than when new and fluid.

'*1* Purified oil $\frac{1}{2}$ part⎫
Water $\qquad\frac{1}{2}$ part⎭ Place in glass trough in the sun.

2 When, after a few days' exposure, a sediment forms, remove the oil and clean the trough.

3 Repeat (*2*) about six times.'[6]

HOW TO REMOVE MUCILAGE AND IMPURITIES

FROM FIXED OILS

Experience has shown that mucilage is the main cause of the yellowing of oils. The excellence of the oil is in proportion to its age and to the absence of mucilage. To purify the oil place it in a large glass funnel with a tap at the end of the tube. Fill it with two thirds of hot water and one third of oil. Stir the liquid several times a day and allow it to settle. Remove the water and repeat the procedure twice.[7]

A little white sand, bread crumbs,[8] or salt added will act as a filter and absorb impurities. Calcined bone [9] and magnesia will increase its drying power.

H. Hubbard's Recipe [10]

Put the oil in a large bottle and mix with an equal volume of salt water. Leave in the open air for about three weeks, shaking well from time to time. Allow to rest for a further three weeks and decant the oil which by this time will be pure.

According to the Heraclius MS [10]

'Put a moderate quantity of lime in the oil and heat it, continually skimming it. Add ceruse to it according to the quantity of oil, and put it in the sun for a month or more stirring it frequently, and note that the longer it remains in the sun the better it will be. Then strain and mix and keep the colours with it.' (Mrs Merrifield's translation.)

H. Hubbard's Recipe with Water and White Copperas [10]

1 White Copperas   1 oz. } Dissolved.
   Pure water   3 oz. }
2 Add 2 lb. Poppy Oil (or other Fixed Oil).
3 Heat the mixture over a fire until the water is reduced to about two thirds or one half its volume.
4 Pour the oil into a dish and leave it for eight days.
5 Draw the oil from the surface with a spoon or skimmer, and place it in a bottle. Expose this to the light for three weeks.

RECIPES FOR BLEACHING OIL

Van Dyck's Method [11]

1 Yolks of two eggs}
   Aqua vitae ½ pt. } Shake well together in a stoppered bottle.
   Linseed oil 1 qt. }
2 Place the filled bottle in the shade and allow the mixture to settle.
3 When bleached, separate the oil from the sediment.

Dietrich Heuss's Method [11]

1 White lead (well ground)} Heat together for about an hour.
   Purified linseed oil   } Stir.
2 Remove the oil from the fire and allow it to settle.
3 The following day the oil will be almost colourless.

Sir Arthur Church's Method

Place in a small linen bag 54 grains of dry powdered manganese borate and hang it in a large carafe containing about 4 pts. and 1 gill of good linseed oil so that the bag is completely covered. Cover the carafe with a wad of cotton wool and leave in a warm place. In two weeks the oil acquires strong drying power.

64

If a glass carafe is used and placed in the sunlight, the oil will be better as it will be lighter. When ready decant into small bottles which should be kept corked.

HOW TO REMOVE ACIDITY FROM FIXED OILS

Oil which has been washed in water and exposed to the sun and to the air becomes very rancid.

WITH ASHES [12]

On clear, warm oak ashes pour four times as much oil. Leave for about a fortnight and strain.

WITH MAGNESIA [12]

Gently boil the oil for three to four hours, removing scum as it forms. Add calcined magnesia by degrees and boil for an hour. Remove the oil from the fire and leave in a covered vessel for three months.

OTHER OILS

ESSENTIAL OILS

Since the excess of slow-drying fixed oils turns certain colours such as white, blue and green, opaque and dark, it is preferable to use essential oils which are lighter. They are very transparent and if properly purified evaporate completely.

The resin-oil temperas of the Venetian and Flemish masters were thinned with essential oils. Pliny and Dioscorides already refer to the distillation of turpentine. In the 8th century Marcus Graccus described the manner of extracting this essential oil.

ETHEREAL OIL OF TURPENTINE

This is a colourless liquid with a characteristic smell. It is obtained by distilling turpentine, rosin and other resins extracted from coniferous trees. A drop of good turpentine essence placed on a sheet of paper will evaporate without leaving a grease mark.

It mixes well with the fixed oils and is the best solvent for resins. It should be kept in a dark place, well stoppered. The residue left after distillation is pitch. Essence of turpentine should be used only for a short time after rectification or it will leave a viscous residue which does not dry and goes black. This oil can be clarified without a second distillation, by adding quicklime and frequently shaking the bottle. Sir Arthur Church recommends keeping a piece of quicklime in every bottle of turpentine as this will hold the sediment formed by yellowed and thickened parts.

Ethereal Oil of Lavender

This is obtained by distilling the blossoms of lavender and spike in water. It is yellowish in colour and has a very strong smell.

A substitute obtained by repeatedly distilling turpentine over lavender blossoms is very often sold under this name. This substitute turns yellow and does not dry as slowly as genuine lavender oil. Spike and lavender oils are most useful for thinning oil varnishes and for emulsion temperas.

Oil of Cloves

This oil goes very yellow. The ethereal oils of lavender and rosemary are preferable since they yellow only very slightly. *Rosemary oil* acts as a solvent for resins and is often used to prepare amber varnish.

Oil of Lemon

This amalgamates perfectly with fatty varnishes without heating, making them very fluid so that the artist can use them in extremely thin coats. It also acts as a siccative in mixtures. It dissolves dry colours and gives cohesion to the various coats of paint.

66

ETHERIC PETROLEUM

This is a mixture of light hydrocarbides, obtained from the first products of petroleum distillation. It is colourless and highly inflammable. It should be kept in well-sealed bottles and used with caution.

Petroleum used in its natural state turns colours black as it leaves a viscous fatty residue. The colours ground with pure petroleum—used by the painters Fernbach and Ludwig—proved unsatisfactory after a very short time. It was used by the Persians and later by the Byzantines.

To purify petroleum for painting purposes first add sulphuric acid and then washing soda. Water should then be added and the mixture well emulsified. A viscous deposit is left.

Rectified *oil of petroleum* penetrates between the various coats of paint and increases cohesion. It should be used with the Vibert varnishes (made with normal resin and oils of petroleum) and not with varnishes made with essential or fixed oils since it will not amalgamate with them but cause precipitation, forming a viscid substance which refuses to dry. It does not turn yellow if mixed with fixed oils.

PETROLEUM DERIVATIVES

White spirits are obtained from petroleum, and vary in volatility: some evaporate in a few seconds and others take several hours or even days. Specially treated they become absolutely colourless. When carefully prepared they do not leave any residue. They rapidly penetrate coats of paint and carry all the resins and oils contained right into the interstices where the previous oil has dried, giving greater cohesion to the various coats of paint.

If the colours contain wax this will help the top layers of brush strokes to amalgamate readily with the undercoat. Since petroleum contains parts which never evaporate, this oil must be refined by very accurate distillation.

Maurice Busset recommends *benzine* as a thinner for oil colours if a quickly drying, mat surface is desired. Its use as a thinner is still in the experimental stage.

Vaseline Oil

This oil should be avoided as it does not dry. Xylol, tetraline, dekalin, which are all petroleum derivatives, are only of interest to the restorer as they are useful for cleaning and restoring; if used as thinners for oil colours they produce dull surfaces of uncertain solidity. Oils extracted from *copaiva* and *elemi* turn yellow in a short time and become a brownish paste; so do oils extracted from pine, fir and pinaster trees. They have all the drawbacks of fixed oils without their qualities.

EMPIRHEUMATIC OILS

Wax Oil

Serves as a thinner for cold wax mural painting. It is obtained by placing equal parts of yellow wax and quicklime into a retort and heating until the contents become red. A little water will flow out at first and then the volatile oil will follow.

ANIMAL OILS

Egg Oil

This is obtained by mashing the yolks of boiled eggs and placing them in sulphuric ether to dissolve their oil content which can be collected when the ether has evaporated. This oil does not turn rancid like other animal oils; it can melt various resins without heat and makes an excellent varnish which, however, is not a good drier. Egg oil mixed with oil varnish produces a brilliant tempera. If mixed with varnish in equal parts it produces a paste which is too dense and cracks. It should be thinned with oil of spike if one wishes to work slowly, and with oil of turpentine if one wants it to dry quickly.

Egg oil can also dissolve copal, affecting it far less than other oils since both have the same boiling temperature (735° F.) and there is no loss of weight. It does not tend to turn yellow and stands up well to damp. It combines excellently with the various petroleum oils.

Hiler, (op. cit., page 158) gives another way of extracting egg oil:

> 'Yolks of eggs (about 250)   5·0 parts
> Distilled water   0·3 part

Beat this together, and heat the mass with constant stirring in a dish on the water bath, or double boiler, until it thickens and a sample exhibits oil upon pressing between the fingers. Squeeze out between hot plates, mix the turbid oil contained with 0·05 part of dehydrated Glauber's salts, shake repeatedly and finally allow to settle. The oil, which must be decanted clear from the sediment, gives a yield of at least 0·5 part of egg oil.'

5

Resins, Balsams, Gums and Waxes

Resins and balsams, as well as gums, are products of natural or artificial secretion by certain plants. The only wax used in painting is beeswax, although there are vegetable and mineral waxes too.

Liquid resins are generally known as balsams. They mix well with ethereal oils and amalgamate with yolk of egg to give tenacity to temperas.

THE VARIOUS KINDS

BALSAMS AND RESINS

Natural turpentine is secreted by various coniferous trees. It consists of two resins and one ethereal oil. *Strasbourg turpentine* (called *olio d'abezzo* in Italy), thickened and bleached, was formerly used to make invaluable varnishes.

Venice turpentine which dries slowly comes from larch (*larix europoea*). If inadequately purified it darkens the picture and produces cracks. Although it dissolves easily, when stiffened and purified it is no longer fragile. Mixed with a fixed oil or an oil of petroleum it becomes very cohesive. It gives stability to verdigris and other pigments which generally deteriorate in contact with the air. It makes mastic varnish more elastic and less susceptible to damp.

Venice turpentine facilitates the process of melting amber and the varnish obtained is more limpid and less coloured.

The *resin balsam* recommended by Lucanus as a medium for colours is only turpentine made viscous through long exposure to the air. This is the fatty essence used in decorating pottery, but it is not wholly reliable as it tends to darken when used with oil paints and varnishes.

Elemi is a semi-transparent resin similar to wax. In former times artists used a variety which came from Ethiopia and India. This resin is softened by the heat of the fingers and easily becomes tacky. The best quality is imported from the Philippine Islands. It is soluble in fixed and volatile oils, spirit and fats. When distilled it yields an aromatic oil with a vitreous and brittle residue. A very small amount (one eighth of the total volume) is blended with varnishes and essences to prevent cracks and 'bloom'. It is used for wax painting and for restoring pictures.

Mastic contains two resins (one soluble and one insoluble in spirit) and some oil which evaporates very little. It produces an excellent varnish for pictures especially if treated with essence of turpentine without heat.

Sandarac is produced by *callitris quadrivalvis*. The best is the pale yellow variety which splinters like glass and is transparent. It was formerly used for fatty varnishes and was confused with amber. Early writers also confused it with the resin of the juniper.

Copaiva balsam comes mainly from Brazil, and consists of 50 per cent resin and 50 per cent essential oil. The oil evaporates completely leaving no sediment; the resin is fluid, very transparent and is not affected by variations in temperature. To test for purity, place a drop on a sheet of ordinary paper. Dry in mild heat: only a hard and shining skin should remain with no trace of grease. Copaiva gives elasticity to varnishes and is most useful for restoring, especially for cleaning pictures.

Karabè or *amber* or *succinite* is a fossil resin. To find a way of dissolving amber without heat is for painters and restorers like the search for the philosopher's stone was for the alchemists. Some restorers claim that they have found the secret, but chemists and scientists hold that it is impossible.

Amber is formed by three different resins, succinic acid, an essential oil and a small quantity of mineral substances. The firm of Block of Antwerp prepares several varnishes which are among the clearest and most solid. Amber can be mixed with colours and temperas but is not recommended as a final varnish for in time it becomes hard and dark.

There are three types: hard, medium and soft. The hard copals produce the most solid varnishes and are more difficult to melt than the soft ones. Varnishes made with copal give great brilliance to colours. They were much used by Cuyp, Teniers, and other Flemish masters.

HARD COPALS

Hard *animé* becomes soft in oil of turpentine but does not dissolve either with heat or without. Subjected to a special treatment it becomes soluble in spirit.

SOFT COPALS

Animé is a soft, opaque, friable resin with a bitter taste. It dissolves in oil of turpentine over heat but is almost insoluble in spirit; unsuitable for painting.

Oriental animé, which is drop shaped, is very brittle. It becomes soft with heat and can be spun into long, thin threads; it is partially soluble in spirit.

Angola copal is orange-red in colour; *Benguela copal* is believed to be a fossil resin.

The copal from *Sierra Leone* varies in colour from pale green to yellow. It is almost entirely soluble without heat in spirit and in oil of turpentine.

Manila copal is found in large yellow-brown lumps.

Dammar dissolves almost completely without heat in oil of turpentine. It consists of two resins and a gum and contains water. It is used for varnishes mixed with resins (such as elemi and copaiva) to counteract brittleness. Dammar dissolved in benzine makes very good fixatives for drawings and pastels. (The proportion is 2 per cent dammar.) A thicker dammar varnish is used for varnishing temperas.

LAC

Lac comes from India and is secreted by *ficus indica, ficus religiosa,* etc., wherever the bark is pierced by the insect *coccus lacca.*

Besides resin it contains a colouring, a wax and a gluten; it is used for spirit varnishes. It is easily bleached but darkens rapidly. Artists who use it to varnish temperas and water-colours are merely condemning their work to darken rapidly.

Benzoin comes from Asia, and is a milky juice which becomes solid and coloured in contact with air. Dissolved in spirit and thinned with water, it can be used in tempering colours instead of milk of figs, but the results are doubtful.

Dragon's blood is a pinky-brown resin, soluble in spirit, which was formerly used as a colour and as a colorizer for certain varnishes. It has little stability, and even in Cennini's day painters were warned to use it with caution.

Asphalt is a fossil resin. Its many defects have already been mentioned when bitumen as a colour was discussed.[1]

GUMS

Gum arabic and *Senegal gum* are used to agglutinate pigments for watercolours. It is difficult to find them in a pure state as they are often adulterated with dextrin. A little boracic acid keeps them from deteriorating. They are often added to glues to strengthen them.

Sarcocolla is a gum resin soluble both in water and spirit. It was already used for painting in Pliny's day. It is bleached and sarcocollin extracted. The watercolour paints prepared with it are rich in tone and dry quickly since they dissolve both in spirit and in water mixed with spirit.

By tempering colours with sarcocollin it becomes possible to glaze gouache paintings whereas it is impossible to do this with plain watercolours.[2] This resin is extracted by making an infusion of sarcocolla (exuded by *poenea mucronata*) in boiling spirit. The liquid is strained and then exposed to light and sun as much as possible. A varnish can be made by dissolving sarcocollin in 60° proof spirit, straining and bleaching it and adding a few drops of glycerine (Vibert).

Tragacanth is similar to sarcocolla and many people confuse them. Reynolds used grounds of gesso and tragacanth which cracked as this gum produces too rigid a mixture. Tragacanth can easily be emulsified with oils; a light solution is used for making fixatives for drawings and pastels and it replaces sarcocolla.

Cherry gum—already mentioned by Theophilus—can also be emulsified with oils and balsams. It was used for temperas and miniatures.

WAXES

Wax is secreted by bees. Bleached beeswax is used for varnishes and in encaustic painting.

It is partially soluble in boiling spirit, completely soluble in ether, in oil of turpentine, in benzine and in carbon sulphide. It was used to agglutinate colours in the ancient technique of encaustic painting and has been used in the various revivals of this technique.[3] A light coat of wax varnish protects the final varnishes of a painting. To bleach and prepare wax, see page 157.

PARAFFIN WAX

Paraffin is a mixture of heavy hydrocarbides, a by-product of the distillation of coal and petroleum. It is soluble in all resin solvents. It was sometimes used as a tempera and as a protective varnish for mural paintings, but the results may be considered rather unsatisfactory.

It was also used in several revivals of encaustic painting by artists who considered it more permanent than beeswax.

SYNTHETIC RESINS

Some firms, like Talens, use synthetic resins for making very light varnishes. These have given satisfactory results.

HOW TO PURIFY RESINS [4]

Resins are purified of (*a*) water, (*b*) crystalline aromatic acids and (*c*) volatile hydrocarbon terpenes, by the following method:

74

1 Powder the resin and mix the particles in a glass retort.
2 Pass a current of steam into the mixture to distil over the terpenes and volatile acids.
3 Add Carbonate of Soda (1 part) to the resinous contents of the retort (100 parts).
4 Shake the mixture and allow it to cool.
5 Filter through a cloth.
6 Wash the purified resin with distilled water.
7 Dry, first in the air, then in a water-oven.

RECIPES FOR TURPENTINE

To prepare thick clear Venice and Strasbourg turpentine, place the pitch in a glass or porcelain vessel, filling only half. Add an extremely pure and strained solution of potash (one quarter potash, three quarters water) and boil continuously for one hour. Remove the pan from the fire and add a little cold water. This will make the turpentine solidify and form a deposit in the bottom of the vessel. Boil the turpentine another four or five times, separating it with cold water every time. This turpentine can now be stored; it is free from fats and very clear.

Another system is to place some solid turpentine in an earthenware vessel, half filling it. Place on an electric ring and when the turpentine swells, plunge the pan into cold water to stop the cooking process.

Heat and cool in this way several times until the turpentine no longer swells in contact with heat. Then pour it into cold water and separate it later.

6

Varnishes and Varnishing

Various types of varnish are used in painting: oil, ethereal, mixed, spirit and albumen varnishes. The artist should avoid those made with elastic gum which darken and become brittle, and those containing cellulose, which have not yet been thoroughly tested.[1]

OIL VARNISHES

These are the most damp-proof, but also the most dense and coloured. They dry more slowly than the others and can therefore be used even on recently painted pictures. They are usually made with amber and copal dissolved in fixed oil. Avoid the cheap types which are made with sandarac, incense and bitumen as they darken the picture.

RESIN ETHEREAL VARNISHES

These generally consist of mastic and dammar dissolved in essential oil of turpentine and petroleum. They dry very rapidly and should not be used over fresh paint as they may cause cracks. A good rule is to wait a whole year before varnishing a picture. If 10 per cent of *Stand Oil* or elemi resin is added the varnishes acquire greater elasticity and resistance to damp and can be used in the same manner as the oil or mixed types.

MIXED VARNISHES

These are generally made with hard resins dissolved in oil

over heat and diluted with essential oils while still warm. They are very solid and resist the damp. A very good mixed varnish was *Ez Zendjabari*, which was tested by the painter Dinet.

SPIRIT VARNISHES

These varnishes are generally used as fixatives for water-colour and tempera paintings, but as they have a solvent action they should never be applied to oil paintings. They produce a shiny surface, dry quickly, yellow badly if they contain lac, and deteriorate in the presence of damp. The use of spirit varnishes originated in the Far East and reached Europe at the end of the 17th century, and became widespread in the 18th, when Jesuit missionaries brought the raw materials from China and taught their use. This type of varnish was applied to prints, maps, furniture, walls and even pictures, but after a few years the temporary gloss vanished leaving a brown and opaque patina. If freed from wax, lac can be used to make spirit varnishes; these are still in an experimental stage but are already proving valuable. Restorers have found them very useful in repairing frescoes damaged by damp as up to the present no other resin has been found capable of hardening in damp places.

The trade now offers light varnishes made of mastic, spirit and lavender which replace those made with lac or sandarac which have proved dangerous. They should be used only for tempera, gouache and watercolour paintings.

ALBUMEN VARNISH

From earliest times painters recommended a varnish consisting of the liquid exuded when white of egg is beaten stiff with a little water and left in a cool place for several hours. It was used as a temporary varnish and removed before applying the final varnish about one year after finishing the picture. This is one of the most harmful types of varnish as in time it becomes hard, opaque and very difficult to remove, and does not protect

77

the painting from atmospheric effects. When careless painters have not removed it before applying the final varnish, the pictures have cracked and flaked.

RECIPES FOR FATTY VARNISHES

Amber Varnish

De Mayerne's method is to make an infusion of pulverized amber in pure spirit. This is left to stand for a long time depending on season, climate, weather: the longer the resin is allowed to stand, the better. A couple of months exposed to sunshine or in a warm place gives good results. It is then made to precipitate by means of distilled water. The powder obtained will dissolve easily in oil of spike at a moderate heat.

A little clear thickened oil may be added. Amber varnishes often darken and burn when melted in oil at a high temperature. Before dissolving amber in oil it is advisable to pulverize it and leave it for a few weeks in an infusion of oil of rosemary and turpentine.

Another method for Amber Varnish[2]

'*1* Dissolve 1 lb. of pulverized amber resin over a charcoal fire.
2 When melted, pour the amber on to an iron plate and reduce it again to powder.
3 Place the powdered amber in an earthen vessel containing linseed oil which has previously been boiled and prepared with litharge.
4 Complete the solution by adding oil or turpentine.'

Alternatively, take 6 parts of melted clear amber and 20 parts of clear cooked oil. Boil together and stir well.

To facilitate the Fusion of Amber

Leave the finely pulverized amber in an infusion of rosemary oil. Make into a paste by adding pure spirit, and when dry make an infusion with oil of turpentine. Grind finely and add some more oil of turpentine, warm, and some Venice turpentine. The resulting liquid will be dense with very little colour.

Libavious's Method for Amber Varnish [3]

1 Linseed oil   3 lbs.⎫
   Burnt alum   ½ oz. ⎬ Mix and boil until it ceases to
   Purified turpentine ½ oz. ⎪ froth.
   Garlic   ½ oz.⎭

2 In another vessel place

   Amber resin   1 lb. ⎫ Melt by heating and stir whilst
   A little oil   ⎭ hot to prevent carbonization.

3 Add mixture 2 to mixture 1 and boil to the consistency of varnish.

Copal Varnish [4]

Copal resin	30 parts
Drying oil	25 parts
Spirits of turpentine	50 parts

1 Place the copal in a vessel capable of holding seven times as much. Fuse it rapidly.
2 Add the drying oil which has been heated to nearly boiling point.
3 Well mix copal and drying oil. Allow mixture to cool a little.
4 Add turpentine.
5 Well mix and cover until temperature drops to 140° F.
6 Strain.

Gerome's Recipe for Copal Varnish [4]

Copal resin mixed with⎫
   Durozier oil   4 parts⎪
Rectified essential oil   ⎬ Mixed by pouring the essential oil
   (e.g. Oil of turpen- ⎪ into the copal mixture and stirring.
   tine)   3 parts⎭

79

SPIRIT VARNISH [4]

Melt over heat:

Strong alcohol	32 parts
Pure Mastic resin	4 parts
Sandarac resin	3 parts
Clear Venice turpentine	2 parts
Coarsely powdered glass	4 parts

ESSENTIAL OIL VARNISHES

DE MAYERNE'S VARNISH

Van Dyck made this varnish by mixing even quantities of essential oil of turpentine and purified Venice turpentine. When binding colours add oil of turpentine in the proportion of one half or one third of the volume of the varnish.

MAESTRO ADAMO'S VARNISH

We owe to De Mayerne [5] the recipe for this varnish which dries in three hours:

Very clear Venice turpentine	$1\frac{1}{2}$ parts
Pulverized mastic	$1\frac{1}{2}$ parts

Melt in a double boiler. When melted add 4 parts of very pure spirits of previously warmed turpentine.

MASTIC VARNISH

This is the recipe suggested by Secco Suardo: 'Take the tears of mastic, wash in water and dry in the sun. Choose the tears for their clearness and transparency and pulverize them in a mortar.

'Put equal quantities of turpentine and mastic in a bottle and leave in the sun, shaking from time to time. If the weather becomes damp, take the bottle indoors or the varnish will become muddy. After a week strain through cotton. At first the liquid which comes through is not clear. As soon as it becomes clear place a funnel underneath to collect the strained liquid. The resulting varnish is extremely clear and will not form a sediment. Add one eighth of bleached oil and leave in the sun to clarify completely.

'If a final varnish is required, dilute this liquid with an equal amount of turpentine; add a larger amount of essential oil if it is to be used as a thinner for oil colours.'

One eighth of elemi resin may be added instead of bleached oil.

Mastic Varnish

Sir Arthur Church gives the following recipe: [6] 'Dissolve 14 parts of ground mastic mixed with 6 parts of fine sand and 44 parts of spirits of turpentine by heating in a water-bath. Pour off into a bottle, cork, and leave to stand until it becomes perfectly clear.' In order to make the varnish less brittle, a little Venice turpentine, Canada balsam, or Elemi resin, or a very little linseed oil may be added. The advantage of mastic as a picture varnish is the ease with which it can be removed without injury to the painted surface below by friction or solvents.

Dammar Varnish

This is made in the same way as mastic varnish. Even after much straining it never becomes completely clear, but when applied to paintings it becomes transparent and does not turn yellow. It is however very soft and friable; even touching it with a finger leaves a mark. In contact with water or with damp it turns white or opaque. It loses these defects if mixed with an equal amount of amber varnish since the latter corrects its friability and prevents oxidation.

Tingry's Varnish

The ingredients are:

Carefully selected and washed mastic 11½ oz.
Venice turpentine 1½ „

Powdered glass	$4\frac{3}{4}$ oz.
Ethereal oil (turpentine, spike)	2·2 lbs.
Powdered camphor	$\frac{1}{2}$ oz.

Put the ingredients into a *bain-Marie* still and heat. The glass dust falls to the bottom forming a layer between the source of heat and the resinous substance, and prevents the latter from sticking to the bottom and becoming coloured.

ROMAIN'S PICTURE VARNISH[7]

This is used especially to varnish temperas.
Dissolve the following in *bain-Marie*:

Choice mastic	13 oz.
Camphor	231 grains
Alcohol	16 oz.
Venice turpentine	$1\frac{1}{2}$,,
Essence of turpentine	$\frac{1}{2}$,,

OPAQUE VARNISH

Melt 1 part of pure beeswax in 3 parts of oil of turpentine. Take 1 part of this solution and add to it 6 parts of mastic or dammar varnish. This is suitable for paintings on a large scale to avoid the large shiny surfaces which occur when the usual varnishes are used. This varnish is however very difficult to handle.

VARNISHES WITH A DISTILLED PETROLEUM BASE

ARMENINI VARNISH[8]

'Some therefore took *olio d'abezzo chiaro* (Strasbourg turpentine) and melted it in a small vessel over a low fire; once melted, they removed the pan from the fire and immediately added an equal quantity of *olio di sasso* (petroleum). Working this by hand they spread it evenly over the picture which had previously been put to warm in the sun. This is held to be the thinnest and most glossy of all varnishes.

'I have seen it used throughout Lombardy by the best artists and I have been told that this is what Correggio and the Parmeggiani used.'

Verri took up this recipe and experimented with it (op. cit., p. 138).

MASTIC AND RECTIFIED PETROLEUM VARNISH

Fill one quarter of a bottle with very pure and transparent mastic and fill up with filtered rectified petroleum. Leave in the sun and after some time decant and filter.

SICCATIVES AND ANTI-SICCATIVES

Galen observed the siccative and astringent properties of white lead and litharge. Heraclius also mentions white lead; minium (red lead) is quoted in 15th-century books of recipes; the Venetian masters added to their oil a powdered glass containing lead which is a harmless siccative. Verdigris, natural lead and litharge,[9] already in use at the end of the 16th century, very soon proved to be bad siccatives as they darkened and destroyed the painting. The siccative most used by the Flemish masters was white copperas.[10] Van Dyck used a siccative made of nut oil cooked with white lead: he only used it when fresh as it loses its properties in about a month. Tintoretto used verdigris as a siccative for some of the pictures which have turned darkest; this practice was taken to Spain by El Greco and is mentioned by Palomino. Litharge is to be avoided: it does not amalgamate with oil and separates, dragging the colour and forming lumps on the picture.

Courtrai siccative is the least harmful of those with a lead base (1 part of oxide of manganese, 3 parts of linseed oil). It should be clarified by the Dinet process, adding three times its volume of sun-bleached oil and leaving it for some months in an uncorked bottle in the light. A minimum application is sufficient to counteract the difference in the drying power of the various colours and to prevent cracking. By mixing $1\frac{1}{4}$ oz. of bleached Courtrai siccative with $1\frac{3}{4}$ pts. of rectified turpentine, a liquid with maximum siccative power is obtained. (Care should be taken not to alter this proportion, since if a greater amount is used the siccative will not help the colours to dry but will form a glutinous residue and cracks and darkening will follow.)

The Harlem and Flamand siccatives are not true siccatives but highly coloured oil varnishes. A good clear siccative mixture can be obtained by blending 2 parts of mastic varnish, 1 part of ethereal oil of turpentine and $\frac{1}{2}$ part of thickened linseed oil.

The use of anti-siccatives is quite as dangerous as that of siccatives: the substances generally used (olive oil, Vaseline oil, resin oil and copaiva) bring into the colours an element which does not dry and which forms a viscous deposit: the only harmless substance is absolutely pure alumina. Mixed with poppy oil a colourless paste is formed which gives solidity to the pigments with which it is mixed. Alumina should of course be used in very small doses.

HOW TO VARNISH A PICTURE

Lay the picture flat. Pour the varnish into a small dish and apply with a thick paint-brush (the type called *queue-de-morue* by the French). If an ethereal varnish is being used, work quickly with brush strokes touching, then cross the brush strokes to give an even coating. It is necessary to work in a dry room where there is no dust; the temperature must be between 60·6 and 80·3° F. The picture can be stood vertically after an hour.

A good way to obtain a thin and even coat is to let the oil varnish fall on to the painting drop by drop, spreading and smoothing it with the fingers as the old masters did. The warmth of the fingers is also very helpful.

As previously stated, ethereal varnishes should be applied at least one year after the completion of the painting; mixed or oil varnishes after at least six months.

The use of temporary varnishes containing albumen, sugar and honey to give brilliancy to the colours is very bad practice.

The dangers of these contracting and hygroscopic substances have already been pointed out.

Do not use clouded varnish. Mix it with a little brick dust and leave it in the sun until it becomes clear again.

It is not advisable to varnish a picture on a damp or rainy day or the varnish will blush and turn opaque. The old masters used to leave the picture in the sun for a while and then apply slightly warmed varnish. They thus avoided all danger of humidity and obtained thin coats of varnish which were extremely glossy and solid.

7
Gilding

The use of gold to enrich pictures dates from the earliest times throughout the East (China, Japan, India, Persia, Phoenicia) and later in Egypt, Greece and Rome. Gold was used for the first icons and during the Middle Ages when it was used for backgrounds and haloes, the latter very often in relief and studded with jewels. Gold was used for manuscripts and paintings of all types, including frescoes. Then, little by little, its use was dropped.

The methods are more or less the same, irrespective of country and period. Gold leaf is applied over a ground of bole or mordant, or the gold is ground to a very fine dust and mixed with vegetable juices and even with ink.[1]

Gold was beaten so finely that from one gold ducat enough leaf could be obtained to cover a surface from 64 to 86 sq. ft.

GILDING TECHNIQUES

Cennini's Technique

'Beat the white of an egg in a glazed basin until absolutely stiff... Pour over it a glass of water, not too full... Leave it to rest and exude overnight. Then grind as much bole as you can with this tempera... Gently rub the places where the gold is to be applied with a little sponge, not too moist... Then with a fairly small minever brush apply a first coat of this bole, thinned to the consistency of water, wherever you wish to gild, to the places you have previously rubbed with the sponge, taking care to get the bole smooth at the end of the

86

brush strokes. Let it stand for a long time; put some more of this bole into your little vessel and give it more body and colour for the second coat . . . Again let it stand; then add more bole to the little vessel and apply a third coat, taking care to spread it evenly with the brush . . . Add still more bole and apply a fourth coat . . . Cover the work with a cloth to protect it from dust. After some time brush the ground thoroughly and smooth out the lumps with a scraper, polish with a piece of linen, or better still, burnish with a tooth.

'Having thus prepared the ground, moisten it with water and a little white of egg, prepared as before, with a minever brush. Lay the sheet of gold leaf on a piece of paper of the same dimensions, handling it with tweezers and place it in position with the gold in contact with the moistened bole; when the gold clings well remove the paper with a rapid movement; press the gold down gently with a little piece of cotton wool and place the next pieces so that they overlap slightly; breathe along the lines where the pieces join so as to make the two sheets of gold leaf unite well and after placing every third piece, press down the first with cotton wool.'[2]

Method given by the Sloan MS

Prepare the ground with gesso, animal glue and albumen in equal quantity: apply three coats with a paint brush. Smooth and burnish the surface. Apply a little glue and delicately place the gold leaf in position pressing it down with a soft piece of cotton wool. When dry burnish with a dog's tooth.

Modern Method

Prime the panel with a mixture of 1 part of glue (prepared with 10 parts of glue to 100 parts of water) and 2 parts of plaster. Apply a second coat and smooth with fine emery paper and pumice.

After polishing well, paint the ground with a solution of alum to make it insoluble. Take some previously prepared bole (mixed with stag suet like the bole sold by Lefranc), make a paste by adding 40 per cent of water and apply a very light even coat. When dry, place the gold leaf in position and press with a very soft paint brush to make it adhere. When absolutely dry burnish the gold with an agate. Instead of the bole prepared with stag suet, Basch-Bordone advises one mixed with soap (231 grains of soap to 2·2 lbs. of bole); according to him the common bole should be kept covered with rain water for about one month.

Gold on Oil Colours

Gold can only be used when painting with oil colours on panels, canvases, copper slabs or walls (not for miniatures or watercolours). Some painters lay gold foil directly on to a preparation made of oil colours (generally yellow or orange), without any mordant, while it is still slightly tacky. The gold leaf is then pressed down with a cotton pad. Other painters mix gold powder with a special medium made with equal quantities of linseed oil and animé resin. Gilding of these types cannot be burnished like those made over a mordant and the surface is generally rather dull.

Gold with Mordant

This is a Byzantine technique. The Mount Athos MS tells us that either garlic juice or a wax emulsion was used. At times the mordant was made with an oil varnish.[3]

Gilding with a Mordant

Recipe by H. Sachs:

Venice turpentine	3 parts
Beeswax	5 parts
Suet	$\frac{1}{3}$ part

Melt over a low fire and apply with a soft brush so that it clings well. When only slightly tacky, apply the gold.

GOLD IN MURAL PAINTING

The painter Girolamo Curti (1576–1632), known as Dentone, used gold lines on frescoes and mural temperas which have withstood time very satisfactorily. He would first apply a mordant made of cooked oil, natural turpentine and yellow wax, blended and brushed on with a thin paint brush while still boiling hot wherever he intended to gild; he would then place the gold leaf in position. This mordant made it adhere well.

GILDING PARCHMENT

Ivrea MS

Ground gold mixed in a solution of cherry gum and vinegar.

'De Coloribus' by Heraclius

Gold was mixed with wine and then with gum and gall; when dry it was burnished with a dog's tooth.

Sloan MS

Temper some ochre with parchment glue mixed with alum and apply to the parchment with a brush. Then place gold leaf in position very carefully and leave it until it adheres perfectly and is completely dry.

Bologna MS [4]

One white of egg beaten with milk of figs, a walnut-sized amount of gum arabic and a little saffron. Leave to stand for one day. Wet the surface to be gilded with this mixture, place the gold leaf in position and press down with a piece of cotton wool. Allow to dry and burnish with a dog's tooth.

This is an excellent preparation. The manuscript also recommends a mixture of white honey, salt and warm water ground with gold leaf.

Gilding Parchment and Gold Inks

Perez de Vargas recommends a solution of gum arabic, copperas (sulphate of iron), white sugar and saffron in equal parts. This solution is used for writing: the gold leaf is then placed over the lettering and adheres to it. When dry it can be burnished.

Tools for Burnishing

Hard stones like agate are most commonly used. They are cut and polished and slightly curved like a dog's tooth. The stone is mounted on a wooden handle. Cennini recommends fine stones like topazes, garnets, sapphires and emeralds. These tools should be kept in a dry place and rubbed with a cloth so as to be warm and dry when used. The ancient manuals recommended burnishing tools made with the actual teeth of dogs, wolves, lions, leopards or other carnivorous animals.

Imitation Gold

From the very first attempts were made to imitate gold by dyeing silver or tin with yellow decoctions or varnishes. Pliny mentions a mixture made chiefly of bull's gall which made bronze look like gold. The Greek papyrus of Leyden (No. 10) gives a more complicated recipe: 1 part celandine, 1 part orpiment, 1 part pure gum and tortoise gall, 5 parts egg, 1 part saffron from Cilicia and resin. This liquid could be used for writing not only on parchment but also on marble.

We find a similar recipe in the *pseudo-Democritus*, in the *Compositiones ad tingenda*, in the *Mappae Claviculae*.

The artist should be wary of the gold paints offered for sale. They are often false and made with bronze dust and very soon turn dark, greenish and spotty.

PART TWO

THE ARTIST'S METHODS

8

Pastels

This technique is one of the simplest: the ground pigment, bound with a light glue and shaped into small crayons, preserves the brilliance of the colours almost perfectly. The softness of the pastels varies according to the amount of gluten contained: they are divided into hard, medium and soft, of which the soft are the most brilliant.

Apart from the preparations and grounds recommended below (pp. 93–4), the mixture used by Latour can be applied to bluish paper. This is composed of yellow ochre and yolk of egg and holds the colours extremely well.

Giuseppe Casciaro used very strong thin grey cardboard. This was prepared with a light coat of white dissolved in water and glue with the addition of sublimate (2 per cent) to prevent mildew.

Sartorio used to apply a coat of rather liquid oil colour, and then evenly sprinkle some very fine sand over this with a sieve. He let this preparation dry and then, while working, fixed the pastel with glue dissolved in water.

PREPARATION OF PASTELS

It is advisable for the artist to prepare his own crayons to obtain the full range of tints desired. The crayons prepared by the trade are often beautiful to look at, soft, smooth and pleasant to work with but do not stand up to the light. Very often the crayons offered for sale are merely little sticks of calcium carbonate dipped in aniline dyes which fade in a very short time. A crayon can be tested by dropping a small piece into pure spirit; if aniline is present the spirit will become tinted. When a crayon made with stable colours is immersed in spirit it does not colour the liquid in any way.

If the artist begins his picture with tempera colours and finishes it with pastels, he should bind his colours with the same medium he has used for his tempera although considerably thinned. If he fails to take this precaution the pastel colours will not adhere properly.

To make pastel crayons carefully wash, decant and grind the coloured powder and then add it to a base which is generally alumina, clay or magnesia. No gluten is necessary for the very light shades which contain a high proportion of clay: water, pure or mixed with a little skimmed milk, is sufficient as a binding medium. For the richer tones some artists prefer water mixed with pure spirit, a little glycerine and gum arabic; others prefer a 3 per cent solution of gum arabic and a little honey.

It is well to remember that an excess of glycerine or honey can produce mildew, while an excess of gum arabic makes the colours brittle.

Thinned temperas, and especially the emulsions containing beeswax, give an enamel brilliance to the colours and also softness of texture. It is not necessary to fix these pastels: in time the action of humidity in the air is sufficient for this purpose.

Certain artificial colours and some very hard ochres should be ground with pure spirit and then put to dry on a brick in the shade. By repeating this operation several times the colours become powdery and friable so that it is easy to knead them as described above.

First prepare the white base using clay which has been well washed, decanted and dried on pieces of earthenware. Some zinc white added to the clay will prevent the light colours from becoming transparent: the paste should be as compact as butter.

All simple colours are made in the same way and are combined with white in varying proportions to obtain several shades of the same colour. The lumps of colour are left on pieces of earthenware for some time to eliminate excess moisture: when the paste is no longer sticky to the touch it is placed on a slab of glass, which delays the drying process and allows it to be shaped into crayons. This is done by cutting little sticks of paste

94

and rolling them on the glass until they become cylindrical. They are then left on the glass until perfectly dry; without this precaution the pastels will be very brittle and crack easily. The paste can also be pressed into special moulds which have been slightly waxed or greased to prevent adhesion.

Do not mix the colour into too stiff a paste or it will crumble while drying. If when dry it proves to be too brittle or breaks, knead it once again with the same gluten. Nowadays finely ground coloured powders, well washed and purified, are to be found on the market, and with these pastel crayons can be easily and quickly made.

COLOURED PIGMENTS TO BE USED FOR PASTELS

Whites: Clay
Zinc white
Talcum powder
Alumina

Yellows: Zinc yellow
Cadmium yellow
Ultramarine yellow
Indian yellow
Mars yellow
Yellow ochres of various tones

Reds: Cadmium red
Madder and alizarin lakes
Red ochres
Mars red

Blues: Ultramarine
Cobalt blue
Cerulean blue

Greens: Oxides of chrome
Green earth

Browns: Umber, raw and burnt
Burnt sienna
Mars browns

95

Violet: Mars and cobalt violet

Blacks: Ivory black

HOW TO WORK WITH PASTELS

There are countless ways of using pastels: the classical technique followed by the 18th-century painters is still the most permanent and rational. In the first stages the colour is applied very thinly to avoid the brittleness caused by a heavy application. The first strokes are then delicately blended with the fingers and made to adhere to the paper; the final strokes are often not blended at all and remain visible.

The colours can be applied with the crayons or with the fingers; when there is a large surface to cover the side of the crayon is used. The first lay in is rubbed with the fingers or with a stump of chamois leather, paper, cork or the pith of the elder tree. Short, hard brushes can also be used for this purpose.

Wrong tones can be dusted off with a rag but care should be taken not to work the surface too much or the pastel will lose its velvety tones and freshness. If the paper becomes shiny through the use of over-hard crayons, roughen it with cuttlebone. Maxence used watercolours for priming and would then roughen the surface by rubbing it with ground calcined bone; other artists made a tempera foundation and finished it with pastels. The classical technique is still to draw directly with crayons on rough tinted paper and blend with the fingers. Russell,[1] who feared the effects of damp, used to glue his paper on to copper sheets or on to canvas and also prepared his own colours. His recipes were found in a little notebook: when he wanted a harder crayon, he substituted turpentine mixed with a little spirit for the thin glue to bind the colours. In Russell's pictures there are still transparent and lively tints, due to the presence of the small amount of resin contained in the raw turpentine with which he mixed his colours, but the clear opacity of ordinary pastels is absent. Where the colours were thickly applied the resin caused cracking, which appeared later.

FIXATIVES

The method of fixing pastels has always been the chief problem
for artists interested in this technique and has given rise to an
infinite number of recipes many of which are absurd. Latour
searched for a fixative all his life: even his contemporaries dis-
agreed on the results he obtained. The Abbé Le Blanc wrote
in 1747: 'Latour's varnish fixes the pastel without damaging
its freshness and it is to be hoped that his works will last as
long as it is humanly possible for the things of this world.'
During that same year Lieudé de Septmanville said the opposite
in his *Reflections of an Amateur*: 'Latour has done his utmost to
find a varnish. This has proved an utter failure and has cost
him the loss of a great number of pictures. It is known that he
has offered a large sum of money to a certain Charmenton who
has boasted that he is able to fix pastels.'

The 18th century produced many new recipes: a certain
Brée claimed that pastels fixed according to his method could
be rubbed with the fingers and even with pumice stone and be
none the worse. An anonymous recipe of the same century
advised covering the painting with very finely powdered gum
arabic, evenly distributed with a sieve. The painting was then
fixed by means of hot steam: a very difficult technique which
transformed the pastel into a gouache with dull tones. The
procedure commonly followed in the 18th century is the one
recommended by Loriot and by Prince San Severo.[2] Latour
himself followed this method which consisted in spraying the
picture with a mixture of water, glue and spirit, applied hot.

This problem of fixatives also interested those who worked
in pastel in the 19th century. Arnaldo Ferraguti found a
formula which allowed a great triptych ($5\frac{1}{2}$ yds. × 2 yds.)
executed in pastel to be exhibited without the protection of
glass. We do not know, however, what its condition was later on
or the formula of the fixative.

In a way the need to fix a pastel is a contradiction in terms
since the operation involves the insertion of a liquid between
the particles of pigment which alters the values of the picture,
and unless this liquid is perfectly transparent and colourless
the pastel darkens and the tone changes.

All fixatives with a lac and spirit base make the whites transparent and the colours dark; those with a glue base make the impasto look like tempera painting without the freshness characteristic of tempera.

If, therefore, solidity without loss of softness is desired, it is advisable to fix the first lay in and to place the final touches over this solid ground. Girardot has observed that pastels fix themselves spontaneously after a certain time through the effect of humidity in the air which acts on the glue used in priming and on the gum contained in the colours.

Many artists use gentler methods such as spraying the back of the picture with skimmed milk, but it should be remembered that certain colours are melted by the fixative and run into those of the undercoat so that the relationships and values of the tones are altered. For this reason it is always better, when the picture is to be fixed from the back, to use cold colours (less soluble) for the first coats, and to reserve the warm tints for the final work.

RECIPES FOR FIXATIVES

A very simple way to fix the colours is to spray the back of the picture with milk, pure water or very thin tempera. There are also solutions of glue, resin and others with a casein base.

GLUE SOLUTION

The following is the recipe given by Loriot, perhaps also used by Latour.

Melt about 150 grains of isinglass in about ¾ pt. of pure water in a double saucepan over a low fire. Strain through fine linen and pour on to a plate while hot.

Add 2 parts of wine spirit to 1 part of glue.

RESIN SOLUTIONS

Melt 31 grains of mastic in 3½ oz. of ether. This can be thinned with a little spirit.

Or dissolve 31 grains of dammar resin in 3½ oz. of benzine; this is really the best fixative as it has least effect on the tones.

Or use Venice turpentine dissolved in spirit (2 per cent) for spraying the picture.

FIXATIVE WITH A CASEIN BASE

(See Mural Pastel, p. 194.)

RAFFAELLI CRAYONS

These colours were shaped into crayons in the same way as pastels; the pigments were bound with coconut butter, Japan wax, a non-siccative oil and suet. Thus they remained soft and easy to handle. But the use of crayons of this type has been abandoned because their components lack adhesiveness and turn dark.

The technique, however, was pleasant. Pastels of a similar type, called *oil pastels*, are now used in America. (See Painting in Oils, p. 144.)

With these pastels, which are eminently suitable for 'divisionism', a hybrid type of painting was obtained, having all the depth of shadow of an oil painting proper and yet the technique of a pastel. The colours were blended with a brush dipped in oil of turpentine. Unfortunately these pastels were used in several cases to retouch and finish oil paintings with the result that the pictures flaked in a very short time.

HOW TO MOUNT PASTELS

Pastel paintings are extremely fragile: any jolt or vibration causes the colours to come away from the ground, and moisture penetrates between the particles of pigment which are not protected by some kind of gluten.

Moreover, the very materials used contribute to the fragility of pastels. The paper is mounted on frames which vibrate at any jolt and are subject to damp; the grounds and fixatives are made with glues which easily rot, hold moisture and decompose. If it is inconvenient to work on paper glued to cardboard because of its lack of elasticity, the artist should mount a canvas primed on the stretcher side and glue the paper to the top. To counteract vibration as far as possible, it is advisable to wedge some cotton wool into the corners of the frame. All the glues used in the preparation and mounting of pastels should be mixed with substances that prevent putrefaction.

It is most important to put the pastel under glass. This is a very delicate operation: the painting should be placed flat on a table over a strong sheet of cardboard with thin strips of wood along the edges, raised like a frame. Wash the glass carefully with spirit and rub with talcum powder to remove all traces of grease and place it so that it rests on the strips of wood and not directly on the painting as this would cause smudges. Fix the glass to the cardboard with pieces of strong adhesive paper.

9
Miniatures

Whether painting on ivory, paper or parchment, the outline should be traced from a previous drawing, as it is not advisable to draw tentatively on delicate surfaces easily damaged by erasures. The lines should be laid down with a thin brush, using sepia or pink. Whatever the stage of the painting it is advisable to let each coat dry completely before applying the next. Some artists use ordinary watercolours or tempera colours: it is, however, advisable to bind the pigments with a solution of gum arabic and candied sugar (the sugar being half the amount of the glue, and sufficient water to produce a syrupy liquid). Naturally the various pigments require different quantities of gum, and the artist should refer to the sections on watercolours and gouache.

To verify whether there is enough gum arabic in the medium, test in the usual manner: apply with a brush to a piece of paper and leave in the sun. If the gum is insufficient, the colour will come off in a fine dust; if there is too much, the colour will be shiny and tend to peel off. The sugar prevents the colours from separating into tiny drops which settle unevenly on surfaces which are greasy by nature, such as ivory and parchment.

Tones can never be obtained with one stroke; they should be built up with successive coats of fluid colour, applied with very short strokes or even with light dabs.

Nowadays very few miniatures are painted with the broad and free brushwork technique of the French school.

MINIATURES ON PARCHMENT:
ILLUMINATING

The parchment should be fixed with several drawing-pins on a smooth, hard board, previously lined with paper. For a small piece of parchment a watercolour block can be used and it is also possible to mount parchment on cardboard, folding it over the edges and gluing it down at the back. The actual surface of the picture must not be glued down as this would destroy its smoothness. The parchment thus mounted is placed between sheets of blotting paper under a heavy weight.

Before beginning to work all grease should be removed from the parchment with ox gall mixed with a little albumen or, according to the rules of the Neapolitan MS, with a light solution of glue and honey applied with cotton wool. (See p. 104.) An anonymous treatise on illumination,[1] written in the 18th century, recommends the use of eel's gall mixed with spirit as this makes the pigments adhere to the parchment so well that flaking is impossible, even if the colour is too thickly applied.

After tracing the drawing, prepare, place and burnish the gold; next, mark the contours and the lettering with a pen. Then paint in the landscape, clothing, hair and so forth; and lastly the flesh, over a light ground composed of white and a little green earth, following the ancient practice described in the Neapolitan MS [2] and in Cennini's treatise.

MINIATURES ON IVORY

Ivory should be backed with white paper stuck on with a very transparent colourless glue (made with gelatine, gum arabic or flour). The ivory should then be affixed to a strong Bristol board to prevent cracking and warping. It should be left to dry for a long time between sheets of blotting paper under a weight.

To obtain a warm tone some artists place gold foil between the ivory and the Bristol board.

MINIATURES ON PAPER

It is possible to paint on paper or Bristol board as one does on ivory by applying a ground of zinc white and glue which is then smoothed with pumice and burnished with agate. It is advisable to waterproof this ground by spraying it with a 4 per cent solution of formalin.

MINIATURES ON ENAMEL

In order to paint on sheets of enamelled metal it is necessary to use colours made with a fusible medium and metal oxides.

The best thinner is essential oil of lavender thickened by exposure to the air. All stages of the work, whether initial or final, must be fixed by firing.

This enamel technique used to be very popular for making copies of famous pictures. Collectors who were worried by the darkening of oil paintings used to commission competent miniature painters to make copies which would preserve all the brilliance of the original colours for posterity.

WATERS AND GLUES NECESSARY
FOR MINIATURE PAINTING
RECIPES GIVEN BY ANCIENT TEXTS

PARCHMENT GLUE

This glue is put to soften in vinegar which is then poured off. The glue is dissolved in water and warmed. A glue made with isinglass is equally effective.

WHITE OF EGG

Remove the white 'tread' and every trace of yolk. Mop up the white with a very clean sponge and squeeze it out, repeating the operation until it no longer sticks to the sponge and runs out as if it were water. It is now ready for use and can be

preserved in a glass phial containing red realgar—a quantity
equal to one or two beans—or a little camphor, or a few cloves,
to prevent deterioration.

Gum Arabic

Break into small pieces, place in a vessel and cover with
water. Place the vessel over hot ashes. When the desired density
is reached, strain through fine cloth. Tragacanth can be used
in place of this but is not as good.

Honey or Sugar Water

Cook white honey over a low fire, remove the scum, add
water and bring to the boil. Add a little white of egg beaten in
plain water and boil, stirring until the water evaporates. Strain
through a fine sieve and preserve in a phial.

Follow the same procedure if using sugar.

A Special Rule to make Excellent Glue for Miniatures[3]

First prepare white of egg with a sponge and then glue water
as previously described. Finally prepare honey water which is
a saturated solution of candied sugar.

Take one part of gum and one of white of egg and mix well
in the phial; add one part—or less—of honey water with sugar
and allow to stand. When the mixture has become clear bind
the colours which, in the hands of an able illuminator or
miniaturist, will be very beautiful.

This glue can also be used when applying gold or silver leaf.

10

Watercolour Painting

Watercolours consist of pigments bound with gum arabic or Senegal gum. Like mural painting, watercolour painting requires sureness of touch and spontaneity in execution since the greatest values of this technique are freshness and transparency. It differs from other types of painting with water as a medium, such as gouache, miniature and tempera, in that the lighter tones are obtained by the addition of water and not of white which would make the colours look chalky and ruin the fluidity of the brushwork. The paper itself provides the highlights in watercolour painting.

The artist needs soft and resilient brushes with fine and flexible points, generally made of sable, swan, badger or minever. In Paris and other cities water, treated with chlorine, fails to dissolve certain colours, and should be distilled or at any rate boiled. Plenty of water should be at hand in two separate containers: one for thinning the colours and the other for rinsing the brushes. A sponge, some blotting paper and fine linen rags are also indispensable for removing or lightening colours.

COLOURS

Watercolour painting allows a very wide range of shades since it includes both vegetable colours and those of mineral or organic composition. Very few contemporary artists prepare their own colours: sap green, indigo, *stil de grain brun* and the lakes are easily found on the market.

Indian yellow is dangerous in oil painting as it has alkaline properties which must be neutralized by the addition of balsam. It can be used with confidence in watercolour, but some pigments which can be safely used for oil painting must be avoided for watercolour if they are sensitive to air and light. One should refrain from using vermilion and white lead which turn brown, synthetic ultramarine which is sensitive to sulphurous gas, and other colours, like cadmium yellow, aureoline, and cobalt yellow, which deteriorate in the presence of damp.

Each separate colour requires a different quantity of glue. Honey, glycerine and sugar are added to make the colours more fluid and adhesive, but if used in excess these ingredients attract moisture and produce mildew. Glycerine and sugar make the colours more soluble and should not be used in the underpainting. The pigments should be bound with genuine gum arabic—very hard to obtain nowadays—or Senegal glue, together with a small quantity of glycerine to give flexibility to the mixture.

For certain colours glue must be used cold, while for others it must be heated to a high temperature. Dextrin should be used with the chrome colours and especially with emerald green. Colours must be sufficiently insoluble to allow the artist to paint without disturbing the underlying coat.

The proportions for tube colours are generally as follows:

For heavy colours, like Naples yellow and the earths: 100 parts of pigment, 15 parts of glycerine, 15 parts of gum solution, 10 parts of water. For lighter colours, such as the lakes: 60 parts of pigment, 25 parts of glycerine, 40 parts of water, 25 parts of gum, and so forth.

The gum solution consists of 20 parts of Senegal gum dissolved in 100 parts of water.

Colours sold in cake form are made with a strong solution of gum (1 part gum, 2 parts water). The paste is pressed into special moulds and dried in mild heat. Some of the dark shades contain arsenic and it is wiser not to suck the paint brush.

When large surfaces are to be covered, put small quantities of glycerine, tragacanth solution or calcium chloride into the water to prevent the colours from drying too rapidly. But these substances have great affinity with water and later on the colours may be affected by moisture contained in the air. Only the slime of snails and the slow-drying liquid made by Vibert are absolutely reliable. These are recommended for tempera as well. (See p. 115.)

FIXING

Damp affects the paper and causes mildew by making the gum ferment. Excessive heat and direct sunlight dry the gums so that they crack and make the colours turn to dust, and many shades fade rapidly if exposed to light.

To avoid these dangers some artists have attempted to fix watercolour paintings, but the result is far worse than the natural damage as almost all fixatives make the painting turn unpleasantly yellow and shiny.

The only fixative that does not affect the colours is that invented by Vibert but the formula is kept secret. However, Hiler has given us the recipe for a very good mixture of the same type. (See pp. 159–60.)

PAINTINGS OF A WATERCOLOUR TYPE

WATERCOLOURS WITH SARCOCOLLA

Watercolours with a sarcocolla base were studied and introduced by Vibert. Pliny[1] mentioned this gum resin and recorded its use by physicians and painters. It is equally soluble in water and spirit but is no longer used.

The gum must first be bleached to extract sarcocollin, the only component of use for painting, which gives the colour great richness and depth of tone. When used in gouache painting, it allows the application of several coats of glaze and the gradual building up of colour. (See recipe, p. 73.)

Colours bound with this gum are preserved in small phials and are covered with a little water and spirit to keep them moist and free from fermentation. When required they are thinned with water and spirit. This makes them dry quickly and enables the artist to paint even on greasy surfaces. These colours are particularly suitable for decorative paintings, posters, etc., but should not be treated with spirit fixatives which would melt and spoil the pictures.

MANNA WATERCOLOUR[2]

Dissolve 1 oz. 40 grains of manna in half a tumbler of boiling water; strain through linen and allow to cool: the result is a smooth whitish gelatine. Grind with the pigment, in equal parts. This paint is more mat than ordinary watercolours and is therefore very useful for touching up and finishing gouache paintings.

ROBERTSON'S METHOD[3]

'C. J. Robertson's watercolour method, for which he received the medal of Isis, from the Society for Encouragement of the Arts, of London, is a process by which one paints on Bristol board which has been glued to a backing which is in turn backed with tinfoil. The ground coat is mixed with a little ox gall. When a coat is finished it is varnished with a solution of gum tragacanth, mixed with a little gum arabic. When this is dry it is worked over, another coat of this solution is applied as thought necessary, and the process is thus carried on as desired.'

When the picture is finished, it is varnished, first with a solution of fish glue, and then with any good picture varnish. The advantages of the method are that the colour, which stays very brilliant and transparent, may be worked over in a way impossible by any ordinary method. A similar method is described by Vibert.

WATERCOLOUR WITH GLYCERINE BASE

Vibert mentions a watercolour with a glycerine base which is fixed by means of heat, but this method is really due to an Italian, Antonio Moretti,[4] who called it 'new encaustic painting' although it had nothing in common with the ancient encaustic technique. (See p. 166.)

The gouache paintings exhibited by M. Pierran in the 1834 *Salon* had all the depth and gloss of oil paintings. This effect was obtained by means of several washes of watercolour mixed with a large amount of gum and fish glue. These paintings have however cracked badly with the passage of time.

PRECAUTIONS NECESSARY IN WATERCOLOUR PAINTING

If in the course of work the paper has been roughened by too much erasure, smooth it with an agate burnisher and a little sandarac powder. Before painting over these patches, cover them with a solution of light glue.

Watercolours should never be directly exposed to the sun or they will fade. They should be kept in a dry place as damp conditions cause mildew and stains.

A watercolour should be mounted under glass, protected at the back with a piece of cardboard waterproofed by means of wax or a spirit lacquer varnish. The glue used for mounting must be of a type that does not putrefy, otherwise it may cause mildew.

Watercolours stored in portfolios should have sheets of grease-proof paper placed between them since certain colours containing sugar or honey turn soft through the action of the moisture in the air. If this precaution is not taken the paintings will stick together.

Mildew can be removed with formalin steam; and grease stains cleansed with a small piece of cotton wool dipped in rectified benzine.

GOUACHE

The term gouache, as used in modern times, indicates a type of painting in which the colours used are bound with glue and in which, unlike pure watercolour, the lighter shades are obtained by the addition of white.

Vasari makes no distinction between gouache and tempera.

In his writings both terms indicate painting on a moist surface with colours having a glue base. A gouache technique was used in the paintings of ancient Egypt, the pigments being bound with tragacanth glue and sometimes with honey.

In the process of drying, gouache colours very often change, becoming light, pearl-like and translucent and look like pastels: this is a typically French technique. (See Boucher, etc.)

At present gouache is widely used for posters, sketches of dresses and costumes, stage designs and illustrations.

The materials used for gouache are canvas or panels of wood and cardboard previously sized to render them non-absorbent. When covering large surfaces with flat colour, the canvas or board should not be kept in a vertical or very inclined position as the colours will run.

GOUACHE COLOURS

These are prepared by grinding the pigments with water and adding glue water (155 grains of Senegal gum dissolved in $3\frac{1}{2}$ oz. of water) and sugar water ($1\frac{3}{4}$ oz. of sugar dissolved in $1\frac{3}{4}$ pts. of water).

The mixtures listed below are typical:

	Pigment	Glue water	Sugar water	Pure water
Blanc d'argent	25	25	2	2
Chrome yellow	50	20	2	2
Venice red	30	7	4	2
Ultramarine blue	25	10	2	2

An excess of gum makes the colours shiny when dry. It is difficult to touch up and finish a gouache picture without getting ugly streaks; for finishing a picture of this type water-colours with manna base are recommended.

POSTERS

For this type of painting the artist should use coloured paper, or paper to which a coat of mat paint has been applied with a roller or atomizer. Some contemporary artists use colours mixed with an egg tempera or with wax emulsions in order to obtain a more solid colour and a greater variety in brush-work.

All these grounds are easily soluble and it is a good idea to fix them first with a solution of 4 per cent gelatine and then one of 4 per cent pure formalin. This treatment is also carried out on the finished gouache pictures to make them more durable. When fixed in this way, gouache underpainting can then be glazed and worked over with colours with a manna base, giving very interesting effects.

Today the colourman sells gouache colours for poster painting. They contain a casein emulsion and, when dry, become completely waterproof.

RECIPES

FIXATIVE FOR WATERCOLOUR

We owe to Hiler the recipe for a very good mixture similar to Vibert's, which is still kept secret.

> Amyl acetate ⎫
> Acetone   ⎬ in equal parts.
> Benzine   ⎭

Dissolve a little pyrixylin in this liquid, in a sufficient quantity to produce a light syrup.

Riffault's varnish:

Sandarac	9 oz.	190 grains
Tears of mastic		380 ,,
Elemi		107 ,,
Venice turpentine	3 oz.	190 ,,
Pure spirit	3 ,,	190 ,,

GUM TRAGACANTH

Put some pulverized tragacanth into a bottle, moisten it with pure spirit and leave it to make an infusion. After several hours add water little by little, shaking the bottle well. There should be 3 or 4 per cent gum in this solution which is excellent for fixing charcoal and pencil drawings.

How to Prepare your own Paper[5]

The recipe given by Goupil consists of:

'Skin glue or parchment size   1 part
Pure white soap   1   ,,
Powdered alum   1   ,,

Melt the glue and the grated soap on a slow fire, stirring until well dissolved. Then add the alum, which on dissolving will turn the mixture milky. Strain and bottle. Spread with a soft brush. The mixture may be diluted with water as desired. If the paper fails to take it well, mix a little ox gall or a few drops of ammonia or alcohol with it.'

How to Obtain Laevulose from Honey[6]

'Pure pale honey is kept partly exposed to the air until it has crystallized and become semi-solid. It is then mixed with four times its own bulk of pure grain alcohol, put into a receptacle and thoroughly shaken from time to time, letting several hours elapse between shakings. The pale yellow alcoholic solution is then filtered. The matter that filters through is a solution of Laevulose with certain impurities which are harmless. If it is desired in a more concentrated form, it is simply evaporated to the desired consistency by leaving it exposed so that the alcohol evaporates.'

How to Purify Ox Gall

Boil $3\frac{1}{2}$ gills of fresh ox gall together with 231 grains of powdered alum. Remove the scum and leave it to boil for some time; when the mixture is cold, bottle and seal it with care. Take the same quantity of ox gall and boil it with 231 grains of common salt. Mix the two liquids together. A dense coloured sediment will then form which must be eliminated by decanting

1 16th-century gilding on a panel: gold haloes and grounds with decorations in relief, engraving and burin work

MATHIAS GRUENEWALD (op. 1483–1529)
The Virgin in the Garden

2 Gold dots take the place of the ancient haloes

FILIPPO LIPPI (1406–1469)
Madonna and Child

3 Miniature on parchment, end of 15th century, Codex T. The flesh is painted over a ground of white lead and green earth

4 Miniature on enamel

s. g. counis (1785–1859)
Portrait of Gabrielle d'Estrées

5 *18th-century gouache on silk*

INDO-PERSIAN ART

6 Pastel on coloured paper
ROSALBA CARRIERA (1675–1757)
Portrait of Amalia Giuseppa, Princess of Modena

7 2nd-century tempera emulsion

EGYPTO-ROMAN ART
Portrait on wood from the coffin of a young woman

8 Oleo-resin painting on panel, with several glazes

JOOS VAN CLEVE (*circa* 1464–1540)
The Death of the Virgin

9 Resin-oil painting, painted rapidly and without retouching

HIERONYMUS BOSCH (*circa* 1450–1516)
The Birth of Christ

10 Oil on canvas (thinned with turpentine)
AUGUSTE RENOIR (1841–1919)
Musk Roses

11 Oil and wax colour, applied with wooden spatula

VINCENT VAN GOGH (1853–1890)
La Guinguette

12 Fresco: the joins reveal the amount done in one day
RAPHAEL (1483–1520) AND PUPILS
The Deluge

13 Gesso ground on panel

LEONARDO DA VINCI (1452–1519)
Annunciation

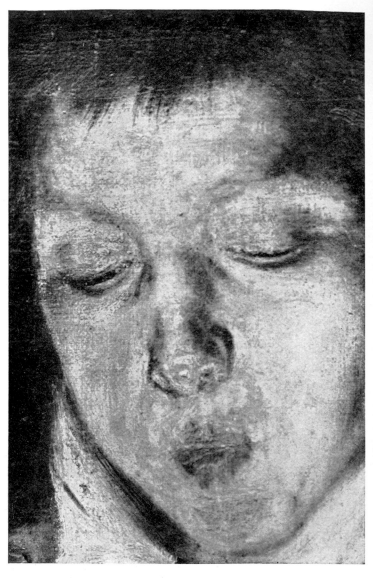

14 Brown oil ground on canvas

ANONYMOUS, 17TH CENTURY
Boy blowing on ember

15 Canvas with almost non-absorbent ground

EL GRECO (1547–1614)
View of Toledo

*16 Reddish ground on canvas: an excess of oil in the
underpainting has made the overpainting contract*

PAOLO VERONESE (1528–1588)
The Youth between Virtue and Vice

*17 Oily grounds: time produces a net-work
of tiny cracks in paintings of this type*

GOYA (1746–1828)
La Maya Vestida

18 Gouache and watercolour on canvas
DÜRER (1471–1528)
St. Philip the Apostle

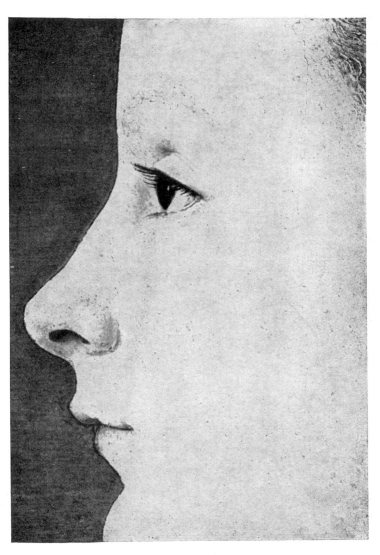

19 Tempera and oleo-resin colours

ANTONIO POLLAIOLO (1443–1496)
Portrait of a Girl

20 Tempera and oleo-resin glazes

MANTEGNA (1431–1506)
The Death of the Virgin

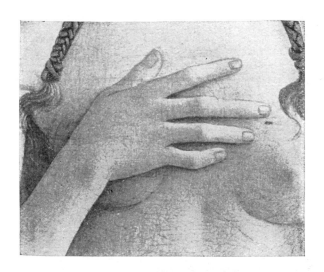

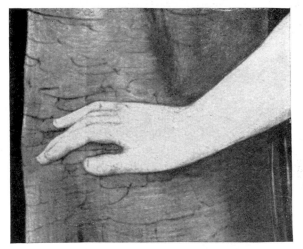

*21 A comparison between the clear modelling obtained with tempera
and the more subtle modelling obtained with oleo-resin media*

BOTTICELLI (1445–1510)
Venus
LUCAS CRANACH (1472–1538)
Venus

22 *Oleo-resin painting on panel: the large cracks are*
because the oily underpainting was painted over too soon

PIERO DELLA FRANCESCA (1416?–1492)
The Nativity

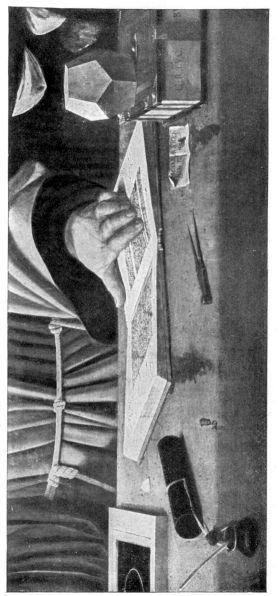

23 Oleo-resin painting of Flemish type

ANONYMOUS, END OF 15TH CENTURY
Alleged portrait of Luca Pacioli

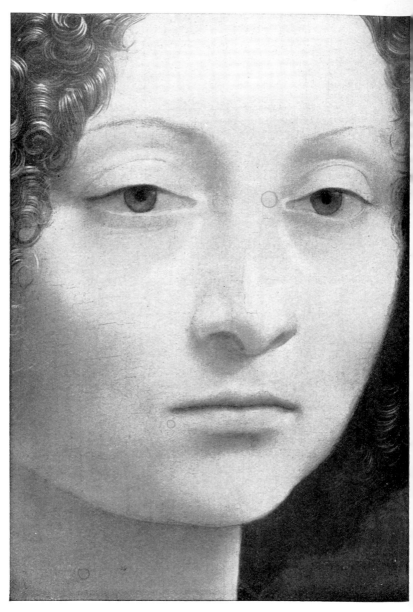

24 Very fluid oleo-resin painting, on panel
LEONARDO DA VINCI (1452–1519)
Portrait

25 Oleo-resin painting on canvas, without preparatory sketch

TINTORETTO (1518–1594)
St. Mary of Egypt

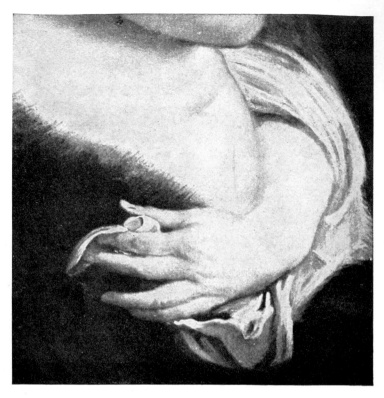

*26 Oleo-resin painting on canvas, with trans-
parent shadows and lights in denser impasto*

RUBENS (1577–1640)
Portrait of Helène Fourment

*27 Oleo-resin painting on canvas: the shadows and
mid-tones are painted with a watercolour technique*

VELASQUEZ (1599–1660)
Portrait of Innocent X

*28 Oleo-resin painting on canvas: slow painting, each coat
applied over a perfectly dry previous coat, with thick impasto*

BERNARDO BELLOTTO (1720–1780)
La Gazzada

29 Oil on canvas with thick impasto

GIORGIO MORANDI
Still life

30 Buon fresco painting over pounced preparatory drawing

PIERO DELLA FRANCESCA (1416?–1492)
The Legend of the Cross

31 Buon fresco on smooth plaster
RAPHAEL (1483–1520)
The Miracle of the Mass at Bolsena

32 Fresco with broad treatment

PONTORMO (1494–1555)
Vertumnus and other gods

the liquid and putting it into a clean bottle. This ox gall will keep for years if stored in a cool, dark place. Eel gall can be prepared by mixing it with an equal quantity of pure spirit. This gall can be used to fix drawings, to remove grease from ivory for miniatures and to improve the fluidity of brushwork when painting on parchment. Gall can also be prepared by boiling with salt and vinegar in the proportion of one tenth of the whole liquid. One part of gall prepared with two of pure spirit, decanted and filtered, makes another excellent preparation.

I I

Tempera Painting

Writers disagree on the meaning of the word tempera: mediaeval authors like Heraclius use it to designate colours ground with water and kneaded into a paste with the addition of organic matter (gums, glue, egg). The word is used with this meaning by Cennini and later by Lomazzo and others, but Vasari uses it for all mixtures of pigments, including those bound with oil and varnish. This has caused much confusion and has given rise to the theory upheld by Berger that the medium used by the Van Eycks was an emulsion of oil and egg, since Vasari calls it a tempera.[1]

Nowadays the term tempera generally indicates painting with emulsions thinned with water and mixed with pigments previously made into a paste with water.

These emulsions can be *natural* (milk, egg, milk of figs); *artificial* (solutions containing gums, egg and varnishes, casein and glue); and *saponified* (fatty oil, soap or wax emulsified by the addition of alkalis).

Since temperas refract the light only slightly, their colour is clearer and more vivid than that of oil paints.

INGREDIENTS OF TEMPERAS

After some time natural emulsions become insoluble in water whereas the artificial ones remain soluble. The most sensitive to damp are those containing glue.

A careful addition of oil, varnish and wax does not affect the cohesiveness of a natural emulsion such as yolk of egg.

Indeed, one can add an equal weight of water and half its weight of fatty oil to a yolk without spoiling the natural emulsion.

Venice turpentine or copaiva balsam give brilliance to the colours but make the brushwork difficult. Certain thinners, such as wine,[2] beer,[3] ox gall and, for mural painting, lime water, improve the cohesiveness of temperas and allow freedom of brushwork.

Milk of figs[4] is the substance which preserves temperas best and holds them together by accelerating the drying process, making the eggs coagulate rapidly. This juice is extracted from the young shoots of the tree, preferably in spring, and is preserved in airtight glass phials to prevent deterioration.

Another easy way to prepare a diluted fig milk is to put young leaves to rot in water and alcohol (one tenth) adding new leaves every day and removing the old ones: after ten days the liquid, which has begun to ferment like wine, is filtered and can be stored in bottles for a long time.

A commercially made drier should not be used as it is merely a saponification with a wax or benzoin base. To delay the drying process, the only harmless substances are Vibert's preparation and snail slime. The manual of Mount Athos advises placing the snail near the flame of a candle, to force it to secrete a good amount of slime which, mixed with the colours, makes them more fluid and slower in drying.

Since there is no danger that colours made with a natural emulsion will desiccate, crack or turn dark, the addition of soap, glycerine, honey and syrups is superfluous—indeed, it may be harmful as these substances may produce mildew.

Applied to a sheet of paper a good tempera should dry without forming a halo of grease and should not form lumps when thinned with water.

Cennini recommends equal parts of pigment and tempera, provided the colours have been ground into a very fluid paste as the pigments require more tempera than oil. The usual practice is to grind them with distilled water and knead them with tempera just before use. Some artists grind the pigments with tempera immediately and preserve the colours in tubes or little glass jars.

According to Max Doerner colours should contain the following percentage of tempera:

	per cent		per cent
Cremnitz white	30	Vermilion	50
Zinc white	50	English red	75
Light cadmium	80	Burnt sienna	180
Dark cadmium	85	Cobalt blue	200
Madder lake	200	Chrome green	220
Golden ochre	80	Burnt red earth	90

HOW TO PRESERVE TEMPERAS

Formalin makes glues, egg and emulsions hard and should not be used, nor should vinegar, phenol and carbol as they affect many pigments. The presence of 1 per cent of vinegar is enough to spoil ultramarine blue. On the contrary, 2 per cent of soda benzoate and 2 or 3 per cent of oil of lavender or cloves or, better still, of cherry laurel preserve temperas without damaging the colours; 30 or 40 grains of pulverized camphor will preserve 1 lb. of tempera for a long time.

30 or 40 grains of cloves can be added to each pound of tempera made with glue or flour. These, added while the mixture is cooking, will prevent mildew. The emulsions should be preserved in a cool, dark place in well-corked bottles.

VARIOUS TYPES OF TEMPERA

UNVARNISHED TEMPERAS

Thin, dry, absorbent grounds are preferable for tempera painting since they preserve all the lightness and opacity of the tones. To make the colours spread easily, keep the ground slightly damp with distilled water sprayed with an atomizer.

On no account should white lead be used for this type of tempera since, unprotected by varnish, it is highly susceptible to atmosphere. Zinc or titanium white should be used instead.

The best mixtures are those made with yolk of egg and milk of figs or emulsions of egg and varnish.

Varnishing a tempera painting presents many difficulties because certain colours, such as the lakes, ultramarine and the chrome oxides, become garish. Others, like white, lose their brilliance. If corrections have been made by overpainting they are bound to show up in time, especially under varnish. Wrong tones should be lightened with a damp sponge or scraped with a very sharp blade.

VARNISHES

A tempera painting can be fixed with glue before varnishing. For this purpose use a 4–5 per cent solution of glue, fixed subsequently with a solution of formalin; otherwise the varnishes, especially those with a spirit base, make the light tones transparent if applied directly to the colours. The picture should be placed in the sun before varnishing, and the varnish itself should be slightly warmed to avoid mildew and oxidization of the resins. Oil varnishes should be used on temperas made with egg or milk of figs. Over temperas made with artificial emulsions thick dammar varnish should be used (1 part of dammar resin to 2 or 3 parts of rectified turpentine), or mastic varnishes or those made with copaiva dissolved in lavender oil.

Mixed Procedure

Temperas finished with oil colours must be thin and very dry. Some artists before finishing fix the tempera with a light coat of varnish. Colours bound with oil or with oil and varnish should be used only as a glaze and not as an impasto as they would spoil the brilliance of the tempera.

The old masters owed their speed in execution and the solidity and luminosity of their colours to this procedure. Underpainting done in tempera dries quickly, and the artist's personal style of brushwork is much better preserved than in oil painting where the colours dry slowly and tend to coagulate. If impasto is used in a tempera painting, thin colours mixed with very little medium should be used or the subsequent brushwork will not cling properly.

These thin temperas dry very quickly and the execution of the picture is therefore very rapid.

This is perhaps the most suitable technique for portraits and landscapes since it allows spontaneous work with light and brilliant tones.

Another mixed procedure, used by the Venetian masters and imported into Flanders by Van Dyck, consisted in painting in oils and finishing with tempera, a very difficult process because a dry colour like tempera does not adhere easily to an oily underpainting and it is therefore necessary to free this latter from grease with garlic juice. The normal practice was to paint the whites and the blues in tempera as they remained cleaner than the same colours bound with oil which invariably turn yellow.

TEMPERA ON GOLD GROUND

Wash the gilt surface with a solution of water (10 parts) and alum (1 part). To obtain good adhesion thin the colours with the same solution.

'A PUTRIDO' TEMPERA

Certain authors such as Max Doerner, Rosa and others, on the strength of a wrong transcription of the Venetian MS in the Marciana Library [5] made by Mrs Merrifield, believed that 'a putrido' painting was a mixture of oil and egg tempera and so started the legend that this medium was used by great Venetian masters like Titian and Veronese. In reality the manuscript mentions among the various techniques the 'a putrido' method, that is to say egg tempera, and discusses oil painting as something quite distinct, but the manuscript never mentions a mixture containing both oil and egg tempera.

Egg Tempera and Egg Emulsion

The egg is used pure to obtain dense, glossy colours for use in thin successive layers. To make clear, light, mat colours suitable for broad, free brushwork, other substances must be added. The ingredients which give this enamel-like quality are oils, resins, balsams and gums, while wine, beer and milk facilitate the brushwork. These substances should be selected and measured with care to avoid altering the cohesion, smoothness and drying power of the emulsion.

In drying the egg forms an elastic and solid substance which, like oil, is insoluble in water. The yolk[6] which contains lecithin, a valuable agent in emulsification, amalgamates well with oil and varnish and can be thinned with water as well as with essential oils. Cennini recommends a tempera made with the yolk alone, shiny and rather difficult to manage, which should be applied with short strokes without blending; a tempera made with yolk well emulsified with albumen, which is more fluid and transparent, but has a tendency to crack if used thickly; and finally a tempera of egg and milk of figs which takes varnish perfectly.

To make a good tempera it is essential that the egg should be fresh, especially when making emulsions. The yolk seems to make the whites yellow at first,[7] but this defect is only temporary because the yolk fades rapidly in the light.

When painting with a tempera of pure egg the first coats should be applied as light glazes and only in the overpainting should the artist draw with his brush. To make sure that the mixture of tempera and egg is perfect, test the colours by brushing them on to a piece of glass. If the mixture is right it will be possible, after twenty-four hours, to remove the colours easily with a palette knife. They should look like elastic skins.

If there is not enough tempera the colours will be dusty-looking, if too much, cracks will be found.

As supports, panels are far better than canvases; the ground should not be too absorbent and the surface should be smoothed until it looks like ivory. Those who dislike the technique of beginning with glazes and finishing with brush strokes but nevertheless wish to obtain all the brilliance peculiar to egg temperas, should use emulsions of egg, oil and varnish, which make an excellent undercoat for oils. Among all those which have been tested the best recipes are those given by Tudor-Hart.

RECIPES

Egg-yolk and Linseed Emulsion [8]

'Ingredients

> Yolk of egg
> Oil of lavender (10 drops to each yolk)
> Linseed oil (washed and sun-clarified in equal quantity to the yolk of egg)
> Water (in quantity, twice the volume of the yolk of egg)

'Separate yolk of egg from the white by rolling the yolk gently from the palm of one hand to the other, wiping free palm between each change. Pinch yolk gently between thumb and index finger, hold it suspended over the grinding slab, puncture and expel the yolk. [Or if this seems too difficult simply strain it through a cloth. *H. Hiler.*] Carefully "mayonnaise" the oil of lavender into the egg-yolk on the grinding slab (by grinding it gradually in with the muller). Collect this "mayonnaise" and place it in a receptacle, keeping it moist with a damp cloth covering it. Then carefully and gradually grind in the linseed oil. The pigments to be used should first be ground in water, sprinkling from time to time with a few drops of water. Collect into a small receptacle, and prevent evaporation by covering with a damp cloth. Measure out an equal volume of linseed oil. Place a small quantity of the egg-and-lavender mixture on the grinding slab, and grind in one drop of the linseed oil in the same manner as directed for the oil of lavender (very gradually and thoroughly). Continue up to four drops. Keep repeating process, alternating egg mixture and oil, till you have a stiff butter-coloured mayonnaise. In this condition it is proper for tempering all pigments with the exception of ultramarine, cobalt, cerulean, and the yellow and orange cadmiums, for which an addition of copal varnish is required as described later on.

120

'For grinding the colours with the medium, the pigments should first be ground in water till evaporated to a stiff paste just sufficiently tractable to move under the muller. The medium is then added in equal bulk to the pigment paste, and mixed up thoroughly with the spatula, after which it is spread out on the grinding slab and ground out smooth with the muller. This is the minimum amount of pigment required for pigments such as white lead, yellow ochre, and most of the earth colours. Others require varying quantities, and all should have the tractability of white lead. Sprinkle with a few drops of water, from time to time, while grinding. These paints can be stored if sealed.'

[NOTE. This emulsion, when required as a medium for diluting pigments while painting, requires the addition of an equal volume of water which should be added in the following manner: Place the emulsion on the grinding slab in a blob. Make a crater in the centre and fill with water (from a thimbleful to a tablespoonful), grind in water gradually until the mixture is smooth and thin enough to flow from a palette knife, then collect it in a receptacle and stir in the remainder of the water. *H. Hiler.*]

MEDIUM FOR TEMPERING ULTRAMARINE, CERULEAN AND THE CADMIUMS[9]

'For tempering these colours and cobalt blue, the medium should be made in the following way.
'Ingredients:

Yolk of egg	Linseed oil
Oil of lavender	Copal varnish

Mix the egg and oil as above. Divide into four equal parts. To three of them grind in an equal volume of linseed oil. To the remaining part grind in a part of copal varnish equal to the quantity of egg it contains. Then grind the two mixtures together, and the emulsion is ready for the above pigments, which should be ground in as described above.'

[NOTE. The grinding of the first quantity of water into the emulsion is an important factor, in order to secure perfect saponification of the oil by the egg, and to produce an emulsion which will not separate out, even after standing for several days. Tudor-Hart does not recommend the casual method of shaking the whole bulk of water and emulsion in a bottle. *H. Hiler.*]

Egg Tempera[10]

Beat three or four eggs for some minutes until emulsified. Add, shaking the mixture well, 386 grains of linseed or poppy seed oil, 386 grains of copal varnish and 15 or 20 grains of carbolic acid (96 per cent). Add little by little 5 oz. of water, shaking all the time.

Mixed egg tempera:[10]

Eggs	3–4
Linseed oil	386 grains
Copal varnish	386 ,,
Water	5 oz.
Carbolic acid (96%)	15–20 grains

Emulsifying as described above.

Recipes by H. Hubbard[11]

The following must not be thinned with water but with essential oils:

A	Linseed oil	1 part
	Venice turpentine	1 ,,
	Yolk of egg	1 ,,

This becomes more transparent while drying.

B	Yolk of egg	2 parts
	Water	3 ,,
	Linseed oil	1 part

This mixture gives the colours more opacity but cracks if thinned with water.

C	Yolk of egg	1 part
	Dutch stand oil	1 ,,

This is thinned with a little oil of turpentine; with this tempera it is possible to use thick, heavy colours without danger of cracks.

These temperas can be used with colours having an essence base when painting or restoring pictures.

Non-cracking tempera thinned with water:

Yolk of egg	2 parts
Water	3 ,,
Stand oil	1 part

Egg tempera for mural painting:
Melt over heat:

Honey	1 part
Vinegar	½ ,,

Add a whole egg to an equal quantity of this mixture.

This tempera, which contains honey, will permit fluid, soft and blended brushwork. Since vinegar damages the blues it is better to substitute strong white wine.

TEMPERA ACCORDING TO FONTANESI [12]

Use 1 yolk of egg and about 1½ oz. of gum arabic dissolved in two thirds of a tumbler of water.

Thoroughly mix the egg and the glue water and allow to stand. Add a teaspoonful of pure spirit or vinegar to prevent putrefaction. Sometimes a pinch of sugar is also added.

Fontanesi used this tempera both warm and cold for the first stage of his landscapes, applying it with heavy brush strokes in a warm monochrome made chiefly with earths. He would then finish with oil colours thinned, it appears, with a varnish with a copal base.

Carrà, who has tried out this tempera (and to him I owe this recipe) recommends that the various ingredients should be added in the order prescribed, as spirit or vinegar added directly to yolk of egg make it coagulate, spoiling the tempera.

RECIPE USED BY THE BENEDICTINES OF BEURON [13]

Mix the following in the given order, stirring all the while and straining finally through a fine sieve:

Eggs (yolk and white well beaten together)		50
Oil		$2\frac{1}{2}$ gills
Essential oil of turpentine	not quite	1 gill
Vinegar		$3\frac{1}{2}$ gills
Water		$3\frac{1}{2}$,,

Dissolve in hot water as much black soap as would fill an egg shell. The soapy water must be cold before it is poured on to the tempera.

This mixture can be kept in bottles for several months and is used, slightly thinned, to bind colours. The picture can be finished either with oil colours or with colours with an egg base.

FATHER PAULINUS'S RECIPE [14]

'The following is the recipe given by Father Paulinus for the tempera as used by the Beuron monks, a branch of the Benedictine Order in the little town of Beuron, Germany. These monks employed it—and employ it still—to paint on well-laid plaster. They used all permanent pigments, except bone or ivory black, preferring mineral black or lampblack in place of these.'

Medium for fat tempera:

> 4 eggs—to which add
> 1 tablespoonful of boiled linseed oil, and
> 1 tablespoonful of vinegar

The white and yolks are well shaken up together. The oil and vinegar being separately mixed and added to the egg, the whole is then thoroughly shaken up and passed through muslin to take out the skins. The medium is kept in a well-corked bottle and mixed with the colours as required, water being used to thin down to the necessary body.

MAXWELL ARMFIELD'S RECIPE [15]

'Shake up yolk of an egg with the same quantity or a trifle less of water. Add enough vinegar to emulsify three or four drops of varnish which are also added to the emulsion.'

Emulsion A. An excellent tempera, fluid and clear, which must not be thinned with water. Use:

Yolk of egg	1 part
Oil, sun-clarified and cleaned with water, or	
Stand oil	1 ,,
Rectified turpentine	⅓ ,,

Emulsion B. Can be thinned with water. Ingredients:

Yolk of egg	2 parts
Water	3 ,,
Clarified oil	1 part

B. Lacher's Recipe [16]

Linseed oil	1 part
Egg	6 parts
Vinegar	12 ,,

For mural painting use the same quantity of milk instead of vinegar.

G. Schudtin's Recipe [17]

Emulsify 4 eggs with four times the volume of oxidized linseed oil which can be contained in half an egg shell not quite full. A dense foam is obtained which should be allowed to stand. Water is added for use with earths, ochres, Cassel earth, etc.

American Recipe

Egg	2 parts
Water	4 ,,
Stand oil	1 part
Dammar varnish	1 ,,

Emulsify the eggs with the water and gradually add the varnish mixed with the oil, beating the whole time.

Ancient Tuscan Recipe

This is an excellent tempera, useful in restoring as well as in painting. It allows the use of washes which are not altered by varnish and which can be easily removed. If too thick, it causes cracks—perhaps that is why it is the favourite tempera of those who fake old masters. It is made by emulsifying the yolk of an egg with an equal amount of melted gum arabic (which should have the same density as the yolk). Spread in a thin layer on a plate and leave in the sun until dry. Keep away from dust and damp: this keeps for some years and is thinned with warm water when required.

Max Doerner's Recipes [18]

Recipe A. Emulsify a whole egg with two thirds of oil and one third of resin varnish to which an equal volume of water has been added.

Recipe B. Emulsify 1 part of egg (whole) with 1 part of oil (Stand oil or fatty varnish) and 2 parts of water.

The egg should be well emulsified with the oil and the water added gradually. A less fatty tempera can be made by using varnishes with an ethereal oil base. Colour bound with this medium can be thinned with water containing glue (5 per cent). The finished painting can be fixed with a solution of formalin (4 per cent).

Secco Suardo's Recipe

Mix:

Yolk of egg	2 parts
Strong white wine	1 part
Skimmed milk	2 parts

Strain through muslin and add a few drops of oil of cloves to prevent putrefaction. Varnish the picture two days after completion with amber varnish thinned with oil of turpentine. A first lay in made with this medium can be finished with colours bound either with oil or varnish.

De Chirico says: 'This, in my opinion, is the safest of the temperas. Of all those I have tested, this has given the best results. It is clear, solid and flexible. When varnished it turns brighter and does not darken; the whites do not change and the colours do not become too opaque from the start. It allows slow work and can be used in a dense impasto with no risk of cracks. It has the same qualities as the tempera made with cooked linseed oil and has the advantage of not being liable to change. Moreover it is very easy to make:

Yolk of egg	1	coffee	spoonful
Poppy oil	2	,,	spoonfuls
Essence of turpentine or of petroleum	1	,,	spoonful
Glycerine, chemically pure	$\frac{1}{2}$	,,	,,
White vinegar	1	,,	,,
Water	1	,,	,, '

TEMPERAS WITH ALBUMEN BASE

Albumen mixed with water containing glue or honey was used when illuminating missals; it produces a brilliant and vitreous impasto, which tends to crack and should never be used with heavy brush strokes.

Albumen mixed with water and alum (water 10 parts, alum 1 part, albumen 30 parts) forms an emulsion which can be used together with oil and resins.

These temperas can be fixed with a solution of tannin (tannic acid 6 per cent) or of formalin (4 per cent), or by warming the picture to a temperature of 155·2° F.

These temperas are often used by forgers of ancient pictures, for which the tendency to crack and the hardness of the impasto are indispensable.

HOW TO PRESERVE ALBUMEN FOR USE

Mix with an equal volume of water, emulsifying well. Place

a small piece of litmus paper in it and add, drop by drop, some diluted acetic acid until you can see the paper changing colour. The albumen keeps better since its alkaline nature is thus neutralized. Strain and preserve in a well-sealed bottle.

GLUE TEMPERA

Very fresh, light paintings can be produced by using colours ground with water, adding to them, at the moment of use, some glue, either animal or vegetable, which has been heated so as to become very liquid. Use a thin ground of an absorbent type, such as gesso or plain sized paper. Glue tempera lends itself specially for stage scenery and decorations on a large scale.

The palette should be of metal, but not aluminium, in order to stand up to heat. The colours are thinned with hot water. It is well to have an electric ring to keep the temperas and the water lukewarm and the palette also can be placed on it if the colours coagulate. Tones may change: some colours fade while drying, others, such as the earths, alter very little; the lakes and blacks do not change at all. Only practice and experience can teach the artist what mixtures of colours can be used safely. This type of tempera painting demands a bold execution and does not allow changes or corrections. The final touches can be applied only with light brush strokes or by means of glazes; if the colours are laid on heavily they will form dark spots in drying and the painting will be spoilt. Before glazing, the painting should be fixed with a light coat of glue applied with an atomizer. When dry, this in turn is fixed by spraying on it a solution of formalin (4 per cent).

Mix the glue and colours in equal proportions, whatever the shade, or there will be greasy spots which will not hold the next coat of colour. This, however, can be remedied by mixing ox gall with the colour which is to cover these spots.

When using this technique it should be remembered that too thick a glue cracks, and too fluid a glue makes the painting dusty-looking and very brittle.

Besides the colours recommended for oils (with the exception of white lead) all the earths can be used, including umber which is excellent when bound with glue although unsatisfactory when used in oil painting. If you wish to delay the drying of the tones, add viscous juices (mistletoe skin, viburnum roots, juice of elder-tree, narcissus or hyacinth bulb) or solutions of sugar and honey, syrup of althea, of jujube and glycerine. However, these substances may turn yellow and they constantly attract moisture.

It is therefore far better to use glue tempera, with all its drawbacks, as the addition of glutens or resins deprives it of its freshness and makes it look like emulsion tempera, but without the enamel-like texture or the solidity imparted by eggs.

For this type of painting, warm solutions of gelatine (6 per cent) which produce light and opaque tones similar to those of pastel should generally be used.

Pure fish glue is rather fragile.[19] It is much improved if mixed with some parchment glue (two thirds of parchment glue and one third of fish glue). Colours can also be tempered with vegetable glues as these resist the action of micro-organisms far better than animal glues, and can be well emulsified with resins and oils: these mixtures, however, do not cling to a greasy ground. Pastes made with flour, starch, rye, potato flour or rice, are prepared by making a smooth dough with a little water; then drop this into boiling water, stirring well.

RECIPES FOR GLUE TEMPERAS

GLUE AND HONEY TEMPERA

This recipe is given by the Strasbourg MS:

'I have here taught extensively how colours must be tempered according to the Greek method with two aqueous vehicles, and how oily grounds are made and how each colour behaves.

'I shall now proceed to teach how all colours can be tempered with glue, for use on panels, walls and canvas, and how one should prepare the glue so that it may keep and not rot. Take scraps of parchment, wash thoroughly and boil in water until a clear glue is obtained with the right degree of adhesiveness. When the glue is cooked place in a basin of vinegar and boil once again. Remove from the fire, strain and allow to cool.

'Glue made in this way will last for a long time. As it will have the density of gelatine, when wishing to temper colours, one should melt a suitable amount in an equal quantity of water, adding a fair amount of honey. Heat well and blend the honey with the glue. With this medium it is possible to bind all colours, in the same manner as the other colours I have spoken of elsewhere, without obtaining either too thick or too thin a paste. All these colours can take varnish and will become so glossy that neither water nor rain will be able to spoil or discolour them.'

The proportions for vegetable pastes are as follows:

FLOUR OR STARCH PASTE

1 oz. 334 grains of flour in 154 grains of water; the dough dissolved in 8 oz. of boiling water.

RYE FLOUR PASTE

154 grains of flour in 154 grains of water; the dough dissolved in 3½–5 oz. of boiling water.

RICE FLOUR PASTE

1 oz. 334 grains of flour in 10½ oz. of water. When cold add half as much oil.

FLOUR PASTE WITH VENICE TURPENTINE

Venice turpentine may be added to the paste described above (1 part of turpentine to 3 or 4 parts of paste). This produces an excellent emulsion, suitable for binding colours as well as for lining pictures.

GLUE TEMPERA

The painter Rapetti, my teacher, used this medium for various decorative paintings, sketches, panels for ceilings, all of which still preserve their freshness of tone.

Water	1¾ pts.
White flour	462–617 grains
Pulverized gum arabic	90–140 ,,
Essence of cherry laurel	10– 15 drops

Boil the glue until it becomes transparent and looks like a syrup, then strain; gum arabic should not be used in excess since it lessens the opacity of the tones.

This is an inexpensive and brilliant tempera which is very suitable for decorative work on a large scale; the colours however alter considerably in drying as do all pigments bound with glues and gums.

INSOLUBLE GLUE TEMPERA[20]

Heat for half an hour, up to a temperature of 406° F.

| Glycerine | 3 oz. 231 grains |
| Potato starch | 93 ,, |

Allow the temperature to drop to 184° F. Add pure alcohol, in the proportion of three times the volume of the mixture, to precipitate the glue. This tempera is thinned with cold water but becomes insoluble when dry. It is adhesive, fluid and smooth. Once dry, it is easy to work over this tempera with glazes without spoiling the tones.

W. OSTWALD'S INSOLUBLE GLUE TEMPERA

Dissolve 154 grains of caustic alkali in 224 cu. in. of water and 3½ oz. of flour paste. Shake until the liquid has a smooth consistency, and after a quarter of an hour add diluted chloridic acid until litmus paper reveals that the glue is no longer alkaline.

The addition of a little benzonaphthol will preserve this tempera which is very clinging and adhesive.

TUDOR-HART'S PARCHMENT SIZE AND LINSEED OIL EMULSION[21]

'Ingredients:

Size made from goat and sheep parchment clippings
Linseed oil

'The size should be made as described by Cennino Cennini in Chapter CX, but, as this is somewhat vague, it may be found useful to add the method which I have evolved, of preparing it so as to produce the most satisfactory result.

'Take one part of goat parchment to four or five of sheep parchment.

[May the author be allowed to interrupt at this point and state that it can be made with sheep parchment, which is the common sort, alone? *H. Hiler*.]

'Place them in a wooden tub, and wash them thoroughly in three or four waters, kneading them and scrubbing them well as a washerwoman scrubs linen. After a final rinsing, draw off the water and wring out the parchment in a linen cloth. Place them back in the wooden tub with a volume of water equal to the mass of wet parchment, and leave them to soak thus for twenty-four hours. Then place the parchment and the water in which it has been soaked in a large glazed earthenware pot (pot-au-feu) which has not been used for any other purpose (the smallest trace of grease will ruin the size).

'Add boiling water, in the proportion of half the quantity of water in which they have soaked, making a proportion in all of one part of wet parchment to one and a half of water.

'Place over a brisk fire, so that the whole of the rounded bottom of the pot is in direct contact with the source of heat, but avoiding as far as possible, direct contact with the flames. Stir slowly with a wooden spoon until the parchment clippings have all curled up, then put a close-fitting lid on the pot and bring to full boiling. The boiling should be continued at intense heat for about two hours, stirring, from time to time, to prevent the clippings from adhering to the sides and bottom of the pot, which must be kept covered between the stirrings. When the water is reduced to about one third its volume, strain off through two thicknesses of muslin, or better still, a thin old linen sheet, and set aside to cool and clarify. By next day it will have set into a tough jelly, and be ready for use. It can be dried, and kept for years by running it into flat-bottomed glazed dishes about an inch deep, and when set, cut into slices, about $\frac{1}{4}$ inch thick, which can then be completely dried by placing the slices on metal gauze or a reed matting, and fanning them in a draught of cold air.'

[NOTE: This method of making glue—somewhat complicated and laborious as it is—provides a glue of very high quality which may be used for grounds, distemper painting, and the emulsion which follows. If there seems too much work connected with its manufacture, substitute ordinary skin glue for it, for any or all of these uses, and the final result will be very similar in every way. *H. Hiler.*]

EMULSION

'This parchment glue dried (or any similar glue in dry form) should be placed in about seven times its weight of water and left to soak for about twelve hours.

'Then melted down and stirred, adding a little more water if evaporation occurs, to keep consistency. If freshly made, a few drops of ammonia may be added while it is being stirred over a slow fire.

[The author begs to advise a double boiler.]

'The chill should be taken off the grinding slab by pouring hot water over it, then it can be heated by spreading a cloth steeped in boiling water over it, and it may be kept warm by pouring boiling water over it from time to time.

'Warm size or glue is poured on to the warmed slab from the double boiler and the linseed oil ground in as for the other emulsions, forming a thick alabaster-like cream. Boiling water should be used for grinding pigments into it. Warm water should be used to dilute it for use as a medium. Equal proportions of size and water.

'Pigments, ground in this emulsion, will keep for a considerable length of time if tubed, but the medium itself will not keep for more than a few days in summer.'

EMULSION OF RYE FLOUR PASTE

Dissolve 4 oz. 180 grains of rye flour in 3·05 cu. in. of very hot water, thin with 6·1 cu. in. of cold water and then with 18·3 cu. in. of hot water. Shake well, incorporating 7·6 cu. in. of linseed oil varnish.

Like egg tempera, pulverized gum arabic dissolved in water (1 part gum, 2 parts water) can be emulsified with oils. Add oil up to double the amount of the tempera. The tempera should not be too oily. This mixture is not as good as the one made with egg and oil, since there is less affinity between gum and oil than between yolk of egg and oil, so that if it is applied to oily grounds it divides into tiny drops. For these emulsions the addition of a small quantity of glycerine is necessary. These temperas are the only ones which are not spoilt by glycerine, but a proportion of 5 per cent of the emulsion should not be exceeded. The result is a light painting like pastel and much more brittle than those done with egg.

Tragacanth and cherry gum can also be emulsified with oil. Boecklin used cherry gum emulsion which was already mentioned by Theophilus, and which confers great transparency and a vitreous quality to the colours but is fragile and produces cracks. Mixed with oil it makes an emulsion which keeps well and can be mixed with egg or casein tempera.

GUM TEMPERA

This recipe by Oreste Mandel requires equal parts of cooked linseed oil and saturated solution of gum arabic. Emulsify with an equal volume of water.

CHERRY GUM TEMPERA[22]

Put into a bottle

> 309 grains of dry cherry gum
> $17\frac{1}{2}$ oz. of water

Leave the bottle in the sun until the gum is dissolved and then strain to remove impurities. The liquid has the consistency of honey. To 3 oz. 230 grains of this tempera add from $1\frac{1}{4}$ oz. to 2 oz. 50 grains of oil or varnish, shaking the bottle to emulsify the liquids.

CASEIN EMULSION

Colours tempered with milk have always been used for painting on walls: this technique will be discussed further in connection with mural painting. In the Middle Ages milk was used to bind certain colours which, like the blues, turned green if bound with egg.[23] The emulsions of casein and lime, commonly used in mural tempera and fixed with a 6 per cent solution of formalin, can be used on cardboard as well. (See p. 37.)

Casein tempera must be thinned because it is so strong and adhesive that, if applied in an excessive quantity, it tears the ground off the surface in the process of drying. Nevertheless it gives tones that are lighter and have more body than those tempered with egg. To emulsify casein with water, the old masters used not only lime but ammonium carbonate, salt of stag's horn and borax.

By adding ammonia to casein it becomes possible to work oils, varnishes and oil of spike into the tempera; soda, potash and borax, which are alkaline, act even better than ammonia. Casein temperas with ammonia have strong adhesive power on both thin and fatty grounds. They should not be preserved in tubes as they form lumps. It is advisable to keep the pigments ground in water and to add the casein only when required. This tempera is thinned with pure water or with water mixed with skimmed milk.

CASEIN TEMPERA

This recipe, given by H. Sachs,[24] requires:

Coagulated milk	$1\frac{1}{2}$ parts
Slaked lime mixed into a stiff paste	1 part
Venice turpentine or oil of spike	$\frac{1}{2}$–1 per cent

Cook this mixture in a double saucepan for two or three hours at a temperature of 85–95° F. Then dilute with 2 or 3 parts of water. This glue keeps its power of adhesion for three or four days. The paints are made fluid by the addition of an equal amount of water and skimmed milk.

135

CASEIN AND LINSEED OIL EMULSION

Another recipe is given by Tudor-Hart. The ingredients are:

Powered casein
Precipitated lime
Linseed oil (washed and purified)

Put the casein on the grinding slab and add lime (one tenth of the volume of casein). Mix well and add sufficient water to make a stiff paste. Then add an equal volume of hot water and mix well with the muller. Thin again thrice, each time with the same volume of hot water, place on fire and boil. Strain through fine muslin and keep warm in a double saucepan. Warm the slab and gradually mix the casein tempera with the oil (one third of the volume of the glue). This emulsion should be similar to that of oil and glue, but, as it also contains lime, one should remember that it easily alters and increases the tone of the lighter coloured pigment.

TEMPERAS WITH SOAP

Many painters follow the practice of adding soap to the tempera to increase its adhesive power and to make it pleasantly thick. The brush strokes flow easily and cling to the ground, even if fatty. But the use of soap is highly dangerous since it darkens the colours in a very short time and even more quickly if the medium contains cooked oil or oils of poor quality.

FATTY TEMPERAS

Certain so-called 'fatty' temperas on the market contain castor oil, olive oil and sodium oleate. Work produced with these substitutes can never be durable.

12

Painting in Oils

The legend that the Van Eyck brothers invented oil painting is no longer accepted: according to Paolo Pino[1] the Romans were acquainted with this technique and used it, especially when decorating shields and arms.

One should not speak of invention but rather of the results of a long and elaborate evolution of oleo-resinous media used in the early Middle Ages for the decoration of arms, stones, walls and finally for works of pure art. One of the reasons for the success and the rapid spread of this method lies in its easy handling and its variety of chromatic effects.

Colours can be superimposed, worked, shaded and corrected without the picture losing its immediacy or its freshness of touch. The artist can use glazes and washes of very fluid colour as in watercolour painting, or apply paint heavily with a palette knife as in encaustic technique. Paintings can be as dry and mat as gouache and tempera, or show a depth and luminosity which no other technique will give them.

There is no one and only technique for painting in oils, as various methods and media have their own specific qualities.

OIL AND RESIN METHOD

The earliest oil painters used mixtures of colour, oil and resin which were thick, slow-drying and difficult to handle, and their use was therefore restricted to the final glazes. The Van Eycks discovered a clear medium, which dried quicker and was more fluid, 'such as painters had always longed for'.[2]

This mixture was made with pigments ground with linseed

or nut oil, amalgamated over heat with hard resins (amber or copal) and thinned with essential oils (apparently lavender, spike or rosemary),[3] oils with different degrees of drying power which allow either a slow technique of finely shaded tones, or the minute, fine, drawn strokes which are possible only with a medium which dries rapidly.

Knowing that the most luminous white was the gesso priming on the supports, painters took advantage of it as much as possible. The final high lights always contained a minimum dose of oil and varnish and were applied thinly. These painters had observed that transparent colours suffered much more than opaque ones when bound with oil and therefore used them with varnish only for glazing and never in impasto.

The oil and resin technique cannot be used on canvas, but on panels, cardboard or similar supports, primed with gesso and size; the ground should be as smooth as ivory and non-absorbent. Canvas and absorbent grounds require an excessive amount of varnish and this in time would make the painting darken and crack.

Paint brushes must be soft: badger, minever, squirrel or sable are suitable. Maurice Busset,[4] who has made a special study of the media of the old masters, advises the painter to use good oil colours, freed from grease by being placed for a long time between sheets of blotting paper and then made fluid again with the following diluent:

Amber or copal varnish	1 part
Essence of lavender	1 ,,

Drying power is increased if essence of petroleum is used instead of essence of lavender. Essence of rosemary makes the colours dry slowly. The painter should draw his picture very carefully when laying it in and use colours thinned to the consistency of watercolours for the shadows; the high lights should be obtained through transparency and the brush strokes fused and finely shaded. Only the final touches should be put in with solid paint, as with the old Flemish masters. Jewel-like paintings of extraordinary vivacity and permanence are thus obtained.

These resin-oil colours can be used for finishing pictures begun in tempera.[5] Some firms, like Blocks of Antwerp, make colours containing from 5 to 10 per cent of amber varnish. They are made into a rather stiff paste which is thinned with essential oils which lend themselves to this technique. On reaching Italy, the Flemish system slowly changed in character, both as regards procedure and medium; to obtain more fluid brushwork the painters gradually diminished the amount of hard resins, using instead soft resins, balsams and essential oils.

The pictures acquired a greater opacity, shadows and lights were painted with coats of equal thickness, as we can see in the paintings of Perugino, Fra Bartolomeo, Raphael, Giulio Romano, Andrea del Sarto, Bronzino, etc. The painters of the Lombard school headed by Leonardo, and those of Parma headed by Correggio obtained, by adding Venice turpentine,[6] colours which could not only be shaded delicately by fusing the tones but could also be used with more solid touches.

The Mussini colours, containing amber, copaiva balsam and turpentine, lend themselves well to this blended half-paste technique.

OIL AND ESSENTIAL OILS METHOD

In the Venetian school, first with Giorgione and then with Titian, Sebastian del Piombo, Tintoretto and Paolo Veronese, pictures were first sketched in with an underpainting in heavy colour on canvas, or on panels primed with gesso and glue so as to be fairly absorbent. Very rarely was the underpainting done in tempera. The chromatic effect was obtained through the power of refraction of the pigments rather than from their transparency and gloss. The colour was rather lean and applied with strong and plastic brushwork. These underpaintings were allowed to stand for months so that the colours might dry perfectly.

The pigments were bound with purified oils and thinned with essential oils; oil varnishes were used only for the final glazes.

Most painters, however, did not use the same resins and thinners for all parts of the picture, but chose the ones which were most suitable for the pigment used locally. The Abbé Requeno observed this in Guercino's pictures, where one finds 'pigments bound with pure oil, with oil and colophony and other resins and gums'.

Reynolds, who made a thorough study of the media of the 16th-century Venetian masters, followed their methods in underpainting with solid colour and finishing with varnish, but unfortunately his mixtures of oils, balsams, resins and waxes were responsible for cracks and darkening in many of his pictures.[7]

Reynolds' mistake lay in using for his underpainting colours too heavily loaded with oils and resins instead of using lean and absorbent colours like the Venetians.

17TH-CENTURY METHODS

Rubens brought together the precepts of the Flemish and Venetian schools. The famous rule 'transparent shadows and impasto light' is ascribed to him. His first paintings were done on panels or canvases less absorbent than those used by the Venetians, mostly white, grey or pale pink. His technique allows spontaneous, rapid and vigorous painting: the shadows are thinned with varnish and applied with a 'wet in wet' method as if they were in watercolour. The lights are put in with thick colour 'applied with a hard brush and with close strokes which can be easily blended by brushing over lightly, without ruffling them. One can then work over this preparation using the bold brushwork which is the hallmark of the great masters'.[8]

According to Maurice Busset[9] a thinner with the same characteristics of the diluent used by Rubens can be obtained by mixing:

Essence of lavender or petroleum	2 parts
Poppy oil	1 part
Amber or copal with oil	1 ,,

Not only the Flemish and Dutch painters, but also English masters like Gainsborough and Lawrence, followed these precepts using the media with slight modifications. The 18th-century French painters, Boucher, Chardin, Fragonard and others, painted with colours which were leaner than those used by the Flemish and thinned their impastos to a greater degree, using essential oils. Like Guardi and Tiepolo in Italy, they thus obtained a clear type of painting, which seems to reflect the light rather than to absorb it.

PURE OIL METHOD

This is the technique used by painters of the last century and by contemporary artists. Many painters use colours straight from the tube, without any thinner.

Working with pure oil lends itself well to paintings which do not need to be finished immediately and to direct painting. The opaque layer of paint acquires great solidity in time, but tends to turn yellow. Colours should always be supplied by reputable manufacturers whose goods are of guaranteed quality, free from adulteration.

In general, the colours found on the market at present contain too much oil, at times one third more than is necessary. The manufacturers do this to prevent the colours from drying in the tube, but as this excess of oil would make the colours run on the palette, they also add wax (20–30 per cent), fat, bacon fat, whale oil. Wax makes the colours opaque and prevents the perfect adhesion of subsequent coats, so that these colours are really suitable only for direct painting. Otherwise they must be thinned with essential oil of petroleum or petroleum varnish which, being akin to wax, holds the various layers of the painting together.

Colours containing fats should be avoided. They are not siccative and produce a viscous mass which dries badly and darkens rapidly. Before starting a picture which is bound to take a long time, it is advisable to place the colours on cardboard or between sheets of blotting paper to remove excess oil and to obtain lean underpainting. The colours can also be placed on a slab of glass and left under water for twenty-four hours.

To regain fluidity the colours are now thinned with essences or mixtures according to the technique preferred. At the end of the day the colours remaining on the palette are transferred to a glass slab and placed in water to avoid their drying and becoming useless.

A very small dose of alumina salt should be added to certain colours, such as vermilion, which have a tendency to run. This does not damage the colours and indeed gives a greater mellowness to the oil.

Should a sketch or a painting have an opaque and greasy appearance due to excess oil in the colours, allow it to dry and then smooth the surface with powdered pumice stone mixed with talc powder or bean flour. This treatment removes all excess oil from the surface, frees the picture from grease and makes it absorbent, thus improving the adhesive power of the finishing touches.

In painting with oil colours it is essential that all colours should dry evenly for if some dry sooner than others there will be tensions and cracks in the various layers since different pigments take a different time in drying. The madders, ivory black and vine black, zinc white and green chrome oxides dry slowly; yellow ochres, cobalt blue and the cadmiums in average time; white lead, Naples yellow, raw sienna earth, and umber dry very quickly.

To hasten the drying process, someone thought of adding substances capable of attracting oxygen which would act on the oil and hasten oxidization. So siccatives came into being. They should be used in minimum quantities and only with dark colours.

The best siccatives are those of Courtrai (treated with the Dinet system, see p. 83) and of Flamand and Harlem which are really fatty varnishes containing resins which harden the colour.

MEDIA AND EMULSIONS

Resin and Wax Colours

There are on the market colours made with a resin and wax base (elemi gluten, Paris gluten, Weimar milk of figs, etc.). We shall discuss them when dealing with encaustic technique and emulsions. (See pp. 183 ff.)

Sérusier reports that Van Gogh worked wax into his colours and spread them on his pictures with wooden spatulas. His colours have preserved their tones almost perfectly.

LUDWIG'S PETROLEUM COLOURS

These turn very dark in time: the resins tend to form a viscous deposit which endangers the good preservation of the painting.

OPAQUE COLOURS

So-called opaque colours are found on the market. They are made with common oil colours mixed with turpentine and Bologna plaster. They are very inferior in quality and have very little covering power.

GUSSOW'S COLOURS

These colours are produced by emulsifying pure soap and a saturated solution of alum over heat and then adding turpentine. This emulsion can be mixed with resins and oils. White thus prepared allows solid and perfect brushwork; unfortunately all other colours are extremely difficult to handle as they become hard and tough within one hour and almost impossible to apply and fuse with a brush.

COLOURS WITH BALSAM

The German apothecary Lucanus in 1834 introduced oil colours containing copaiva balsam.

To give cohesion to the various coats of paint he advocated varnishing the painted part with a mixture of isinglass and shellac. But the excess of balsam and the use of the isinglass and shellac emulsion have darkened the pictures and caused cracks.

BUTTNER'S COLOURS

The colours are mixed with Vaseline oil and should be used

on an absorbent gesso priming. The painter can work slowly and blend his shades well. When he wishes the colours to dry he smears the back of the canvas with a thick paste made with China clay and water. This absorbs the Vaseline which is not siccative. These colours are, however, neither practical in use nor durable.

Students' Colours

There are various colours sold under this denomination. They are made with pigments of poor quality mixed with heavy fluor-spar or alumina. While in use these colours appear to have covering power, but when they dry they lose this quality and become transparent. The fluor-spar tends to make the colours yellow and alters the tones.

Solid Oil Colours and Oil Pastels

These solid colours have been very well received both in England and America, especially for rough sketches and sketches from nature. They are shaped like little cylinders and are used in the same way as pastels on paper, ply-board, cardboard and canvas. If the colour is made into cakes, the technique is similar to that of watercolour. The brush is dipped in turpentine or some other solvent and rubbed on the colour. Very pleasing and unusual effects are obtained but the solidity of the picture is doubtful in view of the fatty substances contained.

In working with oil pastels the shades are blended and fused with oil of turpentine, oil and painting varnish. The best effects are obtained by using paper mounted on cardboard, allowing the white to show through as with watercolours.

Solid oil colours are prepared in the following manner: The pigments are ground with mastic dissolved in an equal amount of oil of turpentine. Once the pastes have dried they are put on a warm grinding slab, and a mixture of 3 parts of spermaceti oil and 1 part poppy oil dissolved over heat are added until the right consistency is obtained. They are then made into little cylinders or cakes as desired and stored.

These colours are similar to the Raffaelli colours discussed on page 99.

Colours Ground with Essential Oils

Rubens held that pigments should be ground with rectified oil of turpentine; some painters are in the habit of grinding them with oil of turpentine before making them into a paste with oil. Modern artists are ignorant of the use of powdered colours simply ground with essential oils: these dilute equally well with temperas with an egg and varnish base, with painting varnishes, fixed oils, emulsions and wax. They are indispensable to the restorer since, unlike oil impastos, they are not subject to alterations of tone, and when mixed with thinned varnish they have the same enamel-like quality as the ancient colours.

Technical Innovations

Modern pictures deteriorate very quickly because of the absurd use of heterogeneous substances. Not only do artists glue to their canvases pieces of paper, material or tin foil, but they also mix sand, sawdust, pieces of tin, glass, wood and cement into the impasto; they mix oil and tempera colours with enamels and synthetic varnishes guided more by caprice than logic.

Klee in some pictures superimposed ten layers of different substances. On a cardboard support he would spread Chinese varnish mixed with oil; on this he would stretch a piece of gauze. Then came the gesso ground, the general tone in watercolour, glue tempera, watercolour once again, a coat of varnish, a fairly heavy coat in oil colours, semi-transparent glazes and finally liquid oil glazes. Because of these stratifications many modern pictures are already the despair of restorers and liners.

In conclusion, to produce a durable oil painting it is necessary:

(a) to use only pure materials;

(b) to employ siccatives as little as possible;

(c) to begin with lean and dry colours, leaving all fatty colours for finishing;

(d) to remember that two thin coats of colour give a richer tone and have more body than one thick coat;[10]

(*e*) to paint only over perfectly dry foundations to avoid the risk of cracks;

(*f*) to thin the colours as little as possible, trying to use them in a rather solid state;

(*g*) to use preferably fatty varnishes for glazes.

THINNERS FOR OIL COLOURS [11]

THINNER	DRYING TIME
Ethereal oil of turpentine	Rapid
Petroleum oils	Few hours
Tetraline	More slowly than turpentine
Siccatives	12 to 24 hours
Linseed oil varnish	12 to 24 ,,
Amber varnish Copal varnish	24 to 36 ,,
Mastic varnish Dammar varnish	If used in a thin coat, 1 to 2 days
Venice turpentine Linseed oil	If used in a thick coat, about 14 days
Oil of rosemary and spike	3 or 4 days
Nut oil	3 or 4 ,,
Poppy oil	4 or 5 ,,
Stand oil (polymerized)	5 or 8 ,,
Oil of cloves	40 days

The rate of drying also depends on the temperature, the season of the year and the type of ground. Ethereal oils confer opacity and fluid colours; fixed oils and oil varnishes give mellowness and brilliance; Venice turpentine and Stand oil produce a vitreous quality and hardness.

MEDIA AND VARNISHES FOR PAINTING

Artists and manufacturers have invented an infinite number of mixtures which are added to the oil colours to give them fluidity, drying power, transparency, brilliance or opacity. These substances, given various names by the trade, such as *media*, pomatums, balsams, *oliesse*, glutens, varnishes, *megilps*,[12] can be very harmful to pictures, since the artist uses and dilutes them without knowing their chemical composition; unless heated, their ingredients may not mix properly with the oil contained in the colours, forming a viscous mass which dries badly, causes cracks and pulls the various coats of colour apart instead of holding them together.

In making a mixture of oils, essences and varnishes for painting, one should use only perfectly pure materials. Varnish should be left in the sun for a long time, and used only when it has become perfectly clear, light and free from sediment.

PAINTING VARNISHES WHICH DRY RAPIDLY

1 VARNISH OF AMBER AND ESSENTIAL OILS

Amber varnish	309 grains
Essential oil of turpentine	618 ,,
Essential oil of lavender	81 ,,

2 VAN DYCK'S VARNISH

Mastic varnish	1 part
Essential oil of turpentine	2 parts

These substances are amalgamated over a low fire. A small quantity of siccative oil is then added (oil cooked with white lead) while the varnish is warm. It should not coagulate, but once cooled should form a whitish jelly.

PAINTING VARNISHES WHICH DRY IN AVERAGE TIME

1 VARNISH OF MASTIC AND OILS

Mastic varnish	309 grains
Essential oil of turpentine	324 ,,
Poppy oil	154 ,,
Essential oil of lavender	81 ,,

2 Turpentine Varnish

Venice turpentine	$3\frac{1}{2}$ oz.
Essential oil of turpentine	3 ,,

This mixture produces vitreous quality and brilliance.

3 Max Doerner's Varnish

Essential oil of turpentine	1 part
Dammar varnish	1 ,,
Polymerized (Stand) oil	1 ,,

4 Consalvo Carelli's Varnish

Essential oil of turpentine	2 oz.
Pure linseed oil	2 ,,
Copal varnish	50 drops

In his letter on the art of painting (Naples 1871), Consalvo Carelli recommends this varnish for glazes and for mixing with colours, warning painters at the same time to beware of those mixtures called *medium*, *oliesse*, *megilps*, etc., which were on the market and which made the pictures of his time crack. Carelli's pictures are very well preserved and the tones have not altered at all.

5 Holman Hunt's Medium [13]

Copal varnish
Poppy oil   } in equal parts, mixed over
Rectified turpentine } mild heat.

In Holman Hunt's pictures the colours are well preserved although slightly darkened.

VARNISHES WHICH DRY SLOWLY

1 Oil Varnish

Poppy oil	386 grains

Essential oil of turpentine   386   ,,
Essential oil of lavender   154   ,,

2 DE MAYERNE'S VARNISH

Amber varnish   1 part
Sun-bleached nut oil   3 parts

OBSERVATIONS ON SOME PAINTING AND RETOUCHING MEDIUMS USED BY PAINTERS AND RESTORERS

MEDIUM	RECIPE	ADVANTAGES	DISADVANTAGES
Armenini's Painting medium	'Dissolve on fire pure mastic with nut oil (enough to cover it), add a small quantity of alum, then filter the varnish through a thin cloth.'	When a very small amount is mixed to oil colours, it gives a hard and glossy surface.	When used too thick causes deep cracks. Stipplings on oil pictures made with this type of varnish are very hard to remove.
De Piles' varnish	A similar recipe to the above was used in 17th and 18th centuries especially for pictures that had to be exposed in open or damp places as it gave a waterproof surface.	Good tractability and bright gloss.	Pictures tend to become brittle with age.
Marcucci's varnish	Turpentine 2 lb. Mastic resin 4 oz. Venice turpentine 6 ,, all dissolved in a warm sand bath. This varnish is used directly with dry pigments.	Used chiefly for decorations exposed to atmosphere.	The same as above.
Wattin's a toil	Silver litharge ½ oz. Burnt white lead ½ ,, Umber earth ¼ ,, Talc ½ ,, Linseed oil 1 lb. all boiled together until a reddish scum appears on the surface. This oil is very thick and has to be thinned with a little turpentine.	Very strong drier which allows the painter to work very quickly.	This oil was one of the main causes of cracking and darkening of so many paintings.
Robertson's medium	Strong copal varnish made with linseed oil and traces of white wax. Used in Italy by many painters who found it a satisfactory and well-balanced medium.	Added to oil colours is very workable and gives easy brush strokes and a silky gloss.	Hardens with age; for this reason it must not be used for stoppings.

American painting mediums (Ralph Mayer, 'The Artist's Handbook' pp. 176–7)	A Stand oil 1 fluid oz.
	    Dammar varnish
	    (heavier than the
	    average) 1 ,, ,,
	    Turpentine 6 ,, ,,
		Good for glazing over egg temperas. Can be added as drier to oil colours.	Tends to yellow with age and to crack through its lack of flexibility; for this reason it is unwise to use it over casein underpainting.

	B Dammar varnish 5 fluid oz.
	    Stand oil 1 ,, ,,
	    Toluol ½ ,, ,,
	    Anhydrous
	    alcohol ½ ,, ,,
		Very workable medium.	If used too thick tends to crack and to get yellow with age.

MEDIUM	RECIPE	ADVANTAGES	DISADVANTAGES
	Stir and shake until clear, then add Turpentine 13 fluid oz.		
	C Dammar varnish 4 fluid oz. Sun-thickened oil 2 ,, ,, Venice turpentine 1 ,, ,, Turpentine 4 ,, ,,	Good for glazing over temperas or to mix with dry pigments with the addition of more turpentine. Can be used by restorers for stoppings over tempera underpainting.	Gets brittle with age in a damp atmosphere.
Japan oil or goldsize	It is a copal oil varnish containing a large amount of siccatives.	Dries very quickly.	It was used by Italian 19th-century restorers; their stoppings got very dark, dull, cracked and difficult to remove.
Guizzardi's restoring medium	Raw linseed oil 4 parts Ground litharge 1 part exposed to the sun for a whole summer, then well decanted and filtered: it was used mixed with oil colours.	Gives the glossy surface of old pictures.	With age it loses the gloss and darkens and cracks.
Another restoring medium	Oil colours blended with a mixture of mastic and amber varnish (1 : 1), thinned with a little turpentine or spike oil, were used by restorers from 18th up to the beginning of 20th century.	Very workable.	With age loses gloss, darkens and cracks.
Modern restoring medium	Dry pigments ground with turpentine and a little oil of spike are mixed with a diluted mastic or synthetic varnish.	Very good 'for stopping alone or used for glazing over egg tempera. Its lack of workability does not encourage overpainting.	Bleaches a little in damp and dark atmosphere.
Soehnée's retouching varnish	Used as oiling out medium for oil pictures or as varnish over temperas before retouching them with oil colours.	None.	One of the most pernicious varnishes: it is affected by damp and gets dull and dark with age.
Junemann's varnish	White shellac 12 parts Borax 4 ,, Water 100 ,, The ingredients are heated all together, very slowly, until the shellac is dissolved and then the varnish is strained.	None.	No permanence.
Delacroix oiling out medium	Oil, water, turpentine in equal quantities are mixed together and shaken well.	Good workability.	The bad preservation of so many pictures of Delacroix is due to this medium as it gives a surface liable to chip and scale.
Dammar emulsion	Dammar resin dissolved in raw linseed oil by exposure to the sun is emulsified with a little water, shaking the mixture well.	Very workable.	This emulsion causes very bad cracks and stains on the surface of the picture.
Ordinary Megilp	A jelly mass is obtained by mixing some mastic varnish with linseed oil.	Megilps dry very quickly and are very workable. The colours acquire a nice enamel gloss.	Complete lack of durability as the colours crack, turn black and are affected by weak cleansing mixtures.

MEDIUM	RECIPE	ADVANTAGES	DISADVANTAGES
Seguier's Megilp	Mastic dissolved in a drying oil was used as picture varnish by Seguier (restorer of the National Gallery, London, *circa* 1824–1856).	None.	With age this varnish became dark and stained the pictures with irregular spots.
Copal Megilp	It is made by adding a little copal to ordinary megilp.	It has a buttery consistency and a shining gloss.	The same erratic behaviour as other megilps.
Pynes' Megilp	A calcium sulphate ground with poppy oil.	A light jelly, very agreeable to work with.	The same as above.
Italian Megilp	Boil slowly 24 parts of nut oil with 12 parts of litharge ground to a very thin powder. Add 1 part of powdered mastic resin. When cold it looks like butter. It was used by 19th-century restorers and recommended by Forni (*Manuale del pittore restauratore*, p. 275).	Very agreeable to work with, in bold strokes or light glazing.	Darkens, blisters and cracks with age.
Flemish Megilp	Mastic 4 parts Alcohol 5 „ dissolved in a water bath, and when the liquid is decanted 1½ parts of white wax are added. The mixture is then dipped into cold water and worked with a wood spatula till all the alcohol is mixed with the water and the wax does not stick any more to the touch.	Mixed with a little siccative oil, gives a very workable medium.	The layers of the pictures painted with this medium tend to blister and flake. Was used by some 19th-century restorers with disastrous effects.
Siccative Megilp	Burnt lead acetate (Sal Saturni) was ground with mastic dissolved in nut oil (1 : 6); adding to the mass a few drops of water a buttery substance was obtained. Used by the Hungarian painter Karl Marko.	None.	The colours become brittle very soon.
Mueller's siccative	The recipe is quoted by Forni (p. 279). One part of mastic or dammar resin is dissolved over heat; then 1 part of hot turpentine is added.	Diluted with turpentine and mixed with oil colours gives a very workable medium.	The colours become brittle very soon.
Haarlem's siccative	Mastic varnish is obtained by dissolving over heat mastic resin and then adding boiling turpentine or spike oil (12 : 12). Then add 1 part of copal varnish and a little more turpentine.	Very good for glazing. It has to be thinned with a little turpentine or spike oil.	Not to be used by restorers as the colours get very hard and difficult to remove when darkened by age.
Courtrai siccative	The old recipe contained: Asphaltum 1 part, amber resin 24 parts, copal resin 12 parts, all well ground into a thin powder that had to be dissolved over heat: then 96 parts of boiling turpentine were added.	Very quick drier: to be used with dark colours, thinned with turpentine.	Darkens with age and cracks if it is not thinned with essential oils.
Water	Water saturated with lead acetate was used as siccative in 19th-century mixing it to oil colours.	None.	Very dangerous medium for erratic effects.

PIGMENT	FILM CHARACTERISTICS
Rapid driers	
Umbers	Tough, flexible
Prussian blue	Hard
Flake or Cremnitz white	Tough, flexible
Aureolin	Hard, erratic
Burnt sienna	Hard, fairly strong
'Average' driers	
Raw sienna	Tough, fairly strong
Cobalt blue	Rather brittle
Cobalt violet	Rather brittle
Red iron oxide (pure)	Strong
Black iron oxide	Strong
Yellow iron oxide	Strong
Cobalt green	Flexible, fairly hard
Chromium oxide	Flexible, fairly hard
Viridian	Flexible, fairly hard
Naples yellow	Strong
Zinc, barium and strontian yellows	Hard, rather brittle
Some native red oxides	Usually brittle
Slow driers	
Other native red oxides	Usually brittle
Green earth	Soft, flexible
Cerulean blue	Soft, non-elastic
Ultramarine	Fairly hard, somewhat brittle
Yellow ochre	Fairly strong
Alizarin	Soft
Very slow driers	
Ivory black	Soft
Emerald green	Fairly hard
Cadmiums	Fairly strong
Vermilion	Strong

Alumina hydrate	Hard and brittle
Zinc oxide	Hard and brittle
Lampblack	Soft
Carbon black	Soft
Van Dyke brown	Soft and weak

HOW TO KNEAD OIL COLOURS

The colours are placed on a porphyry or thick frosted glass grinding slab and kneaded with a very small quantity of oil. The paste thus obtained is then ground with a muller until perfectly smooth. Colours which tend to separate from the oil, such as the blacks, titanium white and others, should first be kneaded with a little pure spirit.

For oleo-resin painting add, during the grinding process, 10 per cent varnish to the amount of oil used. The quantity of oil needed by each pigment varies according to the weight of the pigment itself. The chemist Max Pettenkofer, who made a special study of colours to improve their quality, was the first to try to determine the exact amount of oil needed for each pigment.

In kneading colours preference should be given to oils which are if possible uncooked, clarified, freed from acidity and impurities. (See pp. 63 ff.)

PERCENTAGES OF OIL REQUIRED BY THE VARIOUS PIGMENTS [15]

Lead white	15	Naples yellow	15
Zinc white	30	Indian yellow	100
Chrome yellow	25	Burnt ochre	40
Cadmium yellow	40	Oxides of iron	40
Yellow ochre	60	Cinnabar	20
Raw sienna	200	Madder lake	70
Zinc yellow	40	Minium	15
Barium yellow	30	Ultramarine	40
Strontian yellow	30	Cobalt blue	100

Cobalt violet	40	Opaque chrome green	30
Prussian blue	80	Umber earth	80
Green earth	80	Burnt umber	50
Green cobalt	30	Burnt sienna	180
Brilliant chrome green	100	Ivory black	100

13

Encaustic Painting

Plutarch exalts the merits of encaustic painting thus: 'The sight of a beautiful woman leaves in the heart of an indifferent man an image as fleeting as a painting on water. But in the heart of a lover this image is fixed with fire like an encaustic painting which time can never obliterate.'

The literal meaning of the word 'encaustic' is 'a painting burnt in'. It had a great vogue with Greek and Roman painters and was used up to the first centuries of the Christian era. Then gradually encaustic painting was superseded by temperas and oleo-resin colours.

Here and there, however, later mural paintings or illuminations in missals done with wax colours are found. Interest in this technique was revived during the 17th century. The three systems listed by Pliny,[1] later variously interpreted by scholars and artists, were:

(a) A painting carried out with solid colours mixed with wax, a little oil and resin, modelled with a *cestrum*, a sort of spatula with tooth-like notches, similar in shape to a betony leaf;[2]

(b) A painting on ivory,[3] executed with a *cestrum* or with a *verriculum*, a spatula similar to that used by Silversmiths for skimming melted silver;

(c) A painting carried out with brushes and wax colours made fluid by heating.

The ancient artists knew of other mixtures, not mentioned by Pliny: pigments and wax thinned with essential oils,[4] and those made with saponified wax.[5]

According to Schmidt, the hot wax shrinks in cooling, making the paste very strong and without producing those little lumps which always form in emulsions and cold solutions. The latter lose some of their fragility if fixed by means of heat, and varnished with a hot wax varnish.

True encaustic painting, obtained with heat, gives clear, brilliant and stable results. It is even possible to use colours generally considered fragile, like the vegetable ones, because the wax seems to protect them. The other systems, using cold liquid wax and emulsions, are simpler to use and allow a more varied and rapid execution but are easily damaged by damp.

The most suitable brushes for the hot method are those made of bristle; for the other techniques, without heat and with emulsions, it is best to use badger brushes.

SUPPORTS AND PRIMING

Encaustic can be used on canvas with a gesso ground, on panels, with or without gesso priming, on cardboard and on masonite.

Emulsions containing oil and essential oils can be used also over gesso and oil priming. For all types of vitreous encaustic containing resins, it is best to use wood or masonite coated with a very thin layer of gesso.

HOW TO BLEACH WAX[6]

'Desaint (Vol. I, p. 125) advises bleaching the wax by melting it, adding 20 grammes (309 grains) of nitrate of soda to the quart, and 40 grammes (1 oz. 180 grains) of sulphuric acid diluted in ten times its volume of water. Stir constantly, taking care that the wax is always hot. Let it stand a few minutes, fill the receptacle with very hot water and let cool. Wash well and rinse to eliminate any traces of nitric acid which would make it turn yellow.

'Church's method of bleaching (op. cit., p. 79) is to melt the wax at the lowest temperature possible, and pour it in a slender stream into a cold saturated solution of alum which is being constantly stirred. The wax is thus granulated, and may be bleached by placing it on linen cloths and exposing it for several days to the action of sunlight and dew; or treating it with a dilute chromic-acid solution or with peroxide of hydrogen. All these processes succeed better when the wax is in the form of thin sheets or ribbons. The bleached wax after thorough washing and drying is remelted. Its hardness and its melting point are bettered by this treatment.'

CLASSICAL ENCAUSTIC WITH HEAT[7]

MATERIALS

Of all *heating devices* now available an electric ring is the best, since this medium is extremely inflammable. The ring will serve to prepare the coloured waxes, to keep the palette and the metal spatulas warm and to spread and model the colours.

The *palette* should be of metal with depressions to hold the coloured waxes; it should also have a heat-proof handle so as not to burn one's hands when using it.

WAX

Take purified white wax and melt it with pine resin (half the weight of the wax). Some use Venice turpentine (one third of the weight of the wax) instead of pine resin.

PROPORTION OF WAX AND RESIN (*TO* 3 *PARTS OF COLOUR*)

White lead	18–20 parts	Yellow ochre	40 parts
Vermilion	40 ,,	Rust ochre	40 ,,
Carmine	45 ,,	Ultramarine	40 ,,
Lake	45 ,,	Blue ashes	24 ,,
English red (Light red)	30 ,,	English enamel	15 ,,
Burnt ochre	40 ,,	Green lake	38 ,,
Italian earth	40 ,,	Cologne earth	45 ,,
Naples yellow	16 ,,	Ivory black	40 ,,
Stil de grain	45 ,,	Lampblack	40 ,,

Preparation of Colours

Mix the wax with the resin and pigments and melt in a metal or earthenware vessel, mixing well. Pour still warm into cylindrical moulds. It is possible to make various shades of the same colour. These colours are used like pastels.

Execution

When painting, take some of this coloured paste and place it on a warm palette in one of the depressions. When melted, spread rapidly with a brush. Fuse and model with a hot spatula.

Burns' Method

A. P. Laurie describes the method of the English painter Burns who used to paint with colours mixed with pure wax. The canvas was mounted so that it was possible to warm it by placing its back to the fire. The finished picture was polished with a cloth.

A coat of copal varnish protects the colours from dirt and dust.

Fixing Wax Pictures with Heat

In ancient times encaustic paintings were fixed by bringing them near to a brazier or to any other source of heat. Nowadays, without having recourse to complicated electrical appliances or infra-red lamps as some artists have recommended, it is possible to fix encaustic perfectly by holding a hot electric iron near the picture. The colours melt and become brilliant. Thus they can be easily blended and retouched. When the picture is finished, warm it again to stabilize the medium.

Technique with Wax thinned with Essential Oils

This type of medium was recommended by Count de Caylus, Fabroni, Paillot de Montabert, Knirim, Taubenheim, Fernbach. Arnold Boecklin painted various pictures with a medium of copal, oil of turpentine and wax, sometimes applied directly, with heat, to the canvas or the panel by means of a curved spatula. Durozier, who has made a special study of these encaustics, has placed on the market some products called elemi gluten, or Paris gluten, etc. (See p. 185.) For these paintings many artists use ordinary oil colours, removing the excess oil by washing the colours with benzine or oil of turpentine, and then leaving them for some time between sheets of blotting paper. If too much wax is used as a thinner the colours will not have much covering power. If the wax is insufficient, the painting will dry badly and the tones will be too opaque. The right quantity produces semi-opaque paintings, like the frieze in the Italian House of Parliament painted by Sartorio.

The artist who wishes to produce a lasting work should therefore mix his wax medium directly with the powdered pigments, or with the colour mixed with essential oils. (See pp. 65-6.) The Weimar milk of figs used by some artists is made of saponified wax and essential oils.

SARTORIO'S MIXTURE [8]

Sartorio used to put his colours into little glass jars and cover them with turpentine; after two or three days he would remove the floating liquid and knead the coloured powder with pure wax melted in a double saucepan together with essential oil of turpentine.

Sartorio also used a mixture composed of wax, oil of turpentine and poppy oil in equal parts. If this became hard, he melted it and thinned it again with oil of turpentine. He also used the same amount of medium for every colour so that the picture should be evenly mat.

With this medium he painted the frieze in the Italian House of Parliament; he himself saw that these paintings tended to become yellow and advised artists to take this into account and indeed to take advantage of this amber colouring.

H. HILER'S WAX—OIL OF SPIKE MEDIUM [9]

'A fine medium to use with oil paints which gives them the appearance of tempera in that they dry perfectly mat, is made as follows:

I	Water	10 parts
	Pure white wax	1 part
	Ammonia	

'When the water is boiling shave the wax into it and when the wax is melted, add ammonia drop by drop until the water turns milky, the wax being emulsified. Allow this emulsion to cool and preferably to stand overnight, when the wax will be seen to have separated and come to the top in a cake having the form of the receptacle. Pour off the excess water.

2 Pour enough oil of spike over the wax to cover it, and allow it to dissolve and soften in a warm place for a few days.

3 Add enough rectified turpentine so that the mixture is about the consistency of cream. Bottle, but do not cork for several days so as to allow the excess of ammonia a chance to evaporate. During these operations it is better to stand the ingredients in a warm place while they are amalgamating.

'This medium is splendid for underpainting: turpentine or petrol may be used to dilute it while working. For mural painting it is very interesting, as the colours dry perfectly mat.

'If it separates out somewhat on standing, shake it before using and warm it a little by placing the bottle in hot water.

'Used on paper which has been prepared to receive oil paints by a coating of glue or casein, or a ready-prepared ground, it gives exactly the effect of gouache. Its advantages over gouache are that it is not fragile, being waterproof when dry, and that the colours do not change tone in drying. It took me three years to perfect this apparently simple composition and I consider it an important and very useful formula. Its use permits one to do entirely without gouache or tempera colours.'

The following is *a quick-drying mixture*:

Pure wax	10 parts	
Elemi	5 „	
Linseed oil	10 „	melted over heat.
Essence of		
turpentine	8 „	

KARL ZERBE'S EMULSION [10]

Karl Zerbe is the greatest exponent of wax painting in

America; his emulsions are warmed on a palette with an electric appliance the heat of which can be regulated. The medium is then mixed with dry pigments or tube colours. The painting is done with hot colours on a ground which is also warm, and the result is a surface similar to that obtained by using thin oil colours. If the ground is cold, the painting hardens at once and looks like tempera. To thin the emulsions, use rectified turpentine. Spread with a brush and model with warm spatulas.

Emulsion A (elastic):

Bleached wax	8 parts⎱	melted over
Sun-thickened linseed oil	1 part ⎰	low heat.

Emulsion B:

Bleached wax	8 parts	
Dammar resin	1 part	
Venice turpentine or		
Canada balsam	1	,,

Melt the wax over heat and add the other ingredients leaving the mixture in the heat until all the ingredients have melted completely.

Similar methods are used by other American painters such as Fred Conway, Rifka Angel, Ernst Halberstadt, George Holt, David Haronson, James Penny, Norman Daly, Morris Shulman and others.

Method with Saponified Wax

This procedure was known to the Byzantine painters and was included in various books of recipes of the early Middle Ages, such as the Lucca, Mount Athos and Le-Bègue MSS. The words of this last text have been variously read and interpreted by scholars like Mary Merrifield, Church and some others. The word *flanders* has been translated variously as 'ashes' and as 'glue', giving rise to many types of mixtures. It is not known why others, like Lanchester, added compact slaked lime to the recipe.

Modern recipes for these types of mediums are given by Hilaire Hiler and by the painter Harry Morley. The latter uses them for glazing and for finishing egg temperas. It is well to add a few drops of benzoate of soda to the saponifications containing ammonia and glue to prevent putrefaction, but those containing lime do not need this. Other scholars, such as Lorgna, interpreting Pliny's word *natron* as 'nitre', have concluded that the process of bleaching the wax was a saponification. Lorgna therefore made a mixture of wax, water and nitre to bind the pigments.

Saponifications must be thinned with water and applied cold. They are varnished with warm wax and fixed.

MODERN VERSION OF THE LE-BÈGUE RECIPE[11]

'Take fish glue and skin or parchment glue, about half of each. Soak them overnight and put them, thus swollen up, in a double boiler, and melt them with water until you get a glue of about the consistency of a thin cream when cold.

'As the strengths of different glues vary tremendously, the exact proportions cannot be given, but it is easy to add hot water to thin to the desired consistency.

'The wax is prepared by scraping bleached white virgin wax in little shavings into violently boiling water—about one part of wax to ten of water. I do not use pure unbleached beeswax, as I find it almost impossible to emulsify; the white wax works much better, but of course it must be pure. When the wax is melted in the boiling water, add strong ammonia drop by drop, and you will see that the wax emulsifies, the action taking place quite suddenly. Mix this emulsified "wax milk" with your glue solution, having them both hot. Pour into a bottle, and shake from time to time while cooling. A little linseed oil may be ground into the pigments with this medium, if you favour the putty theory, or a little mastic varnish may be added to the mixture in the bottle and shaken up.

'I use benzoate of soda as a preservative. Carbolic acid precipitated my wax. Very little is needed. About $\frac{1}{2}$ of 1 per cent should be sufficient.'

RECIPE OF THE BYZANTINE MS[12]

Take equal quantities of glue, a strong solution of potash

and white wax. Mix and melt over heat. Add the ground pigment; thin with water when painting.

BERGER'S RECIPE [13]

Bleached wax	100 parts
Potash	10 ,,
Distilled hot water	150 ,,

When cooled this mixture can be thinned with water. A little oil can also be added. Werner of Neustadt gives a similar recipe.

WAX EMULSION [14]

Melt and thoroughly mix in a double boiler 386 grains of bleached wax and 386 grains of turpentine or Venice turpentine.

Into a separate vessel put 154 grains of potash with 8 oz. of water. Warm, mixing in 8 oz. of dammar or mastic varnish. Shake well and then add the wax mixed with turpentine. Add more water until the liquid is twice or thrice its original volume.

This tempera keeps for some time and does not require the addition of disinfectants.

LORGNA'S RECIPE

Melt over heat in an iron vessel 10 to 20 parts wax and 1 part nitre.

Allow to cool and harden; it can be thinned with cold water until the density of milk is obtained.

WAX AND GUM

Some scholars, besides Requeno and Pacchieri, reading in Pliny that sarcocolla was very useful to doctors and painters, thought that the addition of a gum-resin would easily solve the problem of encaustic. Instead of sarcocolla they used mastic or gum arabic.

The colours were ground with a medium of gum, resin, wax and water and were used as oil colours.

White wax	2 parts
Mastic tears	5 ,,

Grind the mastic in a mortar and place in an enamel saucepan over fire together with the wax. Mix until it boils and then throw the hot mass into a basin of cold water.

Grind the pigments with water and mix them thoroughly with this wax paste (3 parts pigment to 1 part wax paste), blending with a pestle on a porphyry slab or in a mortar. These colours are thinned with water.

When the picture is finished varnish with hot melted wax, fix by means of a brazier or a hot iron brought close to the painting.

As supports use canvas, gesso and glue, or paper; cardboard and panels should first be primed with:

Colophony	4 parts
Wax	2 ,,
White lead	enough to make a paste as stiff as oil colours.

Melt over heat and apply several coats with a brush, scraping off the excess with a spatula.

Abbé Requeno mixed the mastic and wax paste directly with the powdered colour, thus making pastes of coloured wax which he then ground down in a mortar and used with water.

HOOKER'S RECIPE[15]

'Dissolve:

Gum arabic 137 grammes (4 oz. 364 grains) in
Cold water 245 grammes (8 ,, 381 ,,)

'When the gum is dissolved, add:

Mastic resin washed and powdered 215 grammes
(7 oz. 256 grains)

'The receptacle, which should be of earthenware, is put on

a slow fire, and when it has boiled a sufficient length of time, it loses its transparency and becomes opaque and like glue; when in this state, add without taking it off the fire:

White wax in pieces 153 grammes (5 oz. 174 grains)

'Stir until the wax is melted; take off the fire, and keep stirring until cold. Strain through a cloth and bottle. If the composition is well made the liquor will be like a cream and the colours, mixed with it, as easily managed as oils. The colours, which are mixed with composition on a porcelain palette and thinned with water, blend readily. When the painting is finished, it is varnished with wax, and when this has cooled, it is melted by means of a heated flat iron. The picture is heated as necessary until all values appear properly: the more frequently heated the better the result. The ground for this painting is made with the same composition. This painting dries promptly, but takes some time to harden. It should be applied in thin and very liquid coats.'

WAX EMULSIONS AND EGG TEMPERA

DOERNER'S TEMPERA

Melt in a double boiler:

Pure white wax	386 grains
Oil of turpentine	386 ,,
Potash	77 ,,
dissolved in water	1 gill

until a smooth, fluid cream is obtained.

This can be emulsified with egg and thinned with water. These temperas should not be varnished: the finished picture can be polished by rubbing with a piece of silk: the colours have a clear and rich quality.

A very pleasing medium, especially effective in decorative paintings, can be obtained by melting in a double boiler 1 part of wax and 2 parts of oil of turpentine, thinning with an equal amount of egg tempera.

Colours thus prepared are especially recommended for large surfaces owing to their clearness.

NEW ENCAUSTIC PAINTING [16]

The painter Antonio Moretti (1810–1892) recommended the use of colours mixed with glycerine. When the painting was finished, he removed the glycerine by washing with water and spirit, this process being based on the physical phenomenon of endosmosis. When the picture was dry, he applied melted wax either to the front or to the back, and then exposed the picture to heat to make the wax penetrate into the colours. The wax seeped in, taking the place of the glycerine and holding together all the molecules of the pigments. The picture was then fixed and became unabsorbent and unalterable.

Moretti added a little gum arabic or dammar to the glycerine. Glycerine allows of the same easy handling as oil.

The ground should be kept damp by spraying with water while painting is proceeding; the colours can be thinned either with water or with spirit. Moretti preferred white paper on which to paint.

It is not as difficult to remove the binding glycerine from the colours as might appear. 36° proof spirit, applied to the back of the paper, is absorbed by the glycerine and combines with it. By repeatedly washing both the right side and the back with a soft sable brush dipped in spirit, the glycerine is eliminated little by little.

This operation can be hastened by gently rubbing the back of the picture with a damp sponge. When the glycerine has been removed completely, melted wax is applied to the back of the picture, keeping the front exposed to heat so that the wax, drawn by the flame, permeates not only the support but the molecules of the pigments as well.

With this technique Antonio Moretti painted many pictures which years later preserved their quality and freshness.

Vibert quotes this technique, without mentioning the author, and calls it watercolour with a glycerine base.

In 1760 Muntz used a similar method, painting with glue

tempera or pastel. The picture was fixed in the course of work and, when finished, had a high gloss. But the difficulty of execution and the visible alteration of the colours permeated by wax make these systems impracticable.

14

Fresco Painting

Fresco requires a resolute and swift hand, but most of all a firm and comprehensive judgement, because while the wall is wet the colours show things in one way, and when the wall has dried they show them in quite another.

VASARI, Introduction

Fresco is the name given to a picture painted over wet lime plaster with colours mixed with pure water. The process takes advantage of the fact that lime mixed with sand and water forms a surface into which colours will penetrate and remain fixed as it dries, thereafter becoming insoluble to water. It is necessary for the surface to dry slowly, since too rapid drying means uneven absorption and causes cracking and flaking.

The building materials, exposure of the wall and position of water pipes must all be taken into consideration. A fresco can be ruined not only by poor materials but also by excess damp, dryness, heat and by violent changes of temperature.

MATERIALS FOR FRESCO PAINTING

COLOURS

Colours not affected by lime must be selected and a number of beautiful and striking tints, such as the copper greens, the cinnabars and orpiment must therefore be avoided.

The most stable tints are those obtained with the ochres and earths, which offer a vast range of yellows, reds, browns and

168

greens. Veronese green earth must be absolutely pure or it will fade in a short time. Yellow ochre should be used in a very fluid state since it produces lifeless and opaque tones if applied too thickly; artists are advised to avoid using it in damp countries as it attracts the moisture in the air and becomes brittle and dark; even the addition of lime water alters its colour and reddens it, but mixed with pure water and used in a liquid state it is a beautiful and brilliant colour.

Among the modern pigments cobalt blue and emerald green have given excellent results. Artificial ultramarine, Indian red and the cadmiums (see tables on pp. 43 ff.) have not yet been thoroughly tested. Natural ultramarine comes off as dust even if applied with tempera over a fresco underpainting made with red or green earths as practised by the old masters.

Naples yellow, unless carefully prepared, also deteriorates. It should be used with lime water only, and this also applies to black, green earth and the lakes. Ivory black, which does not mix easily with water, should first be ground with spirit and then dried. Vermilion should be washed several times with lime water. 'Bianco San Giovanni', made of perfectly pure and buttery slaked lime, is used as white. Zinc white, titanium, clay white and gesso should not be used as they destroy the cohesion of the picture, nor should white lead as it blackens rapidly.

The pigments should be thoroughly ground with water until they become quite fluid, and then kept in glass jars or glazed earthenware vessels; it is advisable to prepare not only the main colours but various shades of each colour and the more commonly used mixtures so as to be able to work with speed. Since the tones alter considerably in drying, it is advisable to experiment with specimens of colour on a piece of mortar or brick over gesso or umber earths. The alteration of colours is not uniform as the light tones dry quicker than the dark ones, some of which, such as burnt umber and burnt sienna, alter very little.

LIST OF COLOURS RECOMMENDED BY HERMAN SACHS FOR PAINTING 'A FRESCO' AND 'A SECCO'

White: Slaked lime

Yellow: Light ochre
Golden ochre
Raw sienna earth*
Naples yellow*

Red: Terra di Pozzuoli
Dark English red
Terra di Treviso
Caput mortuum (oxide of iron)
All burnt ochres including sienna

Brown: Raw umber earth
Burnt umber earth

Green: Oxide of chrome
Cobalt green
Veronese green earth
Bohemian earth
Ultramarine green*

Blue: Natural ultramarine*
Artificial ultramarine*
Cobalt blue

Black: Ivory and vine black.

* The colours marked with an asterisk
should be tested with experiments.

COLOURS FOR FRESCO PAINTING RECOMMENDED BY JAMES WARD [1]

White: Lime white (hydrate of lime)

Yellow: Raw sienna (a ferruginous earth)
Cadmium yellow (cadmium sulphide)

Red: Vermilion (sulphide of mercury) treated with lime
water
Light red (calcined Oxford ochre)
Indian red (ferric peroxide)

Blue: Cobalt blue (phosphate of cobalt and alumina)

170

Green:	Oxide of chromium (anhydrous sesqui oxide of chromium)
	Emerald oxide of chromium (hydrated oxide of chromium and borax)
	Cobalt green (oxides of cobalt and zinc)
Orange:	Burnt sienna (raw sienna calcined)
Brown:	Burnt umber (raw umber calcined earth)
	Raw umber (oxides of iron, manganese and clay)
Black:	Ivory black (charred bones or ivory)

The colours most subject to alteration are ultramarine, light and yellow ochre and green earth. The pigments should always be ground with pure water, not with lime water, as this makes them hard and unusable within a short time.

Lime water should be added to certain colours in the course of work. It should be made freshly every day by placing a little lime in water. This should be allowed to stand until perfectly clear; the skin which forms on the surface must be removed.

BRUSHES

Brushes made of long hog's bristles are generally used. They are rounded in shape and tapered at the point. Some painters prefer those made with calf's hair since they can hold more liquid colour. Martin Knoller recommended that a brush be left to soak in water for some time before use as this makes the colour flow better. To taper a brush wet it and rub it on a dry wall. Brushes which are too hard damage the plaster, especially when it is very fresh.

While working keep a large vessel full of water close at hand. Use this to rinse the brushes and change the water very often. It is best to keep a brush for each colour.

In the preparation of walls for 'a secco' and tempera painting, the dry plaster must be well brushed and freed from all dust. Moisten a section of the wall, apply a thin coat of lime, allow it to set and paint over it while still fresh.

Old plaster must be washed with soap and water to remove all traces of grease. Soap is not harmful and indeed favours the

171

cohesion of the plaster which is generally made with lime, skimmed milk and a little water. The wall itself must naturally be perfectly free from damp or the painting will not cling.

Gesso plaster can be painted after the chalk has dried: the surface must then be painted with a solution of alum,[2] and when this has also dried, brush the plaster well to remove the tiny alum crystals which generally form. After this treatment the plaster will not absorb colours excessively and will become insoluble to the water used in the glazes.

Herman Sachs[3] recommends a good plaster for tempera painting. Coat the *arricciato* (roughcast) with a mixture of slaked lime and water (2 or 3 parts of water to 1 part of lime). Then apply a second coat composed of 2 parts of zinc white and $\frac{1}{2}$ part of tempera, and finally smooth it and make it even.

This surface should then be whitewashed with a solution of lime and pure water (1 : 1).

EXECUTION

CARTOONS

Instead of drawing the general design directly on to the plaster with colour, the old masters very often made a preliminary study on cardboard, on the same scale as the actual fresco; on this they placed the shadows and sometimes even used colour. They drew on large surfaces of sheets of stiff paper glued together, or on sections, and then made holes with a needle, following the contours exactly. Next, they put the drawings in position over the plaster and went over the pricked lines with a little bag of muslin filled with powdered charcoal. With the aid of the marks left on the plaster they outlined their drawing either with a line of colour or by scraping it with a nail or sharp bone. Further sections were prepared in the same way taking care that the edges fitted exactly.

The cartoons were often squared as the squaring made it easier to fit the various sections together.

In modern times the cartoons are drawn and shaded with

charcoal and then fixed with the usual fixatives (see How to fix pastels, p. 97) or with plain skimmed milk. They are then pricked with a special tracing wheel and the drawing is traced through as with the ancient system. Since the joins between the various sections of plaster remain visible,[4] the artist, in making the cartoon, must be careful to plan intelligently so as to avoid joins in light parts, and horizontal or vertical lines. The joins must be concealed in the drapery, along the contours of the figures or architectural elements, in the trees or in the lines of the landscape.

When the drawing has been traced through or marked with a nail on to a section of plaster, the outlines are marked with a thin line of colour. Painting begins when the plaster no longer gives under the pressure of the fingers. As Cennini recommends, the colours must be applied in a very liquid state because a thick impasto suffers from changes of temperature, flakes, and comes off as fine dust. With some colours one must apply several glazes to reach maximum depth. Yellow ochres and red ochres produce strong, deep colours with two coats only, applied as a glaze; cobalt blue and green earth require up to five or six coats. Every painter must experiment since successive coats of paint achieve intensity only up to a certain point; beyond this the excess of pigment does not increase the depth of the tone, but makes the painting drab as in a lean tempera.

Every artist can put on his colours according to his taste and feeling, beginning either with the lights or with the shadows or even covering large areas with local colour and leaving the modelling to a later stage. He must however remember that it is not possible to place light colours over dark ones or vice versa without obtaining dull, dirty and greyish colours as a result.

All corrections must be made immediately by washing or scraping; it is even better to destroy the section of plaster where the mistake has been made by cutting it out with a short, sharp blade. If the need to cut arises, it is best to do this half way through the day for by the evening the plaster will be too hard and even worse the next morning and the painting will not be successful.

The joins between the sections of plaster always remain

slightly visible; it is dangerous to smooth them too much as particles of the newer plaster may get fixed on to the previous coat of plaster which has not yet had time to dry. In time these little splashes make white holes in the paint.

If it is necessary to retouch or strengthen certain colours at the end of the day, one must work with much paler and clearer shades, since retouchings on an almost dry wall darken considerably.

If you wish to obtain a surface smooth as marble, when you have finished work for the day smooth it with a trowel or, better still, with a bottle or marble cylinder, working upwards from right to left and pressing well and evenly. It is advisable to place a strong piece of paper between the painting and the roller. If on the contrary, a rough surface is preferred, beat the damp plaster with a dry brush to roughen it. This, by the way, encourages the absorption of the colours.

In the course of each day's work the piece of wall which is to be plastered on the following day should be moistened from time to time. Apply the plaster next morning and smooth it very carefully to avoid damaging and burning the parts already painted with splashes of lime.

RETOUCHING

Colours with a lime base must not be used for retouching as they alter considerably in the process of drying and it is extremely difficult to calculate this change of tone.

Casein produces colours which change very little. Raphael Mengs recommended skimmed milk mixed with *aqua vitae*.

Max Doerner has obtained very good results in retouching indoor murals with an *emulsion of wax, potash and dammar*. The emulsion must have the consistency of butter when mixed with a little water and the powdered pigment. Some artists fix their retouchings with formalin (4 per cent solution).

Egg tempera, to my mind, is the best. The whole egg is beaten with ten or twenty times its volume of water. The addition of a little honey does no harm to indoor paintings.

Tempera of egg alone should be applied in thin strokes or as a glaze but not heavily. This tempera can also be used out of doors, and is the only one that can produce a shiny surface similar to that of true fresco.

Temperas made with casein and milk may produce spots, and those containing resin and wax may form shiny patches wherever the painting is retouched. Egg tempera mixes well with lime colours and should be thinned with lime water.

Temperas for retouching murals must be thinned far more than those for use on canvas or panels since, according to Cennini, 'if too much tempera is applied, the colour will suddenly burst and tear off the wall'.

PRECAUTIONS

1 Watch the builders when they mix the plaster and do not allow them to add cement, soda or chalk to make it set more rapidly as all these substances spoil the painting.

2 Colours cling far better to a rough ground than to a very smooth one, as the latter is incapable of holding several coats or impastos.

3 Plaster and *arricciato* must always be applied over a wet surface. The maximum thickness of these coats should not exceed $1\frac{1}{2}$ in.

4 The wall can be slightly moistened with an atomizer during work so as to slow down the drying process. It should be remembered that an excess of moisture can make the work easier but also prevent the colours from becoming solid.

5 When working out of doors, one should take care to prevent the sun from shining on the fresh plaster as it becomes unsuitable for painting and its solidity is also impaired. The surface must therefore be protected with curtains or screens to keep off the sun.

6 To be successful, a fresco painter must be able to work quickly and without hesitation, and be acquainted with the properties of his plasters, the action of lime on colours and the varying alterations in tones. Above all he must be capable of sensing the critical moment when the lime begins to lose its power to fix colours so as to work only with extremely fluid colours.

MURAL PAINTING 'A SECCO'

Theophilus Presbyter's Method

This technique is mentioned by Theophilus the monk. It has neither the durability nor the luminosity of the paintings 'a buon fresco' (true fresco), but it is a very easy method as it not only allows of decoration over old plaster but also work over large surfaces without the drawback of having to put on a fresh section of plaster every day and take joins into account. This method is not advisable in industrial cities where the air is full of coal fumes which will affect the painting.

The wall must be in perfect condition without any discolorations caused by damp or saltpetre. If dealing with a damp wall, mix an ordinary plaster and apply it to a rust-proof wire net which can then be fastened to the wall. For this plaster use lime prepared over a wood fire, slaked at least one year before and preserved under water or sand, as for real fresco. It should be buttery and should contain a very small percentage of clay. Some writers, like Theophilus, stressed the need to wet the wall thoroughly with pure water; others, like Schmidt, prescribe the use of lime water; in any case, as and when the colours are required they must be mixed with lime water and applied to a wet wall.

Herman Sachs' Recipe for Plaster

1 part of lime, slaked one year previously and left under ground; $2\frac{1}{2}$ or 3 parts of water.

Apply a first layer and then a second when the first is dry. Before painting, moisten the wall thoroughly with a whitewash made with 1 part of slaked lime and 2 or 3 parts of water.

Temperas for Mural Painting

The following become insoluble and are very reliable: egg tempera (yolk and albumen) emulsified or thinned with clear lime water, casein tempera, flour paste dissolved in spirit,[5] and the bull gluten mentioned by Pliny.

Egg and wax emulsions can be used for indoor painting. Temperas made with gum and those made with flour which contain hygroscopic substances such as syrups, soaps and glycerine are far too fragile and should be avoided.

Lime combined with casein, oil, sugar, albumen, glue and soap produces the temperas classified as insoluble; soaps and glue, being hygroscopic, should be avoided, so should sugar (recommended by Martin Knoller for retouching) because the flies it attracts will soil the painting.

The emulsions of wax and potash tend to crack and flake in drying if the tempera is too thick. These emulsions blend well with fatty oils, varnishes, egg and casein temperas, and can be fixed with a 4 per cent solution of formalin. They are eminently suitable for the decoration of public places where there is a lot of smoke since, once fixed, they can be easily cleaned.

The advantages of painting murals with tempera are that the technique is easy and that it offers a very large range of colours.

All the recipes recommended for tempera painting on canvas can be used, but the mixtures must be made much thinner.

MURAL PAINTING WITH CASEIN [6]

The use of milk in mural painting is a very ancient practice. The Romans used it for plasters and temperas, and primitive American Indians painted the interiors of their huts with ochre thinned with milk.

In fresco painting, milk was mixed with colours which tended to alter; Andrea da Salerno, according to the anonymous author of a manuscript in the Marciana Library, recommends mixing blue with goat's milk as this keeps it from going dark.

In milk temperas the active element is casein, an organic product containing nitrogen, which in the presence of lime forms a soluble caseate of calcium; if oil is added it produces an insoluble calcic soap and the result is a very flexible and solid tempera.

Casein colours are handled more easily over a damp fresco plaster or over a slightly moist whitewash.

Casein should be used only when perfectly fresh and should therefore be extracted from milk day by day. The caseins found on the market should not be used as they often contain glycerine or other noxious ingredients.

One should paint with light glazes as casein makes a rigid and adhesive tempera which causes dense impastos to crack and peel off the wall.

TEMPERA WITH CASEIN BASE[7]

Pour into 1¾ pts. of skimmed milk 6½ oz. of slaked lime and 4½ oz. of poppy oil and stir until an even liquid is obtained. This tempera should be used in a very fluid state and must be thinned with skimmed milk and a little lime water.

TEMPERA WITH CASEIN AND MAGNESIA BASE

This tempera can be used outdoors as it is very solid and adhesive. It produces a caseate of magnesia which becomes insoluble in a very short time. Heavy industrial calcined magnesia is used.

This tempera should have the consistency of a syrup and is made by mixing 11½ oz. of magnesia and 32 oz. of casein together with a little cold water until an even paste is obtained. Mix 1 part of this with 10 parts of mineral colour. Of course, like all other glues made with casein, it should be prepared day by day.

Other recipes can be found on pages 56 and 135.

MURAL TEMPERAS WITH GLUE

These temperas are suitable for whitewashing, interior decorating, painting ceilings and scenery, but do not stand up to damp or washing.

They refuse to take on greasy or oily surfaces so it is advisable to wash the greasy surface with an emulsion of wax and potash. All the mineral colours used in oil painting may be employed so long as one remembers, when binding the colours, that they lose their depth of tone in drying. Thick layers of paint must not be superimposed as this type of painting breaks up if it is too heavy. Parchment glue is normally used to bind the colours.

This is made by soaking the parchment in water until it swells and then dissolving it in a double boiler with the addition of water and alum. It is then strained through muslin and mixed with the pigments ground with water. These colours should be warmed in a double boiler to a temperature between 120° and 150·5° F. and should be used while warm. To give the colours body Meudon white (white clay: carbonate of calcium) can be added mixed with water to the density of a pomatum.

Each colour is made with 3 parts of pigment ground with water and 1 part of glue. Any glue tempera can be made more solid by the addition of 2 parts of oil for every 10 of white tempera colour prepared with plaster. It also becomes more impervious to water if $1\frac{3}{4}$ oz. of alum are added to each $1\frac{3}{4}$ pts. of colour.[8]

In interior decorating the painting is very often done with glues of inferior quality. In time they putrefy and give off harmful fumes which are dangerous to health. To avoid this danger it is as well to add 2·2 lbs. of boracic acid to every 22 gallons of glue paint. This precaution is imperative if new walls and plasters are to be painted.

RECIPES FOR MURAL TEMPERAS WITH GLUE

This type of painting is suitable for decorative purposes because of its quick and easy execution and the cheapness of the materials. By fixing the colour with a 4 per cent solution of formalin a certain solidity can be obtained.

TEMPERA WITH COLOGNE GLUE

Dissolve 2 oz. 50 grains of Cologne glue in $1\frac{3}{4}$ pts. of hot water. By adding pipeclay and water a mixture is obtained which is suitable for priming. The pigments are tempered with this same glue diluted.

Any excess of glue makes the colours shiny and fragile.

PARCHMENT GLUE [9]

Soak clippings of parchment and white leather in hot water

for one day, then boil for five or six hours. Strain through a sieve and allow to stand; unless the weather is too hot, the glue becomes a jelly. For mixing with the pigment, use only the clearest part at the top.

FLUID GLUE

Totain glue	4·4 lbs.
4½% formalin solution	7 oz.
Water	3 gallons 3 pts.
Acetic acid	from 17 oz. to 2 lbs.

In cooling this becomes a jelly which turns fluid again if slightly warmed.

TEMPERAS WITH SYNTHETIC RESINS

The use of polyvinyl or butanic synthetic resins for binding is still in an experimental stage as far as easel or mural painting is concerned.

15

Mural Oil Painting and Other Decorations

Painting with oil colours on the surfaces of walls is a very ancient practice; as early as the 11th century Arnoldo da Villanova describes this system in connection with the multi-coloured decorations which imitate marble. This type of painting is also mentioned in ancient English, French and German documents. It was customary to work either on a wall prepared with a coat of plaster or on smooth stone. Excellent mural paintings were made with oil colours by Sebastian del Piombo, Vasari and Giulio Romano. In the 19th century this technique was revived, especially in France and in England, where climatic conditions make the painting 'a buon fresco' very difficult.

For mural painting the ordinary oil colours must be diluted with essential oils and at times combined with mixtures of wax and resin or with dammar varnish. Colours must not be applied until the underlying coat of paint has dried completely.

PREPARATION OF THE WALL
FOR PAINTING

VASARI'S METHOD

In painting Duke Cosimo's apartments, Vasari followed this method: 'First of all put on the *arricciato* (roughcast) and over this apply a plaster made of lime, ground brick and sand and allow to dry. This done, let the second plaster be made of lime, pulverized brick and iron foam, one part of each, mixed with the necessary quantity of beaten white of egg and linseed oil . . .

Make with this such a solid stucco that no one could wish for a better.' This plaster must be smoothed continually while it dries or cracks will occur.

SEBASTIAN DEL PIOMBO'S PREPARATION

With reference to the *Christ bound to the column* in San Pietro in Montorio by Sebastian del Piombo, Vasari said: 'He exercised so much care that he made his *arricciato* with a measure of mastic and colophony melted over fire and applied to the walls, and he smoothed this with a red hot trowel. For this reason his paintings stand up well to damp and preserve their colours unaltered; with this same mixture he has worked over tufa, marble, mixed grounds, porphyry and very hard slabs on which the painting may thus last for a very long time.'

SYSTEM FOUND IN THE 'VALUABLE SECRETS IN THE ARTS' [1]

Make a plaster with lime and marble or brick dust mixed with linseed oil. Then make a mixture of colophony, mastic and thick varnish; boil, and apply with a hot spatula. On this plaster put a coat of quick-drying colours: chalk, red ochre and other earths, and then paint with colours mixed with varnish.

DARCET AND THÉNARD'S SYSTEM

The chemists Darcet and Thénard recommend this preparation for mural painting in oils:

Wax	1 part
Cooked linseed oil	
(with one tenth of litharge)	3 parts

Heat the mixture and apply hot over a wall which has been warmed so that it will absorb the excess oil. This type of preparation was used for the painting in the cupola of Sainte Geneviève in Paris.

This system appears to be excellent for use over stucco and for preventing the ravages caused by saltpetre.

This artist used the following method for her frescoes at Edinburgh. On the stone walls to which an ordinary plaster of lime had been applied, she spread five coats of zinc white prepared with oil, the first of which was very much thinned with oil of turpentine (each coat being allowed to dry for a week or two). The next coat was thicker, and so on, until the fifth coat which was pure oil colour. This last coat took six weeks to dry.

The painting was then carried out with ordinary oil colours, diluted with oil of turpentine and a little wax (a piece about the size of a hazel nut to every 30 oz. of oil of turpentine).

Mrs Traquair used light red, burnt sienna, yellow ochre, green earth, cobalt blue, natural ultramarine and a little Chinese vermilion; she did not use any black or white as she painted with fluid glazes and made full use of the white ground for the lights as in watercolour painting. These decorations, painted about fifty years ago, have stood up very well to a damp climate and to cleaning with soap and water. As they were varnished with an oil varnish, they have acquired an amber tone. After cleaning, a wax varnish has been applied as a protection.

Cunningham's Emulsion [2]

Thoroughly mix oil and lime water, adding a few drops of oil of turpentine or mastic varnish.

This emulsion can be used either with oil colours or with colours ground with lime water, for decorative paintings on cardboard, masonite panels, and so on.

MURAL ENCAUSTIC PAINTING

During the 19th century encaustic was very often used for mural decorations, especially in Germany and France where the climate makes it difficult to produce solid frescoes by following the classical procedure.

W. von Kaulbach's decorations at the Neues Museum, those by Schnorr at the Munich Residence and those by Rottmann at the new Pinakothek in Munich, are all painted with wax. (The latter were painted with a wax and copal medium.)

In Paris there are frescoes painted with wax colours at the Madeleine (by Coudert, Leon Coignet, Signol, Abel de Puyol), at Saint-Sulpice (by Drolling), at Saint Germain l'Auxerrois (by Coudert), at Sainte Elizabeth (by Alaux), and at Saint-Germain-des-Prés (by Flandrin).

The Cartier process was used by Paillot de Montabert in the church of Saint Vincent de Paul in Paris.

For mural encaustic painting the same colours and mediums suggested for encaustic painting on panels and canvas are used. The system practised by Cross and Henry (see p. 157) is so far the most durable but also the most difficult; this method was perfected by Prof. Schmidt of Munich who used special spatulas and electrical appliances to make the application and fusion of the colours easier. The other impastos made with a base of saponifications and essential oils are not so solid, but they can be improved by fixing with heat and varnishing with a hot wax varnish which is made to soak in by means of heat.

The colours studied by Prof. Urban, called *Monumentalfarben*, can be considered suitable for a kind of encaustic as they are thinned with varnishes and fixed with heat, like the *Spirit fresco* invented by Gambier Parry.

DUROZIER SYSTEM

This procedure is followed in France in preparing walls for wax painting. Mix:

White wax	10 parts
Resin	2 ,,
Essence of turpentine	40 ,,

Warm the wall itself and apply the colours hot; these must be mixed with one of the following mediums:

Elemi gluten which gives flexibility to the coat of colour. The mixture is composed of 1 part of elemi resin, 4 parts of virgin wax, 16 parts of essence of spike, all melted in a double boiler;

Copal gluten which produces a less elastic mixture, deeper in tone. This is made with 1 part of copal, 4 parts of virgin wax, 16 parts of spike, melted in a double boiler;

Paris gluten which has the same qualities as elemi gluten but differs from it in the quality of the wax used. It is made of 1 part of elemi resin, 3 parts of bleached wax, 16 parts of essence of spike, melted in a double boiler.

The essence of spike helps to make the colours opaque and especially to make the first sketches lean; if it is desired to retard drying so as to work slowly, the colours must be thinned with volatile oil of wax instead of spike. (See p. 66.)

Paintings carried out with this medium have a semi-opaque appearance; they can be made shiny by rubbing with a soft wool rag once they have dried.

PROCEDURE OF M. RIDOLFI

Michele Ridolfi used to take 1 part of Smyrna wax and melt it with 4 parts of essential oil of rosemary; he then added 1 part of copal varnish and tempered his colours with the medium thus obtained.

For preparing walls or canvas he thinned this mixture with essential oil of turpentine; and softened the parts to be re-touched with the hot steam of essential oils.

He varnished the finished painting with wax dissolved in spirit and thinned with water and then heated it thoroughly; when it had cooled he polished it with a soft cloth.

COLEBROOK'S ENCAUSTIC METHOD[3]

'Consists in making a ground with slaked and sifted lime, and a little calcined alabaster (fine plaster), which are soaked in water and used for the ground. When this ground is well dried, it is painted in distemper. It is then heated, and while hot varnished with:

White wax	3 parts
White resin	1 part

(the 'white resin' is probably dammar) melted together and

applied to the warmed panel, which is held in a perpendicular position and heated during the application, so that the excess wax which cannot be absorbed by the ground will run off. When cold it is polished.'

RECIPES BY ROTTMANN AND ELGASSER

Linseed oil	1 oz.
Wax	$\frac{1}{2}$,,

The paintings at Munich were painted with this medium.

The excessive oil in this recipe makes stability uncertain. Consalvo Carelli had already noticed that paintings of this type deteriorated in overheated rooms.

RECIPES BY GIOCONDO VIGLIOLI

First recipe:

Melt over heat:

Cooked oil	1 part
White wax	3 parts
Mastic resin	2 ,,

Prime the wall with this mixture: also use it to temper colours, in this case thinning it with oil of turpentine.

Second recipe: To $17\frac{1}{2}$ oz. of wax melted in a sand bath, add $3\frac{3}{4}$ oz. of pulverized mastic; when liquid pour over it boiling water saturated with potash, and allow to cool after the liquids have amalgamated. Remove the excess alkaline water from the wax and mastic; use this medium to temper colours previously ground with water.

WAX VARNISH

Pure wax	$10\frac{1}{2}$ oz.
Alcohol boiling at 105° F.	$2\frac{1}{2}$ pts.

When the mixture is thoroughly melted filter still hot.

When it has cooled and the alcohol has evaporated considerably, mix with $2\frac{1}{2}$ pts. of oil of turpentine.

Spirit Fresco

This was invented by Gambier Parry. This method allows a highly finished execution without producing the opaque colours of tempera painting. *Spirit fresco* is damaged by any moisture contained in the wall, so the plaster must be left to sweat for some months before priming. It is done by soaking the plaster with the mixture used as a medium for the colours, to which has been added half its weight of oil of turpentine. This operation is performed twice. This technique was adopted by Gambier Parry for the mural decorations of St Andrew's chapel in Gloucester Cathedral. The spirit fresco technique was also followed by Lord Leighton and by P. Madox Brown, on canvas subsequently affixed to the wall. It is a very durable type of painting and, if the wall has been prepared with all due precautions, stands up to the weather in damp climates. Lord Leighton's frescoes in the church at Lyndhurst are very well preserved although there is condensation on their surfaces in winter.[4]

According to Gambier Parry the *arricciato* was made of equal parts of lime and sand and was smoothed with a straight-edge so as to obtain a fairly rough surface. After eight months the wall was prepared as stated previously. All the colours suitable for oil painting can be used in dense impasto or as a glaze; the painting can be retouched with light brush strokes or with broad coats of colour.

Recipe for Medium

Thoroughly mix over heat:

Elemi resin	1	oz. 334	grains
Pure white wax	3	,, 231	,,
Oil of spike	7	,, 24	,,
Copal varnish	$17\frac{1}{2}$	,,	

Sir Arthur Church's Recipe

Mix 2 oz. 360 grains of oil of spike and 309 grains of elemi warmed to a temperature of 175·2° F.: add 1 oz. 180 grains of ceresin (white mineral paraffin). When all ingredients have melted, pour in 7 oz. 24 grains of copal varnish (or 5¾ oz. of oil of copal). This medium is less fluid than Gambier Parry's.

To Dilute Colours

Use oil of spike to moisten the plaster surface before painting.

Lord Leighton's Method

Used in the frescoes *The Arts of Peace and War* in the Victoria and Albert Museum and in the church at Lyndhurst.[5]

First a roughcast was applied to the wall: it was made of slaked lime and river sand in equal proportions and was the same thickness as an ordinary roughcast for fresco. This was allowed to 'sweat' for two years before applying a second coat of the same mixture which was left rather rough. After another eight months it was soaked with two coats of *spirit fresco*—the medium used for tempering the colours—thinned with half its volume of oil of turpentine.

STUCCO LUSTRO

The high gloss of the Pompeian wall paintings at one time gave rise to the idea that they had been executed with the same sort of stucco lustro which had a vogue during the Renaissance, especially in Venice. It was used for imitating marble.

Many recipes were invented, all of them based on colours combined with wax, egg or soap. The finished painting was smoothed and polished with a hot trowel or roller.

L. B. Alberti described a method very similar to stucco lustro. It resembled the other hybrid techniques commonly known as encaustic. The painting was done over a plaster of lime and marble dust and finally varnished with mastic and wax dissolved over heat. The varnish was made to soak into the wall with the aid of a small brazier. After polishing, the wall became extraordinarily glossy.

We give various recipes which we think may be useful for decorative painting.

Venetian Method

Apply three coats of plaster composed of lime and marble dust. Paint on the third and smooth it with a trowel. When dry polish it with a varnish made of wax dissolved in turpentine.

Milanese Method

Apply to the wall a stucco of lime and marble dust, and soak it with a solution of wax and soap. Paint with colours mixed with water. When dry, apply the following mixture with a rounded trowel: $3\frac{3}{4}$ oz. of wax, 6 oz. 65 grains of soap and $2\frac{1}{2}$ pts. of water.

Herman Sachs' System [6]

The colours are mixed with water or lime water to a fairly solid consistency and then mixed with the tempera at the moment of use. The colours are the same as have been suggested for 'a secco' painting.

These are the temperas:

1   Egg and lime

Egg	1
Lime	1 oz. 334 grains
Ox gall	231 grains

2   Casein glue

Casein glue	1 part
Fatty varnish	1 ,,
Impasto of stucco (recipe 7)	1 ,,
Ox gall	15–20%

3   Albumen and lime

Albumen	1 part
Lime	1 ,,
Casein glue	1 ,,
Varnish	1 ,,
Lime water	1 ,,
Ox gall	$\frac{1}{2}$–$\frac{2}{3}$ part

4 *Egg*

Egg	1 part
Lime water	1 ,,
Impasto of stucco lustro	1 ,,
Ox gall	$\frac{1}{2}$–$\frac{2}{3}$ part

5 *Albumen and lime water*

Albumen	1 part
Lime	1 ,,
Lime water	1 ,,
Ox gall	1 ,,

6 *Dissolved casein*

Dissolved casein	1 part
Amber and copal varnish	1 ,,
Thick lime	1 ,,
Lime water	1 ,,
Ox gall	1 ,,

7 *Impasto for stucco lustro*

Soapy water (recipe 8)	1 part
Thick lime	1 ,,

8 *Soapy water*

Venetian soap (mottled) dissolved in	1 part
Boiling water	3 parts

Recipes 1 to 6 are used for mixing the colours, for thinning them (in which case they are made more fluid by the addition of 20–80 per cent of water, according to the density desired), and for final glazes. Recipes 7 and 8 serve to make impastos. The roughcast and plaster for this type of painting are applied to dry stone, brick walls or to steel frames about 2 ft. square. (See p. 37.)

The *arricciato* (roughcast) must be made of

Thick slaked lime	1 part
Well-washed gravel	1 ,,
Sand	2 parts

This is spread evenly $\frac{1}{2}$–$\frac{3}{4}$ in. thick.

The plaster is made with 1 part of thick slaked lime and 2 or 3 parts of quartz sand. It is applied $\frac{1}{8}$–$\frac{3}{16}$ in. thick and is worked and smoothed with a straight-edge seven or eight minutes after application. It is allowed to dry for twelve to twenty-four hours, according to climate and temperature.

Over this a marble plaster (rough plaster) is applied, made with 1 part of thick slaked lime and 2 or 3 parts of marble grit; this layer must be $\frac{1}{8}$–$\frac{1}{4}$ in. thick. After ten minutes it is smoothed in the same way as the first plaster.

The third is a fine marble plaster (intonaco): 1 part of slaked lime, 2 or 3 parts of fine marble dust, well mixed and ground in a mortar; it is applied as a coat $\frac{1}{8}$ in. thick or less and smoothed after ten or fifteen minutes. This plaster can be coloured.

COLD SMOOTHING

Wait from ten to fifty minutes, according to the thickness of the wall and the condition of the atmosphere, before smoothing to close the pores of the plaster and give it gloss and compactness.

HOT SMOOTHING

Half an hour or one hour after the cold smoothing, warm the surface with the aid of a brazier or with an electrical appliance and smooth with a hot flat iron. Smooth finished paintings in the same way.

TECHNIQUE OF PAINTING

Wait for fifteen to thirty minutes after smoothing with heat before beginning to paint with colours ground with water and mixed with the tempera a short time before use; the palette must be of metal; the colours can be applied thickly or as a glaze. When the painting is finished apply soapy water as if it were varnish.

If the painting is not too large, it can be polished after twenty or thirty minutes or longer, according to the dimensions and thickness. First polish with a cold iron to give the painting cohesion, and then with a hot iron. It should be kept in mind that if the plaster is too damp, smoothing with a hot iron may bring out excessive moisture which would be harmful to the painting; if too dry, it will not become shiny, but this can be remedied by anointing the colours with olive oil and polishing with a hot iron.

Applying oil or mixtures of glue and oil after a couple of days, as some artists do, lowers the tones and spoils their clearness; it is much better to apply some wax dissolved in oil of turpentine after a few hours and to polish with a rag.

This wax polish should be applied every ten years, removing the old coat by washing with soapy water (1 part of Venetian soap to 12 parts of water).

MINERAL PAINTING

STEREOCHROMY OR WATER GLASS

The early alchemists called silicate *alkahest*; it was supposed to be a universal solvent. In the 18th century it was commonly called *liquide à cailloux*.

Potassium silicate has the property of hardening porous and friable calcareous stones; it also makes gesso as hard as marble. Sprayed on to an 'a secco' fresco, it makes it solid, as it transforms the fatty lime on which the picture is painted into artificial hydraulic lime.

Calcium silicate which is formed in the course of this operation combines with carbonate of lime and produces a substance which hardens rapidly in the air, is waterproof and forms a transparent, vitreous and protective layer over the colours. This technique was studied by Von Fuchs about 1825 and improved by Keim and Rechnagel in Munich. It has been used for mural paintings both out of doors and indoors. Some artists use pastels over grounds prepared for mineral painting and fix the colours with silicate diluted to a density of 20° or 30° Baumé.

PREPARATION OF THE SILICATE

Powdered quartz sand   15 parts

192

| Potassium | 10 parts |
| Powdered coal | 1 part |

This mixture is kept for seven or eight hours in a glass furnace and is then boiled for three or four hours with distilled water, until it forms a colourless syrup.

PLASTER

Over a roughcast of the usual type apply a plaster made with 1 part of lime and 8 parts of fine sand, mixed with marble dust. The mixture must be homogeneous and sufficiently porous to absorb the silicate solution.

Before painting, but only when the plaster is perfectly dry, wash it with fluosilicate to dissolve the crystal layer formed by the calcium carbonate and also to open the pores of the plaster.

The surface is then saturated with the silicate preparation; it hardens in drying but remains perfectly absorbent.

Plaster can also be made with 1 part of lime and 5 or 6 parts of sand. When dry, apply a second coat which should be made with quartz sand. If the fresco is to be out of doors add one third of powdered pumice to the sand. This coat of plaster should not be thicker than $\frac{1}{8}$ in.

Soak with silicate of a density of 20° or 30° Baumé using distilled water as a diluent.

COLOURS

Artificial ultramarine, cobalt blue and green, all the earths and the Mars colours, zinc and baryta white must be ground with distilled water and kept under water.

They must be applied to a damp ground as in 'buon fresco'. It is easier to work on rainy days as this type of painting dries very quickly: the fixing can be left for fine days. Brushwork applied to a dry ground cannot be fixed successfully.

In the past firms like Schirmer of Munich made a study of colours for this type of painting and sold materials so well prepared that the fixing was perfect and there was no alteration of tone.

Painting can be *au premier coup* or left and started again; it can be executed in impasto or with glazes, but each whole section must be completed in one operation. When the painting is dry it is fixed with a warm silicate mixture, sprayed on with an atomizer until the wall is saturated.

A solution of carbonate of ammonia is then applied, and the carbonate of potassium which rapidly forms can be washed off with distilled water.

The painting must dry in an even temperature.

American manufacturers have recently made experiments in order to produce colours with a base of ethyl and alcohol silicates.

TECHNIQUE OF MINERAL PAINTING FOR DECORATIVE PURPOSES [7]

Spread a coat of colourless silicate of a density of 22° Baumé, paint with colours tempered with silicate at 24° Baumé, retouch with colours mixed with silicate at 26° Baumé.

As this painting dries rapidly it is necessary to finish each small section completely as one proceeds.

The colours are shaded while still fresh. The painting must remain opaque; if shiny patches appear, it is a sign that too much silicate is present. These parts must be very carefully washed to remove the excess of silicate.

All colours, with the exception of zinc oxide, must be very finely ground. This type of painting can also be done on zinc, rust-proof iron, glass, stone, brick, gesso, stucco and cement. The colours are non-inflammable and are therefore used for a variety of purposes: for painting huts, scenery, ambulances and so on.

PASTEL FOR MURAL DECORATION [8]

For this type of wall decoration it is necessary to prepare both the wall and the pastels in a special way. The walls, to which plaster has been applied in the usual way, are smeared with a mixture of powdered pumice, lime milk and very fine sawdust of vegetable fibre, which will give elasticity to the ground.

The set of the plaster can be hastened by washing the surface with aerated water.

Stucco walls must be covered with powdered pumice dissolved in starch glue (10 parts of pumice, 8 parts of starch and 100 parts of water). This recipe can be also used in the preparation of cardboard, canvas, panels and paper.

WHITE PASTELS

Barium sulphate (*blanc fixe*) or precipitated clay (*Schlemmkreide*), with a small quantity of kaolin or pipeclay, is better than ordinary clay which breaks up when exposed to the air. Zinc white should not be used as it has a deleterious action on certain organic compounds, nor should white lead which goes black and is very poisonous and dangerous to anyone who breathes its dust.

YELLOW PASTELS

All the earths, the ochres, raw sienna, the cadmium yellows, of which the darker shades are more stable than the lighter, are suitable. Ultramarine yellow and zinc chromate are preferable to light yellow.

BROWN PASTELS

All the umber earths.

RED PASTELS

Burnt ochres, light red, Venice red, cadmium red, madder lake.

BLUE PASTELS

Cobalt and ultramarine.

GREEN PASTELS

All shades of chrome oxide.

Black Pastels

All coal blacks.

The various shades are obtained by adding more or less *blanc fixe*.

Glue for mixing Powdered Colours

Use a light starch glue (309 grains of starch in $1\frac{3}{4}$ pts. of water). Precipitated clay and white must be mixed with a thinner glue (1 part of glue and 3 parts of water). If tragacanth gum is preferred, dissolve 309 grains in $1\frac{3}{4}$ pts. of water and leave in infusion for twenty-four hours in mild heat. White must be diluted as stated above. It is prudent to add a few drops of a solution of benzonaphthol and alcohol to these glues to prevent rotting and mildew.

Technique

Work as on paper but with a denser colour so that the picture does not become drab and evanescent after fixing. Remove excess dust. Shade the colours with the fingers.

Fixing

When the pastel work is completed, fix it using an atomizer with the following solution: mix 309 grains of casein with 62 grains of borax and a few spoonfuls of water. After two or three hours mix this thick syrup with enough water to make a little under half a pint of fixative and add a little less than half a pint of pure alcohol. After a couple of days decant and filter.

If casein is not available take half a pint of skimmed milk and curdle it, wash the solid part well and add 77 grains of borax which will turn the mass into a dense liquid resembling glue. Dilute this as described above, with the same amount of water and alcohol. Fix the work cautiously, little by little, allowing it to dry between the various applications of fixative.

To make the mural pastel waterproof and immune from damp, fix it with a second solution made of alumina acetate (the solution found on the market must be thinned to contain 20 parts of solution to 100 parts of water).

This fixative must always be freshly made as after a time the basic salt of alumina tends to separate.

The artist should keep the atomizers used for fixing free from any trace of casein. These are removed by leaving the atomizers in water and borax after use.

Wall decorations fixed in this manner can be washed with pure water and also cleaned with paraffin wax.

Notes

INTRODUCTION

1 It is interesting to see, among others, the Statute of the painters of Sienna dated 1355, in which it is laid down: 'No one may dare or presume to use in his work anything different from the gold or silver or colours he has promised, such as gold alloy instead of fine gold, tin instead of silver, copper blue instead of ultramarine blue, bice or indigo instead of azure, red earth and minium instead of cinnabar.'

Eastlake quotes a statute of the ancient Dutch government which says: 'The genius of the artist belongs to the nation, so that he has the duty to guarantee the life of the masterpiece he creates for the longest time possible.'

So in times past both governments and corporations insisted upon artists using choice materials and accurate technique.

2 Cennino Cennini (*Libro dell'arte*, chap. 29) gives this advice to the painter: 'Your life must be always methodical, as if you were studying theology, or philosophy, or other sciences.'

3 Stromata, Book VI, 4.

4 The apocryphal book of Enoch, also called *Chema* (whence the terms chemistry and alchemy), was written shortly before the Christian era. It makes the fallen angels the masters of the sciences and of the arts: 'Having fallen in love with the beautiful daughters of mankind, they lived with them, teaching them sorcery, spells, the properties of trees, magical signs, the art of observing the stars . . . the use of colours and how to paint their eyebrows, the art of using precious stones and all manner of colours . . . so that all the world was corrupted. . . .' This information is also quoted by Zosimus of Panopolis in his book of Ismouth, in the apocryphal letter of Osiris, and in Christian authors of the 2nd and 3rd centuries, such as Clement of Alexandria and Tertullian.

5 Medicamen and *venenum* were words commonly used for colours and oily grounds. (See Schoeffer.)

6 Diogenes Laertius attributes to Democritus treatises on the juice of plants on stones, minerals and colours. Seneca (*Epist.* XV) relates that Democritus made a study of the ways to colour glass and soften ivory. These works are lost and only apocryphal derivations remain.

7 For Hippocrates' reproach to doctors who were more interested in art than in science see *De veteri medicina*, quoted by Emeric David in *Recherches sur l'architecture*.

8 Tacitus relates that under Tiberius, Claudius and Vitellius, there were edicts to banish or inflict capital punishment on sorcerers and mathematicians (*Annals*, II, 32; *Annals*, XII, 52). John of Antioch, Suidas and St Procopius (*Acts*) mention the destruction of Egyptian alchemical books that was ordered by Diocletian.

9 Bartolomeo Facio in *De Viris illustribus*, says of Van Eyck: 'Putaturque, multa de colorum proprietatibus invenisse, quae ab antiquis tradita ex Plinii et aliorum auctorum lectione didicerat.'

10 Cennini, op. cit.

11 This we know from manuscripts in the British Museum and at Cambridge belonging to the first half of the 11th century (translated by Berthélot). Especially interesting is an Arabic treatise on painting and calligraphy, the *Umdet-al-Kuttab*, quoted by Berger (*Beiträge*, etc., Vol. I, pp. 60–61).

12 In the 12th century Gherardo da Cremona went to Toledo to learn Arabic.

He began the translation of several works on medicine and alchemy, and brought the manuscripts back to Italy. (See Carbonelli, *Delle fonti storiche dell'alchimia e della chimica in Italia*.) His works spread throughout the West.

13 The Lucca MS, the Venice MS, the Strasbourg MS and others are recipe books of this type.

14 Cennini, apropos of cinnabar, writes: 'This is made through alchemy and you will find many recipes if you go to the friars.' In his *Life* of Perugino, Vasari wrote that the Prior of S. Giusto, a *Gesuato* monk, was very skilled in making blues. The recipes of these fathers are collected in the *Compendio* of Father Alessio, himself a *Gesuato*.

15 The close relationship between letters, medicine, philosophy and art explains how Dante in 1297 became a member of the Guild of Physicians and Apothecaries.

16 In the *De Nobilitate Legum et Medicinae*, Coluccio Salutati says: 'Quod tam juristae quam medico et qui libet artifici scire competit omnes artes.'

17 Marsilio Ficino translated the works of Synesius and those attributed to Hermes Trismegistos; Marco Barbaro annotated, translated and criticized Pliny.

18 'The excellent masters of our time have started a custom, which I would rather call an abuse, of locking themselves up, closing every aperture, when they work, so that barely anybody can see them, and therefore, instead of making art easier, by teaching and demonstrating, they have made it extremely difficult by hiding and keeping their knowledge to themselves. Hence in the past few years, many young men, desirous of attaining excellency and of avoiding the slavery from which they cannot gain anything useful, have taken courageously and resolutely to trying to teach themselves, with long and attentive study, and they have taken to imitating the ordinary examples, such as printed drawings, the works of the good painters, portraits, the ancient sculptures of marble and of bronze.' (Armenini.)

19 See Bibliography, p. 215.

20 Invented by Vincent Monpetit (1713–1800).

CHAPTER 1

1 Oak must be seasoned for at least three years before use. It is preferable to cut panels from old trees, at a time when the sap is not rising. Wood cut in the autumn is more compact than that cut in the spring.

2 See, for example, p. 29, Mixtures against Worm.

3 See Eastlake: *Materials for an History of Oil Painting*.

4 Theophilus recommends leather and canvas. Cennini recommends canvas, as in the Mount Athos MS.

5 Vasari, Milanesi edn., pp. 364–65.

6 Pliny, *Historia Naturalis*, XXXV, notes: 'Nero princeps iusserat, colosseum se pingi, centum quadraginta pedum in linteo', and Boethius (*De Aritmetica*, praef. I): 'Picturae lintea operosis elaborata textrinis . . . materiam praestant.'

7 In the West the first paintings on canvas were standards no doubt. Heraclius also (*De Coloribus*, etc., Chap. XXV) describes how canvas should be prepared for painting.

8 See the instructions of Ph. Bouvier (*Manuel de jeunes artistes et amateurs en peinture*, IX).

9 'And with regard to those colours that you wish to be beautiful, you will at first prepare a perfectly white ground: I am speaking of transparent colours.' Leonardo, *Trattato della Pittura*, Part II, v. 191.

10 Tradition attributes paintings on silk to Guido Reni, but none has reached us.

11 Cennini, speaking of oil colours, says that 'the Germans used them in the same way on iron or stone'.

12 We have found interesting 14th-century reliquaries of brass, painted with oil colours, and others in silver, similarly painted, belonging to the 15th century. (Franco-Italian art of the Aosta valley.)

13 Scanelli gives a curious piece of information: Livio Agresti, of Forlî, is supposed to have painted on silver fabric of his own invention. In the Greppi Belgioioso collection in Milan there is a portrait on silver by a painter of the Rembrandt school.

14 Leon Battista Alberti in his *Trattato della Pittura* (I. 11) says: 'Ivory, jewels and all these precious things are made more precious by the hand of the painter. Gold decorated with painting is paid for with a far greater amount of gold.' Vasari in the *Life* of Sebastian del Piombo says that this painter 'showed how one can paint over silver, copper, tin, and other metals'. Leonardo speaks of a way of painting over thick copper covered with white enamel, different from the ordinary method of painting with a vitreous enamel that must be fired, which he mentions separately.

15 See H. Hubbard, *Materia Pictorica*, Vol. 1, Oil Painting, London, 1939, p. 203.

16 See H. Hubbard, op. cit., p. 93.

17 Oils were used on paper or parchment by Holbein the Younger, Rembrandt, Hans Thoma, Delacroix, etc.

18 A. P. Laurie, *The Painters' Methods and Materials*, New Art Library, London, 1926, pp. 59, 64, 71.

19 H. Hiler, *Notes on the Technique of Painting*, London, 1927, pp. 56 ff.

20 Ralph Mayer, *The Artist's Handbook*, New York, 1940–41–43–45, p. 224; and Faber and Faber, 1951.

21 Max Doerner, *Malmaterial und seine Verwendung im Bilde*, Benjamin Harz (Berlin, Wien), p. 13.

22 Max Doerner, op. cit., p. 22. We recommend only this oily ground because it contains little oil and is free from the defects of the usual oily grounds.

23 See casein tempera, pp. 135–36.

24 See recipes for tempera, pp. 120 ff.

25 See also Max Doerner, op. cit., p. 25.

26 See Max Doerner, ibid.

27 Ralph Mayer, op. cit., pp. 206–7.

CHAPTER 2

1 H. Sachs, *Lehrbuch der Maltechnik*, Berlin, 1927, p. 44.

2 H. Sachs, op. cit., p. 46.

CHAPTER 3

1 Pliny, *Hist. Nat.*, 1. XXXV, ch. 32: 'Quattuor coloribus solis immortalia illa opera fecere: ex albis melino, ex siliceis Attico, ex rubris sinopide Pontica, ex nigris atramento, Apelles. Echion, Melantius, Nichomachus, clarissimi pictores, quum tabulae eorum singulae oppidorum venirent opibus.'

2 The only vegetable colours used for mural painting were the yellow lakes.

3 His recipes for the preparation of white lead, minium and verdigris are similar to those given by Pliny.

4 It is difficult to judge Leonardo's colours as they are often darkened by thick layers of varnish. As to Rubens, Vibert relates that in a storage room of the Antwerp museum there was a trunk containing the colours he used. In Rubens' pictures we find intact the whites (white lead), cinnabars, blacks, lakes, earths, and ochres; we find almost no traces of yellow lakes and vegetable greens, which are very sensitive to cleaning agents such as soap, lyes, solutions of potash which, unfortunately, many restorers still use.

5 See Vibert, *La science de la peinture*.

CHAPTER 4

1 See L. A. Rosa, *La tecnica della pittura dai tempi preistorici ad oggi*, Milan, 1937, p. 167.

2 Codex Atlanticus, folio 4, verso.

3 Codex Atlanticus, folio 9, verso.

4 Codex Atlanticus, folio 262, recto E.

5 Copperas was a sulphate of iron, copper or zinc. White copperas was made of calcined zinc sulphate.

6 H. Hubbard, op. cit., pp. 135–36.

7 Recipe given by Felipe Nuñez of Lisbon, in his *Art of Painting* of 1615.

8 Bread crumbs used by the Flemish painters to purify oil are mentioned by Maestro Adamo. Salt is recommended by Sorg, a pupil of Teniers (De Mayerne).

9 Valentino Bolzano and the Strasbourg manuscript recommend calcined bone.

10 H. Hubbard, op. cit., pp. 112–13.

11 H. Hubbard, op. cit., pp. 117–18.

12 H. Hubbard, op. cit., pp. 115–16.

CHAPTER 5

1 See p. 49.

2 See p. 109.

3 See pp. 155 ff.

4 H. Hubbard, op. cit., p. 211.

CHAPTER 6

1 The varnish made with elastic gum recommended by Secco Suardo in his manual for restorers, has proved in a few years to be bad as it turns black and disintegrates.

2 H. Hubbard, op. cit., pp. 269–70.

3 H. Hubbard, op. cit., p. 268.

4 H. Hubbard, op. cit., p. 272.

5 De Mayerne, *Treatise*, p. 141.

6 A. P. Laurie, op. cit., p. 167.

7 H. Hiler, op. cit., p. 236.

8 *Dei veri precetti della pittura*, 1578, Book II, Chapter IX.

9 This was obtained by heating lead or by calcining nitrate of lead or carbonate of lead. The many recipes were very different.

10 Vitriol of zinc: sulphate of zinc.

CHAPTER 7

1 On this subject there is a very interesting article by Agnes Talbot in the *Transactions* of the Tempera Society (1901–7). The modern methods have been studied by J. Basch-Bordone and Herman Sachs. (See *Bibliography*.)

2 Cennino Cennini, *Libro dell'arte*, Chap. CXXI and resumé of Chap. CXXXIV.

3 See Daniel W. Thompson, *The Materials of Medieval Painting*, Allen & Unwin,

London, 1936, p. 227. 'The standard method, when gold was to be laid upon colours in panel painting, and in wall painting as well, was to use oil mordants. These were in effect *oil varnishes* containing some pigment. They were applied with brushes often in fine lines and touches; and when they were almost dry, so nearly dry that they would not smear or spread, but still retained a little stickiness or "tack", the gold leaf was laid down lightly and the excess of gold was then brushed carefully away.' This method is still used by restorers in repairing small blemishes.

4 This is another recipe found in the Bologna manuscript. It clearly derives from a treatise on alchemy and has an analogy with the recipes of the Leyden papyri. I append it in its easy Latin form: 'Recipe succum celidoniae et pone in ampulla vitrea bene clausa. Ponatur sub fimo equino et ibi maneat per mensem. Postea extrahatur et molletur aliquantum de auro pigmento cum ipso licore et remittitur in fimo per quindecim dies. Tunc erit purificatus. Quando autem vis scribere mitte aliquas guttas decti licoris in coclea aut cornetto, deinde pone unum folium aurifini et liquefac in simul: postea scribe cum penna quod vis et quando erunt siccae, burnias.'

CHAPTER 8

1 J. Russell, *Elements of painting with crayons*, London, 1772.

2 Loriot, *Pastel painting*.

CHAPTER 9

1 See Bibliography, p. 215.

2 According to the Naples MS, entry XV.

3 Naples MS, entry XXXI.

CHAPTER 10

1 *Historia Naturalis*, 1. XIII, ch. XX.

2 Langlois de Longueville, *Peinture au lavis et à l'acquarelle dediée aux dames*.

3 H. Hiler, op. cit., p. 232.

4 There is a pamphlet by A. Moretti on this technique (1810–92).

5 H. Hiler, op. cit., p. 223.

6 H. Hiler, op. cit., p. 230.

CHAPTER 11

1 Tempera derives from the Latin 'temperare' which means 'to mix', hence mixture.

2 Apropos of the use of wine as diluent, Vasari relates the well-known episode of Buffalmacco, already quoted by Pietro di S. Adimaro in his MS 'De coloribus faciendis' of the 13th century.

3 Theophilus and Heraclius mention *cervisia*.

4 Eibner believes milk of figs to be antiseptic as well. Pliny notes: 'Milk of figs makes milk curdle as if it were vinegar' (*Historia Naturalis*, 1. XXIII, ch. 64).

5 See Bibliography, p. 218.

6 Chemical composition of hens' eggs, according to Church:

	Yolk	*White*
Water	51·5	84·8
Albumin, vitellin, etc.	15·0	12·0
Fat or oil	22·0	0·2

	Yolk	*White*
Lecithin, etc.	9·0	Trace
Mineral matter	1·0	0·7
Other substances	1·5	2·3

7 To avoid this temporary yellowing, Cennini recommends using the eggs of city hens which have a paler yolk than country eggs.

8 Tudor-Hart's recipe (See H. Hiler, op. cit , pp. 181 ff.).

9 Tudor-Hart's recipe (See H. Hiler, op. cit., pp. 181 ff.).

10 H. Sachs, op. cit., p. 59. It is advisable to use essence of cherry laurel rather than carbolic acid.

11 H. Hubbard, *Materia pictoria*, Vol. I, pp. 58–59.

12 See: M. Calderini, *Antonio Fontanesi*, Paravia, Turin, 1901.

13 P. Sérusier, *A. B. C. de la Peinture*, Floury, Paris, 1921–42, p. 79.

14 H. Hiler, op. cit., pp. 176–77.

15 Ibid.

16 Ralph Mayer, op. cit., p. 188.

17 From *Die Ei-Tempera*, pp. 71–78.

18 Op. cit., p. 221.

19 De Mayerne notes Van Dyck's failures in using this glue.

20 A. H. Church, *The Chemistry of Paints and Painting*, London, 1890–1901–1915, p. 69.

21 H. Hiler, op. cit., pp. 183–85.

22 H. Sachs, op. cit., p. 60.

23 The Sloan MS advises tempering the blues with goat's or woman's milk.

24 H. Sachs, op. cit., p. 64.

CHAPTER 12

1 Paolo Pino, op. cit.: ' . . . most ancient and one reads in Pliny that painting had been in use six hundred years before being brought to Greece. It is true that it was brought to Italy after the victory of Marcellus in Sicily and that the way to paint with oils was found by Italians . . . and the Romans had Victories painted on their shields . . .' Bartolomeo Facio writes that the Van Eycks were able to perfect the resin-oil mixtures by studying the ancient authors, including Pliny. (See note 9, p. 198.)

2 Vasari.

3 Vasari says: ' . . . although such pictures gave out the pungent smell produced by colours and oils mixed together, especially when they were new.' Van Mander repeats a similar description. The strong smell was caused by the essential oils used as diluents.

4 Op. cit., p. 6.

5 See 17th-Century Methods, p. 140.

6 For oils and varnishes used by Leonardo and Correggio and followers, see pp. 61 ff.

7 Reynolds wrote: 'I have decided my manner of painting: the first and second coat (oil and copaiva) with black, ultramarine and white; the last with yellow ochre, black lake, ultramarine (without white), retouching with white lead and other colours'. (See Rosa, op. cit., p. 12.)

8 So Decamps describes the technique of Rubens. One does not know precisely where he got this information: apparently his source was his master, Nicholas de Largillière, who made a special study of Rubens.

9 Op. cit., p. 105.

10 Dürer in a letter to Jakob Heller, of August 25th, 1509, wrote: 'I know that the panel will keep in a good condition, that for 500 years it will be clean and fresh, because I have taken all due care in painting it', and in another letter of 1508: 'I have painted with the best colours, as I have obtained them, with good ultramarine, with four, five, or six coats of colour. When completed, I have painted it again twice throughout its length.'

11 See Max Doerner, op. cit., p. 162.

12 Megilp (or butter for retouching) is a clear jelly, which is pleasant to use but which can produce darkening and cracks. Pine's *megilp* is a sulphate of calcium mixed with poppy oil. The *Soehnée* varnish contains lac, is not soluble in oil and tends to turn black; it is one of the varnishes which insulate the layers of a picture and cause flaking and cracks.

13 H. Hiler, op. cit., p. 166.

14 See Ralph Mayer, op. cit., pp. 124–25.

15 Max Doerner, op. cit., p. 145.

CHAPTER 13

1 'Encausto pingendo duo fuere antiquitus genera, cera et in ebore cestro, id est vericulo, donec classes pingi coepere, hoc tertium genus accessit resolutis igni ceris penicillo utendi, quae pictura navibus, nec sole, nec sale ventisve corrumpitur,' Pliny, *Historia Naturalis*, 1. XXV, ch. 149.

2 Cestro was the betony or serratula.

3 The outline was incised on ivory and was then encrusted with wax colour. The *chiaroscuro* was applied with fine strokes, as can be seen on a little box in the British Museum.

4 Naphtha, turpentine (pissinum) are described by Pliny and Dioscorides.

5 Serenus Sammonicus (2nd century before Christ) tells of wax made soluble by means of lye. This must have been similar to the wax mentioned in some Egyptian papyri (1300 B.C.), which read: 'Take wax which is soluble in water.' Rosa, op. cit., p. 297, note 4.

6 H. Hiler, op. cit., pp. 201–2.

7 Revived in 1884 by the chemists Cross and Henry. (See Bibliography.)

8 See Moreau Vauthier—Ojetti, op. cit., p. 111.

9 H. Hiler, op. cit., pp. 207–8.

10 F. Pratt and B. Fizell, *Encaustic, Materials and Methods*, pp. 33–34.

11 H. Hiler, op. cit., pp. 196 ff.

12 Quoted by Didron, op. cit., p. 44.

13 Berger, *Beiträge zur Entwicklungsgeschichte der Maltechnik. Die Maltechnik des Altertums*, Vol. I, p. 100.

14 H. Sachs, op. cit., p. 60.

15 H. Hiler, op. cit., pp. 204–5.

16 Antonio Moretti, *Note sopra la nuova pittura encaustica*.

CHAPTER 14

1 James Ward, *Fresco painting, its art and technique*, Chapman Hall, London, 1904, p. 17.

2 Dissolve 2 oz. 205 grains of glue, 93 grains of alum in $1\frac{3}{4}$ pts. of water over heat.

3 H. Sachs, op. cit., p. 42.

4 In the ancient frescoes we can tell from the joins how much was done in one day. In Raphael's *School of Athens*, almost every figure was completed in one day, thirty-seven days in all. This is also true of Michelangelo's gigantic figures on the ceiling of the Sistine Chapel. Paolo Veronese completed as much as two figures a day in his *Olympus* at Maser.

5 See pp. 120, 129, 134.

6 Cadet de Vaux, *Sur la peinture au lait.*

7 Derived from Cadet de Vaux, op. cit.

8 F. Margival, *Détrempes et badigeons.*

9 *Dictionnaire de l'industrie,* 1776.

CHAPTER 15

1 '*Valuable Secrets in the Arts and Trades*', London, 1780.

2 H. Hiler, op. cit., p. 171.

3 H. Hiler, op. cit., p. 205.

4 J. Ward, op. cit., p. 32.

5 J. Ward, ibid.

6 H. Sachs, op. cit., pp. 51 ff.

7 Nimdeau, *Entrepreneur de peinture.*

8 W. Ostwald, *Das monumentale und dekorative Pastell,* Leipzig, 1912.

Glossary

OF TERMS NOT EXPLAINED IN THE TEXT

Alla prima painting. Direct painting, laying-in and finishing at once, without scumbling, glazing or retouching.

Backing. Protection to prevent atmospheric damage to canvas, panels, cardboard or paper.

Badger or *blender.* Badger brushes are used to blend wet colours softly into one another.

Balsam. Fluid resins like Venice or Strasbourg turpentine, copal, elemi, were called balsams, and mostly used to protect fugitive pigments.

Blanch, Bloom, Blush. The dull bluish cloudy appearance that covers the varnish, called chanci in French. *Blanch* is the misty film that covers a varnish when a strong solvent is used to clean a picture. *Bloom* is caused by inferior materials in the varnish, or by damp on an old picture. *Blush* is the bluish cloud which develops on the surface of newly varnished pictures in damp weather. At an early stage the surface can still be rubbed with a silk rag to restore the shine. If the blush has already worked into the film of the varnish, a little wax polish will remove the cloudiness. Alternatively, the picture can be put in the sun, rubbed with a silk rag and re-varnished with a warm oil varnish.

Body colour. Colours made with pigments that have a good covering power.

Bole or *bolus.* An earthy clay, white, red or yellow, rather oily; formerly used in preparations for gilding; mostly adopted by French painters in 17th–18th centuries for their primings; caused bad cracking and blistering.

Burnisher. A tool made from polished metal or hard stone such as agate, used to burnish the primings or gold layers.

Chiaroscuro. The light and shade contrast in a picture. The term also applies to monochrome pictures.

Copperas. A metallic oxide used as siccative. Sulphates of copper, lead, zinc, or iron were formerly added to boiling oils and varnishes to increase their drying properties.

Cradling, grating, parqueting. Methods of reinforcing the backs of wood panels to prevent or repair splitting and warping. Cardboard and pressed wood panels can also be reinforced to prevent bending.

Diluent. Thin liquid, such as water or essential oils, used to dilute temperas, varnishes or oils, to obtain very thin absorbent layers of colour.

Emulsion. Emulsions used for painting are prepared by mixing an oily fat substance with water by means of another substance combining both.

Fixative. A liquid binding agent which is sprayed on to drawings or pastels to make them more permanent.

Flat colour. A layer of colour uniform in brilliance, tonality and value.

Gelatine or *isinglass.* A transparent and colourless glue mostly made from bones, membranes or fish bladders.

Gouge. A hollow steel cutting tool used to remove knots and other parts of a panel which exude resin.

Ground. The prepared surface on which the colours are laid.

Impasto. The method of laying on colour thickly.

Lacquer. A varnish stained with a transparent yellow or brown colour, generally made with shellac dissolved in alcohol.

Lay-in. The first quick layer of paint which can be finished or remain as a sketch.

Lecithin. This natural emulsifying agent is found in yolk of egg; it swells quickly in water and helps to combine the yolk with oils and varnishes.

Litmus paper. A paper prepared with litmus (blue colouring matter), without size, used for testing the acidity of oils, glues, temperas.

Local colour. The precise colour of an object, not modified by light, shade or distance.

Medium or *binder.* A vehicle such as tempera, oils, varnish, etc., which, blending with the pigments, causes adhesion to support.

Mordant. A sticky medium applied to a surface to be gilded to make it tacky so that the gold foil adheres firmly to the ground.

Mucilage. A gummy solution contained in oils; it must be eliminated as it absorbs moisture and causes deterioration.

Oiling-out. Rubbing lightly with a drying oil or a retouching varnish parts of an oil painting which have 'sunk in' during the drying process.

Patina. An artificial coating imitating the golden-brown colours of old varnishes. Some forgers obtain a patina with glue or gum solutions mixed with decoctions of soot, ashes, bistre, saffron, liquorice, tobacco, the green outer shell of walnuts. Others simply use brown coloured varnishes.

Priming. A mat ground which sometimes contains coloured pigments, but a minimum of oil and varnish.

Relining or *lining.* Backing a picture painted on paper or canvas, cementing it with an adhesive substance to a new canvas. Used for repairing or to give protection and strength to the original support.

Saponification. The action of alkali on oils which converts them into a soapy substance.

Scumbling. Painting with thin layers of opaque colours thinned mostly with essential oils on a wet surface.

Sinking-in. Oil colours during their drying process are liable to become opaque and dull in small patches or on the whole surface of the picture. The painter has to 'oil-out' the parts that have sunk to judge their hue before retouching and finishing the picture.

Slice or *scraper*. Metal or hardwood instrument used for scraping grounds, stucco, colours. The wooden ones are used by many painters for laying primings.

Stamp or *punch*. Small instrument with an ornament at one end, used for stamping decorations on a gold background or on the gilded ornaments of primitive pictures.

Stretcher. The wooden frame upon which the canvas is stretched.

Stucco. A plaster made with lime and fine sand, used for decorating or coating walls.

Stump. A leather or paper instrument rolled in the form of a pencil and tapered at the ends, used to lay or to smooth the touches in drawings, chalks, pastels.

Tempering. The word was formerly used to describe the process of combining dry pigments with a medium.

Tip. Generally made with camel hair set between cards, used to lift the gold leaf from the cushion and to lay it on to the bole or mordant.

Tooth or *grain*. The roughened or absorbent quality of a surface which favours the application and adhesion of paint.

Viscous. Sticky, glutinous.

Volatile. Evaporating readily.

Wash. A transparent layer of very diluted watercolour or ink.

Wedges or *key*. To control the tension of a canvas, flat triangular pieces of wood, called wedges, are inserted in the corners of the stretcher and hammered in, if the canvas tends to become loose.

Wet-in-wet. Method of working on a wet surface: the brush strokes can be blended gently to produce an even surface. See Holman Hunt's preparation, p. 23.

Bibliography

ANCIENT AND MEDIAEVAL TREATISES

Theophrastus of Ephesus, *Treatise on stones*, translated by Turnèbe (Paris, 1574); in 1577 a Greek and Latin translation; English translated by S. Hill (Davis, London, 1774). The same recipes (how to prepare white lead, cinnabar, lapis lazuli, orpiment and how to purify the ochres) are to be found in Pliny and Vitruvius.   315 B.C.

Vitruvius Marcus Pollio, *De Architectura, Libri decem*. There are many editions, of the 15th and 16th centuries; among them that of Daniele Barbaro and that of Cesariani; there are also many editions of the 17th and 18th centuries, mainly published in Venice or in Paris; among those of the last century that of Schneider (Leipzig, 1807) and that of Orsini (Perugia, 1802) must be mentioned, translated into English and annotated by F. Granger (Putnam, New York, 1931–34).   27 B.C.?

Pliny C. the Second, *Historia Naturalis*, 1. 37. There are many editions of the 15th and 16th centuries, and some of the 17th century (see Hardouin) which concern painting techniques in particular. Pliny derives his information from many sources which have been lost. The chapters on history of art have been translated into English by E. K. Jex-Blake (Macmillan, London, 1896).   1 cent. A.D.

Dioscorides, *De re medica* (Venice, 1499–1516). *De medicinali*   1–2 cent.

207

materia (Venice, 1538; Basileae, 1542). During the Middle Ages painters learnt from him how to perfect materials and how to purify oils.

Galen Claudius, *Opera omnia*. In Greek, Venetiis, Aldus, 1525; in Latin, Venetiis, Vagrisius, 1562. He reports the use of coloured glazes over blue-green and brown grounds, used by painters to avoid the glare of white gesso grounds (Book X). *2 cent.*

Anonymous, *The Greek papyri of Leyden* (Leemans, Leyden, 1885; see also Berthélot). In the 5th and in the 10th centuries there are recipes similar to those of Pliny, Dioscorides, etc. *3 cent.*

Zosimus of Panopolis, *Treatise* in XII books. MSS in Syriac in Cambridge University, 15th-century translation. *5 cent.*

Aetius of Amida, *De re medica*, publ. J. Cornarius, Lugduni, 1549; Venetiis, 1563. He observes that nut oil was also used by gilders and encaustic painters. *5-6 cent.*

Paulus Aegineta, *De re medica, Libri VII* (Venice, 1528). *5-6 cent.*

Anonymous, *Ivrea* MS (Biblioteca Capitolare). Recipes of Roman origin; teaches how to write in gold and silver and to dye parchment with purple; quotes tempera of cherry gum. *7 cent.*

Isidore of Seville, *Origines vel Etymologiae*. A kind of encyclopedia in which colours are listed. *7 cent.*

Anonymous, *Compositiones ad tingenda* (MS of the Biblioteca Capitolare of Lucca, MSS 490). Published by L. A. Muratori in *Antiquitates Italicae Medii Aevi*. Many recipes are of Byzantine derivation; others are taken from Pliny, Dioscorides, from the Leyden papyri, from Isidore of Seville. *7-8 cent.*

Anonymous, *Chimica* (called *of Moses*). A collection of Greek alchemists. See Berthélot. *7-8 cent.*

Anonymous, *Mappae claviculae* (MSS 6514, National Library, Paris, another in the Schlestadt Library, and another from the 12th century in London). Recipes for colours and dyes.

Anonymous, *Liber sacerdotum* (Latin MS 6514, National Library, Paris). See Berthélot, *La Chimie au Moyen Age* (Paris, 1893). *10 cent.*

Anonymous, *Liber septuaginta Jo.* (MS 7156, National Library, Paris). Translated from Arabic by Rinaldo da Cremona. *10 cent.*

Heraclius Presbyter, *De Coloribus et artibus romanorum* (Brit. Mus., Sloane 1754). English translation published by Mary Merrifield (*Ancient practice of painting*, 1849), in Latin and German by A. Ilg (*Quellenschriften*, etc., 1873). *10 cent.*

Ruggero, called Theophilus Presbyter, *Diversarum artium schedula*. There are various ancient MSS, among which the Harley MS 3915 published by R. Hendrie, London, 1847, by A. Ilg in *Quellenschriften*, etc. (Vienna, 1876). A 15th-century MS from the Montpellier school of medicine, now in the Sorbonne, is a derivation of the *Treatise* of Theophilus and is called *Liber Diversarum Artium*. *11-12 cent.*

Anonymous, *Tractatus de coloribus illuminatorum seu pictorum* (Brit. Mus., Sloane 1754). Translated by D. V. Rampson, jr., in the magazine *Speculum* (1. I, p. 280). The precepts have a strict analogy with those of Pietro di Sant'Adimaro. *13-14 cent.*

Pietro di Sant'Adimaro, *De coloribus faciendis* (Latin MS in the National Library, Paris, No. 6741). Derives from Theophilus; edited in Latin and English by Mary Merrifield (*Ancient practice of painting*, 1849). *13 cent.*

Alcherius Johannes, *De coloribus diversis modis tractatus*. (See Jehan   *14 cent.*
le Bègue.)

Scot, Michael, *Manuscript* of Gonville and Caius College (MS
181), published by W. Singer (*Michael Scot and Alchemy*, I mis.
XIII, 1929). Contains an interesting recipe on preparation of
ultramarine blue.

Bacon, Roger, *De coloribus per artem faciendis*, *De secretis operibus
artis et naturae*. The greater part of Bacon's works was collected
and published in *Theatrum Chemicum* (Frankfurt, 1620). The
information is taken from Egyptian and Arabic alchemists.

Dyonisus Presbyter, *Mount Athos MS* (*Hermenea*).[1] Translated by   *12 cent.*
Durand in *Manuel d'Iconographic sacrée de Didron* (Paris, 1885).   Other parts
The recipes for temperas, plasters, glues, etc., are still used   perhaps later.
unchanged from the 10th century to this day in orthodox
convents.

Anonymous Bernese, *De clarea*. Published by D. V. Thompson, jr.,   *12–14 cent.*
in Technical Studies, I (1932).

Albertus Magnus, *Compositum de compositis, super libros mineralium*.
Published at Augsburg, 1519.
Delle cose minerali e metalliche. Translated by Pietro Lauro
(Venice, 1557–1558). The information is taken from Aristotle,
Hermes, Avicenna; he teaches how to prepare noble azure,
minium, ceruse, almost perfectly.

Robert or Albert the German, *Venetian MS* (*Receipts and Direc-*   *14 cent.*
tions of curing Diseases, dyeing, making Glass, etc., Brit. Mus.,
Sloane MS No. 416). According to Eastlake the name Robert
is to be ascribed to a copyist's error, because directly afterwards the MS speaks of an azure 'secundum dotrinas Alberti
Magni, ordinis fratrum predicatorum', a derivation therefore
from the writings of St. Albert. We find again some of the
recipes in Rosselli's *Segreti*. Of interest is the description of
false tapestries painted with tempera and of painting on glass.
Published by Mary Merrifield.

St Thomas Aquinas, *Opera Omnia*. (Rome, 1570; Venice, 1592,
etc.) Repeats ideas and recipes of St Albert the Great.

Anonymous, *Manoscritto napoletano de arte illuminandi* (Naples,   *14 cent.*
National Library, MS XII, E.27). Quotes Pliny and St Albert   copy of
the Great; collects the tradition of lost ancient treatises and   older text.
makes an excellent précis of the procedures of the Benedictine
school; very clear and valuable recipes. Translated and transcribed by Salazzaro, Lecoy de la Marche, Dimier, Berger,
Daniel Varney Thompson, George Heard Hamilton.

D'Ascalo, Saladino, *Compendium aromatarium* (Augsburg, 1485).   *15 cent.*
This Neapolitan doctor who lived at the beginning of the 15th
century teaches how to preserve substances which decay.

De Beauvais, Vincent, *Speculum Naturale*. Quotes the same col-   *15 cent.*
ours as Pliny.

Le-Bègue, Jehan, *Tabula de vocabulis sinonimis et equivocis colorum*   *15 cent.*
(National Library, Paris, Latin MS No. 6741).
Experimenta coloribus. Transcribes Heraclius, teaches how to
prepare oil for tempering all kinds of colours and how to make
a wax saponification. He also transcribes the MS of Pietro di
Sant'Adimaro and that of Giovanni Alcherio of Milan: *De
coloribus ad pingenda*, etc., of 1398. Alcherio analysed and

---

[1] Victor Hugo has thus defined this manuscript: '*Tout s'y trouve mêlé et combiné dans une puissante et
singulière unité: l'art, la poésie, la religion: pour les uns c'est une étude, pour les autres une contemplation.*'

examined the painting technique of Jacques Coene, a miniaturist and artist of Bruges who lived in Paris. Transcribed and
translated by Mary Merrifield (op. cit., Vol. I, p. 32).

Anonymous, *Libro dei colori*, Bologna MS (San Salvatore   15 *cent.*
Library, MS No. 165). Egyptian origin of some recipes (see
Leyden papyri); close analogy with Leonardo's recipes. Important for the preparation of vegetable colours. Transcribed
and published by Mary Merrifield (op. cit., II, 595) and published by Olindo Guerrini and Corrado Ricci at Bologna in
1887.

Cennino Cennini, *Libro dell'arte*. MSS in Florence: Mediceo
No. 23 at the Laurenziana Library, No. 2190 at the Riccar-
diana Library. In the Vatican Library Ottoboni MS, the
most complete, published by G. Tambroni in 1921; a more
correct edition published by G. and C. Milanesi in 1859; even
better the edition by Renzo Simi in 1913. Translated into English by Mary Merrifield and Christian G. Herringam (London,
1899), into French by Victor Mottez (Paris, same date), into
German by Albert Ilg with interesting notes. It is the clearest,
simplest and most practical of the ancient treatises.

Anonymous, *Strasbourg MS* (A VI, No. 19). The original was   15 *cent.*
burnt in 1870. In the National Gallery, London, there is the
copy made by Eastlake. It deals with medicine and painting
technique and contains excellent recipes for colours, temperas,
gilding, derived from the Venetian MS, the Montpellier MS,
and from Pietro di Sant'Adimaro.

Anonymous, *Liber illuministrarium*, etc. A fragment published by   15–16 *cent.*
Rockinger (*Abhandl. d. hist. Ges.*, etc., Munich, 1872). The
MS is in the Stadtsbibliothek of Munich (German MS No.
821).

Ketham, John, *Collection of recipes* (Brit. Mus., Sloane MS No.   15 *cent.*
345). This doctor, who lived in the second half of the 15th
century, lived near the native village of the Van Eycks. His
book of recipes contains writings revealing their methods of
preparing linseed oil and amber varnish.

Facio, Bartolomeo, *De viribus illustribus*. The MS is dated 1456   15 *cent.*
and was published in Florence by Abbé Mehus in 1745.

Ambrogio di Ser Pietro, *Ricepte daffare più colori*. The MS is in   15 *cent.*
Sienna (MS 11–19, fol. 99r–105r) and is dated 1462.

Magister Johannis De Burgundia, *Pratica physicalia*. MS at   15 *cent.*
Oxford (Bodleian MS Raoul D. 251), edited by Herbert
Schöffler in *Beiträge zur Mittelenglischen Medizinliteratur* (Halle,
1919).

Maestro Bernardo, *Liber quartus eiusdem magistri Bernardi*   15 *cent.*
Trevirensis in quo tractatur de collis, de maculis et bondis et de con-
ficiendis pellibus. Unpublished MS (Oxford, Bodleian MS
Canonici, mis. 128). Contains recipes for glue similar to
those of other MSS of the same time.

RENAISSANCE TREATISES

Alberti, Leon Battista, *De Pictura*.   Basilaeae, 1540
De re aedificatoria. Partially translated into German by   Amsterdami
H. Ganischek in *Quellenschriften*, etc., Vol. XI, Vienna, 1881.   1549
Translated into Italian by Bartoli (*Opuscoli morali*, Venice,
1568), edited by Du Fresne (Paris, 1651), into English by
Leoni in 1829.

Alessio Piemontese (Padre) *Doni segreti . . . havuti da un rev. padre gesuato pratico et eccellente.* Recipes for medicines, varnishes, oils, colours, etc., transcribed in many later works, chiefly French and English. Translated into English from the French by W. Ward (London, 1558) and from Italian by W. Androse (London, 1568–69); French edition by C. Laudré (Paris, 1573). — Venice, 1555, 1557

Anonymous, *Ricettario dell'arte e università dei medici e speziali*, called *Ricettario fiorentino*. MS. — Florence, 1573

Anonymous, *Trattato dell'affinare l'oro e l'argento*. MS in the Marciana Library (It. IV 48). Contains many recipes of interest to painters, including the description of an amber varnish.

Armenini, Gian Battista, *Dei veri precetti della pittura*, etc. A mine of information, especially for fresco painters. — Ravenna, 1587 / Venice, 1578

Biondo, Michelangelo, *Trattato di pittura veneziana*. Translated into German and annotated by Albert Ilg (*Quellenschriften*, etc.). Speaks of colours and media of his time. — Venice, 1549

Biringuccio, Vannuccio, *Pyrotechnia*. Treats also of colours, distillation, turpentine, extraction of oils, gums, and waxes, etc. — Venice, 1540, 1550, 1558, 1559

Bolz (or Bolzano), Valentin De Rupac, *Art und Weise allerhand Farben zu bereiten*. Has close analogy to the Strasbourg MS. *Illuminierbuch*, about illuminating. — Frankfurt a.M., 1562 / Hamburg, 1646 / Basel, 1546, 1549

Borghini, *Riposo*. Information on fresco, corresponding to that given by Vasari. — 1584

Cardano, Girolamo, *De subtilitate*, L. XXI, Bâle, 1550; Lugduni, 1559; French translated by R. Leblanc, 1559. — Norimbergae, 1550

De Varga, Perez, *De re metallica*. Recipes for gilding. — Madrid, 1569

Dolce, Ludovico, *Dialogo della pittura*, called the *Aretino*. In Italian and French (Florence, 1735). Translated into English by W. Brown (London, 1770). Translated into German by C. Cerri in *Quellenschriften*, II, 1871 (Vienna). *Dialogo dei colori*. Explains the terminology of colours, media and mixtures then current. — 1557

Dürer, Albrecht, *The symmetry of human bodies*. The technique of this master is studied better by consulting his letters and notes than by reading the treatises which remain. — Venice, 1591

Fioravanti, Leonardo, *Del compendio dei segreti razionali*. The secrets derive from those of P. Alessio. Treats of colours, varnishes, oils, glues, stucco. English translated by J. Hester (London, 1582). — Venice, 1564, 1571

Hollanda, Francisco (De), *De la pintura antiqua*, etc. Castilian translation by M. Denis, 1563. Edited by Vasconcellos at Oporto in 1896, translated into German in *Quellenschriften* (Vienna, 1899). Printed in Madrid by J. Ratés in 1921. The works of Francisco de Hollanda, published in Portuguese, are found in the Spanish version with an introduction, translation and notes by A. Pellizzari (Perrella, Naples, 1915). — 1548

Laguna, Andreas (De), *Annotationes in Dioscoridem* (*Dioscorides traduzido, illustrado, por A. de L.*), Salamanca, 1560; Valencia, 1636, 1695. — London, 1554 / Lyons, 1559

211

Leonardo da Vinci, *Trattato della pittura* (Vatican Library Urbinate, No. 1270). English translation in Italian and English, by G. P. Richter, (London, 1721, 1796, 1882); French translation by Fréart de Cambray (Paris, 1651, 1716, etc.); Dutch translation by W. Goerce (Amsterdam, 1682); German translation by G. Bohmsen (Nuremberg, 1724–47, etc.); Italian and German translation by H. Ludwig (*Quellenschriften*, etc., XV–XVIII) (Vienna, 1882, 1888).
Codex Atlanticus contains notes and recipes similar to those of the Bologna MS, therefore of Egyptian origin. — Paris, 1650–51, 1704; Bologna, 1786; Florence, 1792; Milan, 1804–57, etc.

Libavius, Andreas, *Singularia*. Recipes for dissolving resins and making varnishes. — Frankfurt, 1599–1601

Lomazzo, *Trattato della pittura*. Translated into English by R. Haydocke, quoted also by Mary Merrifield.
Tempio della pittura. The advice on proportions and distribution of lights is more useful than the technical advice. — Milan, 1584

Marco da Siena, *Manuscript*. Treats of painters who painted murals in fresco and in oils. — 1550

Mattioli, P. A. *Commentarii in libris Dioscoridis*, etc. — Venice, 1565

Monjosus, *Gallus romanae Hospes*. A short treatise on the painting and sculpture of ancient times, reprinted in the Helzevirian Vitruvius of 1649. — 1585

Morato, Fulvio Pellegrino, *Del significato dei colori*. — Venice, 1545

Occolti, Coronato Da Canedolo, *Trattato dei colori*. He speaks about the occult meaning of colours, not of media and technique. — 1568

Oldanis, *Ars sive doctrina de transmutatione metallorum*. The most ancient among Italian chemical-alchemical encyclopedias. It describes the preparation of the lakes and the extraction of oil from eggs. — 16 cent.

Pino, Paolo, *Dialogo di pittura*. Speaks of the various painting techniques, their merits and defects. — Venice, 1548

Porta, Giovan Battista (Della), *Magia naturalis*, Libri XX. Translated into English (*Natural Magic*). Tells how to melt amber, Lugduni, 1644. — Naples, 1558–59
De distillationibus, Libri IX. — Rome, 1608

Portius, Simon, *Libellus de coloribus*. — Florence, 1548

Rosselli, Timoteo (Don), *Della summa dei secreti universali*. — Venice, 1575

Rossetti, Ventura, *Plico dell'arte dei tintori*. Translated into French and edited in 1716 in Paris. — Venice, 1548

Tottil, Richard, *Art of limming*, etc. Recipes for glues, temperas, gilding, preparation of colours. — London, 1573, 1596

Vasari, Giorgio, *Vite dei più eccellenti pittori*, etc. The Florence edition of 1568 contains information on several Flemish masters. The best edition is that revised and annotated by Milanesi (Florence, 1878). English translation by F. Foster, London, 1850, by G. P. Richter, London, 1885, translation of the introduction to the Three Arts by Miss Maclehose, London, 1907; French translation by Jeauron and Leclauché, Paris, 1839–42; German translation by L. S. Schorn and E. Forster, Stuttgart and Tübingen, 1832–49. Both in the general introduction and in the single lives, this text gives valuable information on painting technique. — Florence, 1550, 1568; Bologna, 1647; Rome, 1759–1760; Leghorn, 1767, 1772, etc.

Auda, F. D., *Breve compendio di meravigliosi segreti.* Rome, 1663

Baldinucci, F., *Vocabolario toscano dell'arte del disegno, Discorsi sulla* Florence, 1681
pittura, Vite degli artisti italiani e stranieri, Cominciamento e pro- Florence, 1681
gresso dell'arte di intagliare in rame, Vite dei principali incisori.

Ballart, Christophe, *Traité de la miniature.* Translated into Paris, 1672
German and published at Leipzig in 1703. Lyons, 1679

Bates, J., *Mysteries of Nature and Art.* London, 1654

Bie, Cornelis De., *Het gulden cabinet van de edele vry schilder const.* Lier, 1661

Birelli, G. B., *Secreti.* Interesting recipes for the preparation of Florence, 1601
oils. German and Dutch translation (*Segreet Boeck*), Frankfurt
a.M., 1603.

Bisogno, D. F., *Trattato della pittura.* Taken almost entirely from Venice, 1642
Armenini.

Boschini, Marco, *Le ricche miniere della pittura veneziana, Carta del* Venice, 1664
navegar pitoresco. In eight cantos or 'winds'. These works are
full of episodes from the lives of famous artists.

Bosse, Abraham, *Le peintre converti aux règles précises de son* Paris, 1666,
art, etc. 1667

Boyle, Robertus, *Experimenta et considerationes de coloribus.* Con- London, 1664
tains documents of great interest concerning the chemical Rotterdam,
aspect of painting. 1671

Brenneri, Elia, *Nomenclatura trilinguis, germina, specimina colorum,* Holnuall, 1680
simplicium exhibens, quibus artificiis utuntur.

Brown, Alex, *Ars pictoria.* London, 1675

Bulengerus, *De pictura, plastica, statuaria.* Lyons, 1627

Caneparius, P. M., *De atramentis cuiuscumque generis.* Venice, 1619

Cespedes, Paolo, *Manuscripts.* On painting, quoted by Pacheco.

Corneille, J. B., *Les éléments de la peinture pratique.* Paris, 1684

De Mayerne, Theodore Tuquet, *Pictoria, sculptoria, tinctoria* 1620
et quae subalternarium artium spectantia, etc. MS (Sloane, MS
No. 2052) published by Berger in *Beiträge,* etc. (Munich,
1901).

De Piles, R., *Conversation sur la connaissance de la peinture.* Paris, 1677
Les premiers éléments de la peinture pratique. The 1776 edition was Paris, 1684
edited by Jombert. These works are very useful and informa-
tive about the mannerists.

Du Cange, *Glossarium med. et inf.* Paris, 1678
Glossarium med. et inf. graec. Lyons, 1688

Du Fresnoy, C. A., *De arte graphica.* Published by Mignard, Paris, 1668,
translated into French and annotated by De Piles: poses the 1684
main problems of the science of colours, deriving his knowledge from Leonardo. *De arte graphica* was translated into
Italian and published in Rome with the title *Dell'arte della*
pittura (Rome, 1713), and several times into English, in
London (London, 1716); one edition bears notes by Reynolds
(York, 1783). There is also a German translation (Berlin,
1699).

Dupuy, Bernard De Grez, *Traité sur la peinture pour en apprendre la* Toulouse, 1699
théorie et la perfectionner dans la pratique.
Traité sur la fresque. Paris, 1700

Felibien, A., *De l'origine de la peinture*, etc. *Des principes de l'archi-*   Paris, 1660
tecture, de la sculpture, de la peinture.

Fludd, (Robertus De Fluctibus), *Tractatus de arte picturae.*   Frankfurt a.M., 1624

Gautiers, H., *Art de laver ou nouvelle manière de peindre le papier.*   Lyons, 1684

Geier, Jean Daniel, *Mélanges curieux.* Information on the manu-   1689
facture of varnishes.

Gerhardt of Bruges, *Inleyding tot de Praktik der algemeene Schilder-*   Amsterdam, *konst.* Published by W. Goeree. Translated into German under   1694
the title *Illuminien oder Erleuchterei Kunst*, etc., Hamburg, 1678.

Junii, Francisci, *De pictura veterum, Libri tres.* More useful to the   Rotterdam, critic and the scholar than to the painter. A work full of quota-   1694
tions of ancient Latin and Greek texts, much praised by
Rubens.

Love, Marley Christopher, *Collectanea chymica leydensia.* Repeats   Lugduni Bata-
the information given by Padre Alessio.   vorum, 1684

Mander, Carel van, *Het Schilder-Boeck*, etc. (book of painters).   Harlem, 1604, French translation by H. Hymans.   1884

Nuñez, Felipe, *Arte de pintura.* Repeats recipes from the com-   Lisbon, 1615
pendium of Padre Alessio.

Ottonelli (Padre), *Trattato della pittura e scoltura*, etc. Written in   Florence, 1652
collaboration with Pietro da Cortona.

Pacheco, Francisco, *Arte de la pintura, su Antiguedad y Granderos*,   Seville, 1649
etc. Brought to Spain the technical precepts of the Italian
school. Many of the recipes are still among the most rational
and practical.

Perrot, Catherine, *Traité de la miniature.*   1625

Pomet, Pierre, *Histoire générale des drogues.*   Paris, 1694

Pozzo, Andrea (Padre), *Perspectiva pictorum et architectorum,*   Rome, 1693
Andreae Putei. Latin-Italian (Rome, 1790); Latin-English,
translated by J. Jones (London, 1707), known as *The Jesuits
perspective.*

Ridolfi, Carlo, *Le meraviglie dell'arte.*   Venice, 1648

Rosa, Salvatore, *La Pittura* (a satire). This is the first polemical
writing in the history of art criticism; it shows up crudely the
lack of seriousness and conscientiousness of the art schools and
profession.

Rubens, Pieter Paul, *Letters.* De Piles describes the artistic
thought and technique of Rubens.

Ruland, Martin, *Lexicon Alchemial.*   1612

Salmasius, Claudius, *Plinianae exercitationes.*   Utrecht, 1629, 1689

Sanderson, Sir W., *Graphicae* (*The use of pen and pencil or the most*   London, 1658
excellent art of painting).

Sandrart, Joachim von, *Deutsche Akademie der edeln Bau, Bild-und*   Nuremberg, *Mahlerung-Künste.*   1675, 1679

Scannelli, Francesco, *Il microcosmo della pittura.* One of the first   Cesena, 1657
treatises for collectors and antiquarians.

Schoeffer, Johannes, *Graphicae, id est de arte pingendi Liber singu-*   Nuremberg, *laris.* Very valuable for the interpretation of ancient texts.   1669

Scroheder, *Pharmakopeia medico chymica leydensis.*   Lugduni Bata-
  vorum, 1684

Smith, John, *The Art of Painting in Oil* (*Introduction to the art of painting and varnishing*).   London, 1687, 1685–87, 1701, 1705, 1723

Smith, Marshall, *The Art of Painting*, etc. Describes the practices of the Flemish, Italian and German masters.   London, 1692

Volpati, Gian Battista, *Modo da tener nel dipinger*. MS in the Bassano Library. *La verità pittorica rittamente svelata* (Marc. It. IV, 132).

Wecheri (or Wecker) Hans Jakob, De secretis, Books XVII, English translation by Dr Read (London, 1660).   Bâle, 1604

ANONYMOUS TREATISES

A Proper Treatise, Wherein is briefly set forth the art of leinning.   London, 1626

Trattato del disegno e della pittura in miniatura.   Venice, 1668

Traité de la miniature pour apprendre sans maître. Speaks of miniatures painted both with oil colours and watercolours; a meticulous description of techniques and materials; it is the best book and all the most recent works derive from it.   Paris, 1672

Livre des secrets pour faire la peinture.   1682

Secreet Boeck (*Waer en vele diverache secreten gebracht zyn tot Dordrecht*). Dutch translation of G. B. Birelli's *Secreti*.   1601

Description of varnishes. In the writings of several Jesuit missionaries in China, towards the middle 17th century, there are descriptions of varnishes used at first in the East and then in France and Italy, especially for maps, prints, furniture, decorative panels, pictures. Father Martino Martini describes one of these varnishes in the Chinese atlas, and Father Coronelli a varnish made of juniper gum, turpentine, lavender and alcohol, which is very beautiful but turns dark with time (*Epitome cronographica, 1. III, c. 32*). Other missionaries who studied varnishes were: Father Jehan Zahn, Father Vannham, Father Le Compte, Father Bonomi (who introduced them into Tuscany), Father Albert Tiskonski. Father Rizzari made a special study of oils.

18TH-CENTURY TREATISES

Algarotti, Francesco, *Saggio sopra la pittura*. Contains excellent advice for artists.   Leghorn, 1749

Astori, Gianmaria, *Della pittura a cera con l'encausto*.   Venice, 1786

Bachelier, *L'Histoire et le secret de la peinture en cire*.   1749

Backmann, J., *Beiträge zur Geschichte der Erfindungen*. Translated into English by A. Johnston (London, 1797–1814, and in an abridged form in 1823).   Leipzig, 1782, 1805

Bancroft, C., *Experimental Researches Concerning the Philosophy of Permanent Colours*.   London, 1794, 1813

Bardwell, *Practice of Painting and Perspective*.   London, 1756

Beltramini, *Due discorsi sulla mestica della pittura*.   Imola, 1796

Bonanni, *Trattato sulla vernice*.   Bologna, 1786

Boyle, R., *The Painters' Companion*.   London, 1762
    Experiments and Considerations Touching Colours, etc.   Florence, 1854

Budberg, De, *Essay sur l'époque de la découverte de la peinture à l'huile (Versuch über das Alter der Oelmalerei zur Vertheidigung des Vasari)*.   Göttingen, 1792

Caracciolo, Antonio, *Livre des quatre couleurs*.   Paris, 1759

Carvalho y Iampayo, Diego, De, *Memoria sobre a formaçao natural das côres*.   Madrid, 1791

Cavaceppi, *Trattato sull'arte di restaurare gli antichi*.   Rome, 1799

Caylus, A. C. P., Comte de, *Du genre et de l'espèce des peintures anciennes*, etc. *Mémoire de l'Académie des Inscriptions*, Vol. XII.   Paris, 1771

Chiusole, A., *Dell'arte pittorica*, 8 books.   Venice, 1768

Crespi (Canonico), *Lettere sulla pittura, scultura, sulla maniera di pulire i quadri*, etc.   Rome, 1769

Croekers, J. Melchior, *Wohlanführender Maler*. How to paint with oils, pastel, fresco.   Jena, 1778

D'André, Bardon, *Traité de la peinture*.   Paris, 1765

Degny de Marcenay, *Traité du coloris*.   Paris

Delaval, E. H., *An Experimental Enquiry into the Causes of Changes of Colours*, etc. French translation (Paris, 1779). Italian translation. (Bologna, 1779; Milan, 1779).   London, 1777

Delavoy et Mignot, *Traité de la miniature, pour apprendre à peindre sans maître*.   undated

Diderot, *Essay sur la peinture (Histoire et secrets de la peinture en cire)*.   Paris, 1755

Dossie, R., *The Handmaid of the Arts*.   London, 1758, 1767, 1796

Durand, David, *Histoire de la peinture ancienne*. A recapitulation of Pliny's *Historia Naturalis*, Book XXXV, with Latin text.   London, 1725

Elsum, G., *The Art of Painting after the Italian Manner*.   London, 1703

Fabbroni, G., *Antichità, vantaggi e metodo della pittura encausta*.   Rome, 1797

Faujaz de St Fond, *Studi sulla calce, sulla durata degli intonachi, ricerche sulla pozzolana*.   undated

Ferrand, *Traité sur la peinture en émail et miniature*.   Paris, 1721

Fouquet, M. Le, *Traité de la peinture en miniature*.   Den Haag, 1708

Franchi, *La teoria della pittura, ovvero trattato delle materie più necessarie per apprendere con fondamento quest'arte*.   Lucca, 1739

Garcia de la Huerta, Pedro, Don, *Comentarios de la pintura encaustica del Pincel*.   Madrid, 1726

Gauthier, H. *L'art de laver, ou la nouvelle manière de peindre sur papier*.   Brussels, 1708

Guevara, F. Don, *Comentarios de la pintura*.   Madrid, 1788

Guidotti, Angelo Maria, *Nuovo trattato di vernici all'uso della China usate in Francia ed in Inghilterra*.   Bologna, 1764

Hartman, Melchior Philippus, *Dissertatio de succino*.   Lugduni, 1710

Hodory de Hoda, Karl, *Ars delineandi coloribusque localibus adumbrandi*.   1790

Hymans, H., *L'idée du peintre parfait*. Italian translation (Turin, 1767).   London, 1707

Lairesse, Gerard, *Het groot schilderboeck*, etc. (*Le grand livre des peintres, ou l'art de peindre*), French translation (Paris, 1787); (*A Treatise on the art of painting revised with an essay by W. M. Crevig*), English translation (London, 1817).   Amsterdam, 1707

Lessing, G. E., *Vom Alter der Oelmalerei*.   Brunswick, 1774

Lorgna, *Un discorso sulla cera punica e il natron*.   Verona, 1785

Loriot, *La pittura a pastello.*

Massoul, Constant de, *A Treatise on the Art of Painting* (English London, 1797
edition).

Mayol, *Introduction à la miniature.* Amsterdam,
1771

Mengs, Raphael, *Opere complete*, translated into Italian. Of Bassano, 1783
special interest the practical lessons in painting, and the reflections on the different colours of flesh, etc.

Milizia, Francesco, *Dizionario delle belle arti e del disegno.* Largely Bassano, 1797
derived from the *Enciclopedia Metodica.* This writer edited the
works of Mengs with the help of d'Azara.

Montany (D'Arclais de), *Traité des couleurs pour la peinture en émail* Paris, 1765
et sur porcelaine.

Munts, J. H., *Encaustic*, etc. Speaks of the method of the Count London, 1760
of Caylus and deals with fixatives for pastel.

Orellana, F. V., *Tratado de Barnices y colores.* Valencia, 1755

Orlandi, Fra Pellegrino Antonio, *L'abbecedario pittorico.* Bologna, 1719

Palomino del Velasco, *El museo pictorico y escala optica* (1. IX). Madrid, 1724
Four books are about the practice and history of painting; the
information is taken from Theophilus, Dürer, Vignola, Du
Fresnoy, Pacheco. It is an encyclopedia of painting full of
valuable technical information.

Petitot, J., *Lettera al figlio per servirgli da guida nella pittura a smalto.* Paris, 1759

Pictorius, J. B., *Die mit vielen . . . Geheimnissen angefüllte Illuminier-* Nuremberg,
kunst, etc. 1713

Raspe, R. E., *A critical Essay on Oil Painting*, edited by H. London, 1781
Goldney.

Reifesthen (or Renfesthen), *Sur l'art de peindre en pastel à la cire* 1757
(Journal étranger, Févr., 1757)

Rejon de Sylva, Diego Antonio, *La pintura.* Segovia, 1785

Requeno, Vincenzo, Don, *Saggio sul ristabilimento dell'arte di* Parma, 1787
dipingere all'encausto degli antichi.

Reynolds, Joshua, Sir, *Discourses Delivered to the Students of the* Bassano, 1789
Royal Academy. Edited by Fry in 1905. Italian translation.

Richardson (Père et Fils), *Traité de la peinture et de la sculpture.* Amsterdam,
1728

Riem, Andreas, *Ueber die Malerei der Alten.* Berlin, 1789

Russell, John, *Elements of painting with crayons.* This painter's London, 1772
special technique has been mentioned in the chapter dealing
with pastels.

Stockars, *Specimen inaugurale de succino.* How to dissolve amber to Leyden, 1760
make varnishes.

Torri, Luigi, *Osservazioni intorno alla cera punica.* Verona, 1786

Tripier Devaux, *Secrets des arts et des métiers. Traité de l'art de faire* Paris, 1790
des vernis.

Violet, *Traité sur l'art de peindre en miniature.* Paris, 1788

Walpole, *Anecdotes on painting.* London, 1786

Wathelet, *L'art de peindre.* In verse, Italian translation by undated
Caranucio.

Watin, *L'art du peintre vernisseur.* This is the most valuable book Paris, 1772
for decorative painting; it contains the practical advice of an

excellent technician, instructions on how to cure cases of poisoning from colours and the interesting *Mémoire* of Father d'Incarville on Chinese varnish painting.

Williams, M., *An essay on the mechanic of oil painting with receipts.* Bath, 1787
Of interest with regard to preparing colours.

Winckelmann, *Trattato del restauro.* Not completely published. 1763
Contains a history of ancient art.

Zanetti, Anton Maria, *Della pittura veneziana.* Venice, 1774

ANONYMOUS TREATISES

L'idea del perfetto pittore. A brief work which describes very super- Venice, 1771
ficially the various methods of painting.

Antologia dell'arte pittorica. Augusta, 1784

Secrets concernant les arts et les métiers. Very similar to the Egyptian Avignon, 1737–
and mediaeval books of recipes; brings to mind the *Com-* 1743
pendium of Father Alessio; contains recipes for cooking, for
engraving, for the fusion of metals, the making of wine and
vinegar, the composition of varnishes, colours and oils, for oil
mural painting and miniatures, all very well described. This
book is the source of Watin (*Secrets de la nature de l'art*), the
Enciclopedia medica pittorica chimica, etc.

Valuable Secrets in the Arts and Trades. This work derives from the London, 1780
Avignon book and therefore from Padre Alessio.

The Art of Drawing and Painting in Watercolour. London, 1732

Instruction sur l'art de peindre en miniature. Leipzig, 1752

Painting in Miniature. London, 1757

Trattato di Miniatura. Derived from contemporary French Milan, 1758–77
sources.

Moyen de devenir peintre en trois heures. Paris, 1757

Anweisung zum Miniaturmalen. Leipzig, 1766

Traité de la peinture au pastel, etc. Paris, 1789

Le vernisseur parfait. Interesting recipes for etching, edited by Paris, 1771
Ch. A. Jombert.

Hortus sanitatis. Gives neither name of author nor place of print- undated
ing; repeats the information given by Dioscorides; was used
by 18th-century scholars in the researches as to materials suitable for encaustic.

19TH-CENTURY TREATISES

Adeline, *Art Dictionary* London, 1891

Andrew, J., *La peinture au pastel mise à la portée de tout le monde.* Paris, 1859

Anonymous, *An Account of a New Process of Painting* (2 parts). London, 1821

Bachellier, C. A., *École de la miniature.* Paris, 1814

Bacskay, M. T., *Vegyeszeti Titkok.* Budapest, 1894

Baes, E., *Recherches sur les couleurs employées par les peintres depuis* Brussels, 1821–
l'antiquité jusqu' à nos jours. 1883

Bagin, Ch., *Petit traité ou méthode de peinture au pastel.* Paris, 1849

Baseggio, G. B., *Per preparare tele colori ed altro spettante alla pittura.* Bassano, 1847
Transcribes Volpato's MS.

Baurassé, G. G., *Translation with notes from the Treatise of Theo-* Paris, 1851
philus.

218

Berger, E., *Die Maltechnik des Altertums nach den Quellen, Funden, chemischen Analysen und eigenen Versuchen.*   Munich, 1893–1894, 1901
Quellen und Technik der Fresco, Oel und Temperamalerei des Mittelalters, etc.   Munich, 1897
Quellen für Maltechnik Während der Renaissance, etc. (For Berger's other works see *Treatises of the twentieth century*.)

Bermudez, G. A. Cean., *Dialogo sobre el arte de la pintura.*   Seville, 1819

Berthélot, M., *Les origines de l'alchimie. Collection des anciens alchimistes grecs. La chimie au moyen âge.*   Paris, 1875
  Paris, 1887–88
  Paris, 1893

Bienchy, A., *La peinture chez les égyptiens.*   Limoges, 1868

Blanc, Charles, *Grammaire des arts du dessin: La Peinture.*   Paris, 1860

Boettiger, C. A., *Essai sur l'archéologie de la peinture.*   Dresden, 1811

Bouvier, G., *Handbook for Oil Painting.*   London, 1885

Bouvier, Ph., *Manuel des jeunes artistes et amateurs en peinture.* Good advice, partly derived from Wattin. English translation with the addition of writings of Mérimée, De Montabert, etc. (New York, 1845); German translation, revised by Berger (Leipzig, 1910).   Paris, 1827

Boyleau, E., *Le livre des métiers.*   Paris, 1837

Brockhaus, *Die Kunst in den Athos-Klöstern.*   Leipzig, 1891

Brou, Charles, *La peinture à l'huile avant les Van Eyck (Revue Universelle des Beaux Arts).*   1857

Burnet, J., *A Practical Treatise on Painting* (3 parts). French translation by P. C. van Geel (Paris, 1835).   London, 1827

Burtin, François Xavier, *Traité théorique et pratique des connaissances nécessaires aux amateurs de tableaux.*   Valenciennes, 1846

Cadet de Vaux, A., *Mémoire sur la peinture au lait (Nouveau procédé de peinture).*   Paris, 1811

Calau, B., *Eludorische Malerei,* etc. (*Gazzetta letteraria,* p. 750).   Halle, 1868

Carelli, Consalvo, *Lettera sull'arte di dipingere.*   Naples, 1874

Carpentier, P., *Notes sur la peinture à la cire,* etc.   Paris, 1875

Carrer, Luigi, *Ammaestramenti per la pittura fatti da vari scrittori.* Writings by G. P. Cavazzoni, Zanotti, Leon Battista Alberti, Leonardo, Armenini, Lomazzo, etc.   Venice, 1839

Chaptal, J., *Chimie applicable aux arts.*   Paris, 1807

Chevreuil, M. E., *Recherches expérimentales sur la peinture à l'huile* (Mémoire de l'Académie des Sciences, Vol. XXII.)   Paris, 1850

Church, A. H., *The Chemistry of Paints and Painting.* A classical text for students of painting technique. Translated into German by M. and W. Ostwald.   London, 1890, 1901–15   Munich, 1908

Collier, J., Hon., *Manual of oil painting* (8 vol.)   London, 1886

Couillier, P. H. J., *Considérations sur l'altération des couleurs dans les tableaux peints à l'huile.*   Paris, 1824

Cremer, F. G., *Beiträge zur Technik der Monumental-Malerfarben.* Of interest for anyone wishing to study the technique of silicate painting.   Düsseldorf, 1892–95
Vollstaendige Anleitung zur Frescomalerei.   Düsseldorf, 1891
Studien zur Geschichte der Oelfarbenmalerei.   Düsseldorf, 1895

Cross et Henry, *L'encaustique et les autres procédés de la peinture chez les anciens.* One of the most serious and documented works on this subject.   Paris, 1884

Crowninschield, F., *Mural Painting*.   Boston, 1887

Davy, H., *Some Experiments and Observations on the Colours used in*   London, 1815
Painting by the Ancients (Phil. Trans. C. V.).

Dehaisnes (Chanoine), *Histoire de l'art dans la Flandre, l'Artois et*   1886
le Hainaut. A richly documented work.

Delacroix, E., *Journal*.   Paris, 1845
Deon, Horsin, *De la conservation et de la restauration des tableaux*.   Paris, 1851
Very little technical knowledge and barbarous methods of
cleaning and restoring.

De Vecchio, Buonaiuto, *Cenni sul modo di dipingere, di dorare, di*   Venice, 1842
verniciare, di stuccare, di tingere.

Didron, A. N., *Manuel d'iconographie chrétienne, grecque et latine*. (See   Paris, 1843
Durand.)

Dolent, J., *Petit manuel d'art à l'usage des ignorants: La Peinture*.   Paris, 1851

Donner, Otto, *Die erhaltenen antiken Wandmalereien in technischer*   Leipzig, 1869
Beziehung.   (reprint)
Ueber Technisches in der Malerei der Alten, etc.   Munich, 1855

Duhamel Dumoriceau, *L'art de faire les colles*.   Paris, 1812

Durozier, A. M., *Notices sur la peinture à la cire*, etc.   Paris, 1838
Manuel de peinture à la cire.   Paris, 1848

Eastlake, Sir Charles, *Materials for an History of Oil Painting*.   London, 1847–
Italian translation by G. Bezzi. A valuable book, with a richly   1849–69
documented German translation by G. Hesse (Vienna, 1907).

Ebers, Georg, *Antike Porträts. Die Hellenistischen Bildnisse aus dem*   Leipzig, 1893
Fayum.

Eitelberger von Edelberg, R., *Quellenschriften für Kunstgeschichte*   Vienna, 1871
und Kunsttechnik, etc.

Emeric David T. B., *Histoire de la peinture au moyen âge*.   Paris, 1863
Discours historiques sur la peinture moderne.   Paris, 1812

Fabroni, A., *Antichità vantaggi e metodo della pittura ad encausto*   Venice, 1800
(Lecture).
Ricerche chimiche sopra le miniature di un antico manoscritto (Atti,   Siena, 1841
Accademia, Vol. X).

Federici, *Memorie trevigiane sulle opere di disegno*.   Venice, 1863

Fernbach, *Die enkaustische Malerei*.   Munich, 1845
Die Oelmalerei, etc.   Munich, 1843

Field, G., *Chromatography*. Brought up to date by G. Scott Taylor   London, 1841
and newly published (Winsor & Newton).

Fielding, T. H., *On Painting in Oil and Watercolour*.   London, 1839

Fillon, B., *Description de la villa et du tombeau d'une femme artiste*   Fontenay, 1849
gallo-romaine découverte à St-Médard des prés.

Fischerd, L., *Die Technik der Oelmalerei*.   Vienna, 1898

Forni, Ulisse, *Manuale del pittore restauratore*. Excellent for every-   Florence, 1866
thing concerning the consolidation, transport and restoration
of mural painting.

Forster, E., *Beiträge zur neueren Kunstgeschichte*.   Leipzig, 1835

Frimmel, Th., *Handbuch der Gemäldekunde*.   Leipzig, 1894

Gambier Parry, T., *The Spirit Fresco Painting. An account of the*   London, 1883
process.

Gaye, G., *Carteggio inedito di artisti dei secoli XIV, XV, XVI*, etc.   Florence,
                                                                      1839–40

Geiger, P. L., *Chemische Untersuchung altaegyptischer und altroem-*   Carlsruhe,
ischer Farben, etc.   1826

Goethe, W., *Beiträge zur Farbenlehre.*   1810
    Optik.
    Reflections and information on ancient pictures in Venice, on
    Leonardo's *Last Supper*, etc., scattered in many works, in
    which he speaks admirably about art, as a technician, as a
    critic and as a writer.

Goupil, *Traité général de la peinture à l'huile.*   Bailly
    Of interest as he describes the technique of contemporary
    artists, such as David, Ingres, Horace Vernet, etc.
    L'aquarelle et le lavis.   Paris, undated
    Le pastel simplifié et perfectionné.   Paris, 1881

Guaita, L., *La scienza dei colori e la pittura.*   Milan, 1893

Guichard, E., *La grammaire de la couleur.*   Paris, 1882

Haefer, F., *Histoire de la chimie.*   Paris, 1842–43

Halphen, G., *Couleurs et vernis.*   1895

Hamerton, P. G., *The Graphic Arts*, etc.   London, 1882

Hareux, E., *Cours complet de peinture à l'huile* (2 vol.)   Paris, undated

Hayter, C., *An Introduction to perspective, practical geometry, drawing* London, 1845
    and painting, etc.

Hollaender, E., *Translations of Heraclius, Theophilus, Cennini*, with   Vienna, 1881
    notes (*Quellenschriften*, etc.)

Holmes, Sir Charles, *Notes on the Science of Picture Making.*   London, 1893

Jeenes, G. C., *Guide and Advice to Young Painters.*   London, 1893

Jozan, J., *Du pastel*, etc.   Paris, 1858

Keim, A. W., *Die Mineralmalerei.* Explains the technique of   Vienna, 1881
    mural painting with silicate.

Knirim, F., *Die Harzmalerei der Alten*, etc.   Leipzig, 1839
    Technische Mitteilungen für Malerei. A collection of writings
    founded in 1884 and published for over thirty-six years.
    Die Malertechnik des Klassischen Altertums, etc.   Munich, 1845

Kopp, H., *Beiträge zur Geschichte der Chimie.*   Braunschweig,
                                                       1869

Kulmann, *Découverte de l'emploi du silicate de potasse dans la peinture*
    des murailles (*Revue Universelle des Arts*, Vol. V, p. 82).

Landerer, X., *Ueber Malerei und Farben der alten Griechen.*   Leipzig, 1840

Larochenoire, J., de, *Le pastel appris seul avec sept couleurs.*   Paris, 1852

Latronne, *Lettres d'un antiquaire à un artiste sur l'emploi de la pein-* Paris, 1834
    ture murale.

Lattilla, E., *A Treatise on Fresco, Encaustic and Tempera Painting.*   London, 1842

Lecoy de la Marche, A., *Les manuscrits et la miniature.*   Paris, 1884
    L'art d'enluminer, Transcription of the Naples MS.   Paris, 1890

Lefort, Jules, *Chimie des couleurs pour la peinture à l'eau et à l'huile.* Paris, 1855
    Interesting as it also discusses the toxicology of colours.

Leslie, C. R., *A Handbook for Young Painters.*   London, 1855

Linton, W., *Ancient and Modern Colours from the Earliest Periods to*   London, 1852
    the Present Time, with their chemical and artistic properties (Long-
    man).

Lloyd, F., *Practical Guide to Scene-painting and Painting in Dis-*   London, 1879
    temper.

Lucanus, F. G., *Vollständige Anteilung zur Erhaltung der Gemälde.*   Halberstadt,
                                                       1842–56

Ludwig, H., *Grundsätze der Oelmalerei*, etc. *Technik der Oelmalerei* (2 vol.).   Leipzig, 1893

Mansion, *Lettres sur la miniature*. Interesting writings by this pupil of Isabey.   Paris, 1823

Marcucci, L., *Saggio analitico chimico sopra i colori minerali*, etc.   Rome, 1813

Melignan, *Traité sur la peinture en miniature*.   Paris, 1818

Mérimée, J. F., *De la peinture à l'huile*. English translation by W. B. Sarsfield Taylor.   Paris, 1830, 1839

Merrifield, Mary, *Original Treatises Dating from the XII to the XVIII Centuries on the Art of Painting* (2 vol.)   London, 1849
The Art of Fresco Painting as practised by the old Italian and Spanish masters. A valuable transcription of ancient MSS.   London, 1846

Montabert, Paillot, De, *Histoire de la peinture* (9 vol.). An important work, rich in documents.   Paris, 1829

Mottez, Victor, *Translations* from the *Libro dell'arte* by Cennini, with notes on fresco also taken from the Mount Athos MS.   Paris–Lille, 1858

Oughton, F., *Notebook on Oil Colour Technique*.   London, 1892

Paléologue, Maurice, *L'art chinois*.

Palmieri, P., *Ricerche chimiche sopra dodici colori solidi trovati a Pompei*.   1875

Pelouze, *Secrets modernes des arts et des métiers*.

Petrini, *Della pittura degli antichi*.   Florence, 1873

Pettenkofer, Max von, *Ueber Oelfarbe*.   Braunschweig, undated.

Prange, *L'art de restaurer et de conserver les vieux tableaux*. Rather empirical precepts and advice.

Recouvreur, A., *Grammaire du peintre*.   Paris, 1890

Ridolfi, Michele, *Scritti vari*, regarding the Arts.   Lucca, 1844

Rivot et Chantoney, *Considérations générales de la composition des mortiers*. Useful for the fresco painter.   Paris, 1856

Robert, K., *Le pastel*.   Paris, 1890

Rood, O. N., *Théorie scientifique des couleurs et leur application à l'art et à l'industrie*.   Paris, 1881

Roret, *Manuel*. A manual compiled by M. Constant, Vignier, Langlois de Longueville, Durozier, entitled: *Miniature, gouache, lavis, sépia, aquarelle et peinture à la cire*.   Paris, 1845

Salazzaro, Demetrio, *L'arte della miniatura nel XIV secolo*, a transcription of the Naples MS.   Naples, 1877

Secco Suardo, G., *Pensieri sulla pittura ad encausto, ad olio e a tempera*.   Turin, 1870
Il restauratore dei dipinti.   Milan, 1866

Seroux d'Agincourt, *Storia d'arte*.   Prato, 1827

Shaw, Henry, *The Art of Illumination as Practised During the Middle Ages*. Describes materials and procedures of various artists.   London, 1870

Soehnee, C. F., *Recherches nouvelles sur les procédés de la peinture des anciens*.   Paris, 1810, 1822

Standage, H. C., *Use and Abuse of Colour in Oil Painting*.   London, 1892
Artists' Manual of Pigments.   London, 1887
Handbook of Chemical and Artistic Qualities of Watercolours Pigments.   1891

Sully, T., *Hints to Young Painters and the Process of Portrait-Painting*. Of interest as it describes the techniques of contemporary American artists.   Philadelphia, 1873

Taylor Sarsfield, B. S., *A Manual of Fresco and Encaustic Painting.* London, 1843
One of the most complete and intelligent writings on mural
painting written in England.

Terry, G., *Pigments, Paint and Painting* London, 1893
The Painters and Varnishers Guide, etc. London, 1816

Teyssedre, *Art de décorer les apartements contenant les compositions et* London, 1821
l'application des enduits, etc.

Tingry, P. F., *Traité theorique et pratique sur l'art de faire et appliquer* Geneva, 1803
les vernis.

Tyrwitt, R. S. J., *Handbook of Pictorial Art.* Clarendon, 1875

Verri, G., *Saggio elementare sul disegno*, etc. (with some advice as to Milan, 1814
the use of oil colours).

Vibert, J., *La science de la peinture.* English translation. (London, Paris, 1891
1892.) Previati's book derives from this treatise.

Vichon, *Notices sur les peintures à fresque qu'il a exécutées dans la* Paris, 1822
chapelle de Saint-Maurice à Saint-Sulpice à Paris (Le Moniteur,
17 Déc.)

Vignoli, Giocondo, *Del dipingere a fresco sull'intonaco greco-romano.* Parma, 1885
Practical advice of a good technician.

Wyatt, M. Digby, *The Art of Illumination as Practised in Europe* London, 1890
from the Earliest Times.

20TH-CENTURY TREATISES

Abendschein, Albert, *The Secrets of Old Masters.* About the New York,
materials of old masters and their use. 1905

Alston, R. W., *Painter's idiom.* London, 1954

Andes, L. E., *Oil Colours and Printers' Ink.* A useful and practical London, 1931
manual.
Vegetable Fats and Oils, translated from German (4th edition). London, 1925

Backner, *The A. B. C. of Japanese Art.* London, 1922

Ballò, E., *Az olajfestés mestersége.* Budapest, 1914
Technik der Oelmalerei. Leipzig, 1924,
1935

Baltus, G. M., *The Technics of Painting.* Glasgow–
London, 1912

Barnes, C. A., *Art in Painting.* undated

Basch-Bordone, J., *Handbuch der Konservierung und Restaurierung* Munich, 1921
alter Gemälde. Contains good advice for the restoring of
pictures.

Battaglini, D., *Il consigliere dell'artista.* Milan,
undated

Baudouin, Paul, *La fresque, sa technique, ses applications.* A clear Paris, 1914
and practical book by an authority with a deep knowledge of
fresco.

Bellanger, C., *L'art de peindre.* Paris, 1909–11

Berger, E., *Die Technik der römisch-pompejanischen Wandmalerei,* 1906
etc.
Böcklins Technik.

Binyon, L., *Painting in Asia.* London, 1908

Block, G., *Compendium.* English and French translation, 1922–26. Antwerp, 1904

Blumer, *Die Maltechnik des Altertums.* 1908

Boizey, M., *La science des couleurs et l'art de la peinture.*   Paris, 1923

Breitscheidel, O., *Die Technik der römisch-campanischen Wand-*   Munich, 1911
malerei, etc.

Breton, G. A., *La peinture et le but. Les lois essentielles. Les moyens,*   Paris, 1904
etc.

Brown, W. N., *Workshop Wrinkles for Decorators, Painters and*   London, 1901
Others.

Burroughs, A., *Art Criticism from a Laboratory.*   Boston, 1938

Busset, Maurice, *La technique moderne du tableau*, etc.   Paris, 1929

Cadet Gassicourt, *Dictionnaire de chimie.*   Riffault, 1924

Cartaillac, E., and Breuil, H., *Peinture et gravure murale des cavernes*   Monaco, 1906
paléolitiques, etc. English translation by A. H. Keane, under
the title: *Varnishes, their chemistry and manufacture* (London,
1923).

Coffignier, Ch., *Les vernis.*
Les couleurs et les peintures.   1924
Manuel du peintre (2 vol.: I *Couleurs et enduits*; II *Peintures et*   1925
enduits). A work for craftsmen and manufacturers of colours.

Constable, W. G., *The painter's workshop.*   New York, 1953

Dalbon, Charles, *Les origines de la peinture à l'huile.* An excellent   Paris, 1904
book, well documented.

De Chirico, Giorgio, *Piccolo trattato di tecnica pittorica.* The value   Milan, 1928
of this work lies in showing De Chirico's methods: from the
preservation of his pictures one will judge the value of his
precepts.

Dimier, L., *L'art de l'enluminure.* A translation of the Naples MS.   Paris, 1927

Dinet, E., *Les fléaux de la peinture.* Discusses the diseases of pictures,   Paris, 1926
due to bad technique or bad preservation.

Doerner, Max., *Malmaterial und seine Verwendung im Bilde.* English   Berlin–Vienna,
translation by E. Neuhaus, under the title: *The materials of the*   1921–22–27
Artist and their use in painting (London, 1935; New York, 1934).

Dolz, F. P., *Iniciacion a la tecnica de la pintura.*   Barcelona, 1947

Doust, L. A., *A manual on Pastel Painting.*   London, 1933

Dumas, Horace, *La physique des couleurs et la peinture.*   Paris, 1930

Dupont, *Les essences de therebentine.*   1926

Eibner, Alexander, *Zur Entwicklung der Technik der Oelmalerei*   Munich, 1908
vom Mittelalter bis in die Neuzeit.
Ueber Fette, Oele, etc.   Munich, 1920
Die Oelfarbe in Kunst und Handwerk.   Munich, 1920
Entwicklung und Werkstoffe der Wandmalerei vom Altertum bis   Munich, 1926
zur Neuzeit.

Eibner, A., and Trillich, H., *Die Ei-Tempera.*   Munich, 1926

Erhardt, A., *Die Kunst der Malerei* (3rd edition edited by   Leipzig, 1910
E. Berger).

Fasani, A., *Éléments de peinture murale*, with a preface by Le   Paris, 1951
Corbusier. Deals with media suitable for modern paintings.

Fierens, P., *La peinture et les peintres.* Contains a very important   Brussels, 1916
bibliography.

Fiorilli, C., *I dipintori a Firenze nell'arte dei medici, speziali, merciai*   1920
(Italian Historical Archives, A. 78, Vol. 11).

Fischer, M. J., *The Permanent Palette.* Interesting glossary and   Mountain Lake
bibliography.   Park, Mary-
                                                                                                land, 1930

224

Fleury, P., *Traité classique du peintre décorateur.*   Paris, 1905
Histoire générale de l'art décoratif, etc.
Nouveau traité usuel de la peinture en bâtiments, décor et décorations. 1898
Friedlein, E., *Tempera und Temperatechnik.*   Munich, 1906
Friend, G. M., *An Introduction to Chemistry of Painting.* New York, 1910
Frimmel, Th. von, *Gemäldekunde* (2nd edition, 3rd edition). Leipzig, 1904,
    1920

Ganz, W. H., *Practical Hints on Painting.*   London, 1905
Gardner, H. A., *Painting* (Material technique) *Physical and* Washington
Chemical Examination of Paints, Varnishes, Lacquers and Colours. undated
This treatise has been defined as 'the Bible of pictorial
chemistry'.

Gaston-Gerard, *Peinture à l'huile enseigné par l'aspect. Mélange et* Paris, 1928
association des couleurs. Peinture à l'huile et peinture à l'eau.

Gettens, R. S., and Stout, G., *Painting materials.* A fundamental New York, 1942,
work.   1943, 1946,
    1947

Gouillon, *Traité méthodique de la fabrication des vernis.* 1924
Goulinat, J. G., *La technique des peintres.* Paris, 1922,
    1926

Heaton, Noël, *Outlines of paint technology.* London, 1928
Volatile solvents and thinners. New York, 1926
Hebing, C., *Vergoldung und Bronzierung.* Munich, 1907
Praktischer Ratgeber der Dekorationsmalerei. Munich, 1920
Hildebrand, H., *Wandmalerei, ihr Wesen und ihre Gesetze.* Berlin, 1920
Hiler, Hilaire, *Notes on the Technique of Painting.* Pleasant, easy, London, 1927
and full of valuable advice.
New edition. London, 1948
Hiscot Gardner, D., *The XX century book of receipts, formulas and* London, 1910
processes.

Hopkins, A. A., *The Scientific American Encyclopaedia of Formulas.* New York, 1935
Hubbard, Hesketh, *Materia pictoria*, Vol. I, *Oil painting.* An London, 1939,
excellent collection of recipes. 1948
Hurst, G. H., *Painters' Colours, Oils and Varnishes.* London, 1901
5th edition corrected by Noël Heaton. Philadelphia,
    1906
    London, 1913

Jantzen, H., *Farbenwahl.* The choice of colours of the Dutch Parchim I. M.,
school in the 18th century. 1912
Kiesling, E., *Wesen und Technik der Malerei.* Leipzig, 1921
Kroh, F., *Technik der Oelmalerei.* Leipzig, 1921
Lange, N. A., *Handbook of Chemistry.* Sandusky, Ohio,
    undated

Lapparent, P. de, *Les altérations des couleurs.* Paris, 1923
Laurie, A. P., *Simple Rules for Painting in Oils.* 1932, 1955
Materials of the painters' Craft in Europe and in Egypt. Excellent London, New
bibliography. York, Edin-
    burgh, 1910
    London, 1926

The Pigments and the Vehicles of the Old Masters. Cambridge,
    1910
The Pigments and the Mediums of the Old Masters (with a special London, 1914
chapter on the microphotographic study of brushwork).

225

Greek and Roman Methods of Painting.   London, 1926–
                                                                                1935

The Painters' Methods and Materials.   London, 1935
New Light on Old Masters. A valuable book, full of technical   1935
and historical information.

Linke, Fr., *Die Malerfarben, Mal- und Bindemittel und ihre Verwend-*   Esslingen, 1908
ung in der Maltechnik.

Linzi, Carlo, *La tecnica della pittura e dei colori.* Personal theories   Milan, 1930
and ideas which do not correspond with historical tradition.

Lippmann, E. von, *Entstehung und Ausbreitung der Alchemie.*   Berlin, 1919

Liron, *Contreplaqués et colles à la caséine.*   1928

Loumier, G., *Les traditions techniques de la peinture médiévale.*   Brussels, 1914,
                                                                                1920

Also a translation by the same author of the Berne anonymous   Berne, 1908
writer, under the title: *Un traité de peinture du moyen âge.*

Lowe, A., and De Beer, G., *Manuel sur la peinture à l'huile, ses*   Brussels, 1917
matériaux, ses supports et sa technique, etc.

Lucas, A., *Ancient Egyptian materials and industries.*   London, 1934

Margival, F., *Les peintures.*   Paris, 1912
Peintures.   1928
Lacques et vernis.   1928
Couleurs et pigments.   1930

Maroger, G., *The secrets, formulas and techniques of the Masters*: the   New York, 1948
author presents personal opinions, not supported by scientific
data.

Mayer, Ralph, *The Artist's Handbook.* A very important work,   New York, 1940,
full of scrupulously verified technical advice.   1941, 1943,
                                                                                1945
                                                                                London, 1951

Montagne, Saint Hubert H., *The Art of Fresco Painting, Pure*   Paris, 1923
Technique and Actual Renaissance. Lectures given at the Ameri-
can School at Fontainebleau.

Moreau Vauthier, Ch., *La peinture.*   Paris, 1912–13
English translation under title: *The technique of painting,* with
preface by E. Dinet (London, 1923); Italian translation with
additions by Ugo Ojetti (Bergamo, 1913). An excellent book
of divulgation.

Morrel, R. S., *Varnishes and their Components.*   London, 1923

Morrel, R. S., and Wood, H. R., *The Chemistry of Drying Oils.*   New York, 1925

Nemberg, A., *Die Technik des Altertums.*   Leipzig, 1920

Neubauer, R., *Die Flächenkräfte.*   Greifswald,
                                                                                1913

Nicholls, B., *Painting in Oils.*   London, 1938

Nicolay, G. de, *Les principes de la peinture d'après les maîtres.*   Meulon–Tours,
                                                                                1929

Ostwald, W., *Malerbriefe.* English translation by W. H. Morse   Leipzig, 1903
(*Letters to a painter*) (Boston, 1906).
Das monumentale Pastell. On the use of pastels for mural paint-   Leipzig, 1905,
ing.   1912

Parry, E. S., and Coste, S. H., *Gum and resins: The chemistry of*   London, 1902
pigments.

Partington, J. R., *Origin and Development of Applied Chemistry.*   London, 1935

Pecheu, *Les couleurs, les matières colorantes, les mordants en teinture.*   1920

Petrie, Sir W. Flinders, *Arts and Crafts of Ancient Egypt*.   Edinburgh, 1909

Piot, René, *Les palettes de Delacroix*.   Paris, 1931

Piva, G., *Manuale pratico di tecnica pittorica*.   Milan, 1951

Popp, G., *Martin Knoller*. Concerning Knoller's technique of mural painting.   Munich, 1908

Pratt, F., and Fizell, B., *Encaustic. Materials and Methods*.   New York, 1949

Previati, G., *La tecnica della pittura*. Derived from Vibert.   Turin, 1923

Raehlmann, *Ueber ultramikroskopische Untersuchungen von Farbstoffen und ihre physikalisch-physiologische Bedeutung*.   1904-05
Ueber die Maltechnik der Alten.   Berlin, 1910

Ronchetti, *La pittura murale*.   Milan, 1922
Manuale per i dilettanti di pittura.   Milan, 1904

Rosa, L. A., *La tecnica della pittura dai tempi preistorici ad oggi*.   Milan, 1937

Rose, Fr., *Die Mineralfarben*.   Leipzig, 1916

Ruhemann, H., and Kemp, E. M., *The artist at work*. A short study showing a deep knowledge of media.   Harmonds-worth, 1951

Sabin, A. H., *The Industrial and Artistic Technology of Paint and Varnish*.   New York, 1905

Sachs, Herman, *Lehrbuch der Maltechnik*. Excellent and clear recipes.   Berlin, 1927

Schmid, H., *Enkaustik und Fresko auf antiker Grundlage*.   Munich, 1926

Schrodterk, Schroeder, *Malgrunde der Italienischen Renaissance*.

Schultze, R., *Die Technik der Malerei*. The part concerning encaustic is very interesting.   Leipzig, 1920

Sérusier, P., *A. B. C. de la peinture*.   Paris, 1921, 1942

Sims, Ch., *Picture Making. Technique and Inspiration*.   New York, 1935

Solomon, Solomon, *The Practice of Oil Painting*, etc.   London, 1919

Speed, H., *The Science and Practice of Oil Painting*.   London, 1924

Steinbach, H., *Die Praxis des Dekorationsmalers*.   Munich, 1913

Taubes, F., *The Mastery of Oil painting, a practical and comprehensive guide of the techniques of Masters*.   London, 1953

Thompson Varney, Daniel, Jr., *On the Chemistry of Ancient Assyrians*.   London, 1925
De Clarea. From the anonymous treatise of Berne. (Technical Studies, I.)   New Haven, 1932
The Craftsman's Handbook. An excellent translation of Cennini's *Libro dell'Arte*.   New Haven, 1933
The Practice of Tempera Painting. Based on Cennini.   New Haven, 1936

The materials of mediaeval Painting   London, 1936

Thompson Varney, Daniel, Jr., and Hamilton, G. H., *An anonymous XIV Century Treatise: De Arte illuminandi*. An excellently annotated translation of the Naples MS.   London–Oxford, 1933

Tikkanen, J., *Studie ueber die Farbengebung in der mittelalterlichen Buchmalerei*.   Helsinki, 1933

Toch, M., *The Chemistry and Technology of Mixed Paints*.   New York, 1907
Materials to paint Permanent Pictures.   1922
How to paint Permanent Pictures.   1922
Chemistry and Technology of Paints (3rd edition)   1925

Tschirsch, A., and Stock, E., *Die Harze*.   Berlin, 1903

227

Venturini-Papari, T., *L'arte della pittura ad encausto e degli stucchi*   Rome, 1901
    del tempo di Augusto.

Wanderpoel, E. N., *Colour Problem*. A manual for students.   New York, 1903

Ward, James, *History and methods of Ancient and Modern Painting*.   London, 1913–
                                                                          1921

Weber, F. W., *Artists' pigments*.   New York, 1932

Wehlte, K., *Wandmalerei*. Good recipes for 'a secco', tempera   Berlin, 1938,
    and encaustic painting.   1946

Wild, A. Martin De, *The Scientific Examination of Pictures*.   London, 1929
    Dictionary of Colour   New York,
                                                                          1930–31

Williams, Terrick, *The Art of Pastel*.   New York, 1937

Wolff, *Die Farbe im Altertum*.   1913
    Manuel de Laboratoire pour l'industrie des vernis et des couleurs.   1926

Wyzema, Theodore De, *Peintres de jadis et d'aujourd'hui*.   Paris, 1903

Zerr, G., and Rubencamp, R., *A Treatise on Colour Manufacture*.   London, 1908

228